PEACEMAKING AND DEMOCRATISATION IN AFRICA

COVER: The graphic on the cover is adapted from the work, "The Arising," by Carla Stetson. Reproduced with permission. Artwork by Sange Graphics and Expert Printers.

PEACEMAKING AND DEMOCRATISATION IN AFRICA
Theoretical Perspectives and Church Initiatives

Edited by

Hizkias Assefa
and
George Wachira

East African Educational Publishers
Nairobi • Kampala

Published by
East African Educational Publishers Ltd.
Brick Court, Mpaka Road/Woodvale Grove
Westlands
P.O. Box 45314, Nairobi, Kenya

East African Educational Publishers Ltd.
Pioneer House, Jinja Road
P.O. Box 11542, Kampala, Uganda

© Nairobi Peace Initiative (NPI) 1996

First published 1996

ISBN 9966-46-837-4

The opinions expressed in this publication are solely those of the individual contributors and do not necessarily represent the views of NPI, AACC or AMECEA, the original organisers of the symposium.

Typeset by
Dataforce Ltd.
Muthithi House, Muthithi Road
Westlands
P.O. Box 26543, Nairobi

Printed in Kenya by
Fotoform Limited
Muthithi House, Muthithi Road
Westlands
P.O. Box 14681, Nairobi

Contents

Preface   *vii*

Foreword   *ix*

Introduction   1

1. The Crisis of Neo-colonialism in Africa and the Contemporary Democratic Challenge
   Kwesi Prah   7

2. Good Governance for Development: Perspectives from the African Traditional Cultural Heritage
   Timothy G. Kiogora   23

3. Churches and the Reconstruction of Society for Democracy: Some Insights from the African Heritage
   Jesse N.K. Mugambi   34

4. Peace and Reconciliation As a Paradigm: A Philosophy of Peace and Its Implications for Conflict, Governance and Economic Growth in Africa
   Hizkias Assefa   42

5. Religious Leaders, Peacemaking and Social Change: Some Theological Perspectives
   Laurenti Magesa   72

6. The Churches' Involvement in the Democratisation Process in Kenya
   Agnes C. Abuom   95

7. From Independence to Multiparty Democracy in Zambia: A Personal View from Inside the Church
   Foston Dziko Sakala   117

8. Churches and the Struggle for Democracy in Zaire
   Philippe B. Kabongo-Mbaya   130

9. The Christian Council of Churches in Madagascar (FFKM) and Its Commitment to Social Change
   Josoa Rakotonirainy 153

10. Peacemaking and Social Change in South Africa: The Challenge of the Church
    John Lamola 179

11. The Demands of God's Faithfulness: A Case Study of Peacemaking in Mozambique
    Dinis S. Sengulane and Jaime Pedro Gonçalves 192

Appendix I: Summary of Discussions   211
Appendix II: Joint Statement of Symposium Participants   216
Appendix III: Description of the Sponsoring Agencies   224
Appendix IV: Aggregated Responses from the Symposium
                Evaluation Form   226
Appendix V: Symposium Participants   229

Index   235

About the Contributors   241

Preface

This book was born in 1992 as the germ of an idea. In our work with Nairobi Peace Initiative, we were acutely aware that in the previous three years many African countries had started bravely down the road to "democracy" after years of single-party rule. All over the continent, NGOs, human-rights organisations and political activists had taken up the call for change. As the work of "democratisation" evolved, we noticed that a large number of churchmen and churchwomen also had become centrally involved in Africa's political processes—tentatively at first but eventually gathering strength in roles as varied as peacemakers, mediators, shapers of policy and something very closely resembling political leaders. How did they manage to juggle their churches' spiritual calling with the rough-and-tumble demands of political struggle and high-level societal mediation? Could members of the clergy assume new roles within the political sphere without grievously compromising their primary roles within the church? Was their involvement coincidental or the result of careful preparation?

Without a doubt, the initiative church leaders had displayed was impressive. The energy and strength evident in the church's committed action offered hope in a landscape largely devoid, these last fifteen years, of innovative leadership in any field. As we began to look around, we realised that church leaders in many African countries had decided to journey with their fellow citizens along the rocky road to democratisation. In Benin, South Africa, Mozambique and at least a half dozen other countries, the church, in different ways and at different times, had chosen to take up the people's struggle for peaceful change. Perhaps the church, with its moral authority in a political environment distinctly lacking in trust and goodwill, had something to offer that should be investigated in depth?

And so, before this book, came a symposium. Theoretical concept papers and case studies of church involvement in peacemaking and democratisation in various countries were presented to the symposium participants, who gathered in Nyeri, Kenya, in mid-1993. Not all of our questions were answered, but both the presenters and participants shed enough light on their subject that we felt their insights should be shared in book form.

We would like to thank the individual contributors for producing their case studies and conceptual papers, as well as all the participants in the symposium for honouring our invitation.

We would also like to thank the following: Nairobi Peace Initiative Steering Committee members—Kabiru Kinyanjui, Samuel Kobia and Harold Miller, for their support during preparations for the symposium; and José Chipenda and Peter Lwaminda, General-Secretaries of the All Africa Conference of Churches (AACC) and the Association of Member Episcopal Conferences of Eastern Africa (AMECEA) respectively, for agreeing to co-sponsor the symposium with NPI. Our thanks also go to Jesse Mugambi, Agnes Chepkwony Abuom, Grace Imathiu, Michael Chege, Kabiru Kinyanjui and Laurenti Magesa for serving on the advisory committee for the symposium. Thanks are also due to Peter Lwaminda and Mutombo Mulami for serving on the symposium steering committee. Additional thanks to Jesse Mugambi and Harold Miller for synthesising the symposium participants' discussions and drafting the "Joint Statement of Symposium Participants," which appears as Appendix II.

The symposium and the preparation of the papers published in this book were made possible by a major grant from the Ford Foundation, Zimbabwe. Other organisations that contributed towards the symposium expenses were the Interchurch Fund for International Development Canada, Norwegian Church Aid, Lutheran World Relief, Danish Church Aid, Sweden Church Mission, United Church of Canada, Diakonisches Werk and Benevolentia. We are most grateful to all of them.

Very special thanks are due to our NPI colleagues: Florence Mpaayei, who was cheerfully involved at every stage in the preparation of both the symposium and this book, and Emmanuel Bombande who helped immensely by proofreading and correcting French translations. Both were an invaluable source of support and encouragement. We also register our deep appreciation to Carla Stetson for kindly allowing us to use her work, "The Arising", free of charge on the cover of the book

Finally, we are indebted to Lisa Lawley Nesbitt, whose editorial skills and hard work have greatly improved the papers in this volume.

Hizkias Assefa
George Wachira
Nairobi Peace Initiative
September 1996

Foreword

Most readers of this book will be familiar with Africa's transformation in the international media, over the course of the last century, from the Dark Continent to the Awakening Giant and then to the Doomed Continent.

Africa is indeed in trouble. Too many of her people are suffering, and the expectations built up during her countries' first three decades of independence have not been fulfilled.

Those who have good memories will recall the period 1960 to 1980 as a time of rising expectations. During this period, the word *development* was equated with peace, and poverty was seen as the harbinger of conflict. The World Bank and the International Monetary Fund, launched in 1945, were widely accepted as the financial institutions with the capacity to eradicate poverty and protect Africa from communism.

Now the situation has changed. Discussions regarding the limits to growth brought realism to the economic field. "Structural adjustments," introduced into the vocabulary of the 1980s, were expected to alleviate but not eliminate poverty. In the 1990s, economic theorists advocate the politics of the market-place, considered universally appropriate to the Brave New World.

The recent wind of change that has brought democracy to Africa places the market-place at the centre of the political game. Public protests that started in Benin in 1989 fundamentally challenged the legitimacy of African dictators, whether civil or military. Today, multiparty politics—legal in 42 of the 48 countries of tropical Africa—is associated with strengthening civil society and facilitating privatisation of each country's economy.

Yet between September 1990 and October 1991, when popular participation in African politics was greatest, ten heads of state in Africa were either voted out, toppled, exiled or murdered. Up until 1992, multiparty elections were reasonably well tolerated in Africa, but they soon became points of severe tension. Elections have been accompanied by disputes, as in Algeria and Nigeria; ethnic clashes in Kenya; loss of lives and destruction of property in Togo and Angola; a military coup in Burundi; and unprecedented carnage in Rwanda. With the exception of South Africa, it has become the rule for parties to petition for an election re-run as soon as defeat seems imminent. It seems clear that the current multiparty experiment will continue to be a problem until the politics of the market-place is replaced by a political theory appropriate to the needs of the people of our continent.

Concern about the changes currently underway inspired the Nairobi Peace Initiative, AMECEA and the All Africa Conference of Churches to sponsor a unique symposium. Its participants were drawn from churches in Eastern and Southern Africa, and their task was to explore the role of religious leaders in peacemaking and social change processes in their region.

As a continent in crisis, Africa faces a variety of internal and external threats—to life, to justice, to peace, to the environment, to the unity of the church, to the family, to tolerance. All of these are due to the struggle for power, a desperate grasping for diminishing resources. We are being consumed by hatred, ethnic conflict and brutal violence. The Bible affirms that all these things come from desires that battle within us: "Where do all the fights and quarrels among you come from? They come from your desires for pleasure, which are constantly fighting within you. You want things, but cannot get them, so you quarrel and fight. You do not have what you want because you do not ask God for it. And when you ask, you do not receive it, because your motives are bad."

Yet it is possible to imagine in Africa a democracy based on the belief that there is plenty for all, that one person's success is not achieved at the expense of others. A democracy suitable for Africa excludes no one; it invites everyone to participate in the struggle for survival. Such a democracy will emphasise the holistic character of life and respect for traditional authority and the values of the extended family in society, holding all authority accountable to God. A suitable democracy will emphasise just relationships within community. It will respect the rights and dignity of individuals and of people in and beyond individual families, at the same time holding each person accountable to others in a renewed dedication to the goal of African unity.

The symposium that this book documents began a dialogue that may prove crucial in reformulating a democracy that not only will work in the African context, but will, in the words of Nelson Mandela, "reinforce humanity's belief in justice, strengthen its confidence in the nobility of the human soul and sustain all our hopes for a glorious life for all." Glorious life everywhere begins with respect for life and the healing of wounds of the past. Glorious life continues when united leaders pledge to help each other, participating jointly in the liberation of the victims of oppression from the bondage of poverty, deprivation and insecurity—when all citizens commit themselves to the construction of a society in which people individually and collectively walk tall without fear or intimidation in their hearts, assured of their inalienable right to human dignity.

The crises Africa faces today must not divide church leaders; they demand unity in action based on Christian conviction. Today, the church and its leaders must come near to God: "We must humble ourselves before the Lord and be lifted up." Our allegiance should no longer be based on a broken witness manifested in denominational trivialities or other short-term, tangible goals such as salaries and benefits. We are called to "examine collectively the possibilities for surprise-rich futures," to stand against new powers and principalities, and to work earnestly for peace and justice in our countries. Our ecumenism should combine affirmation of our faith in God, Christian brotherhood and sisterhood, and submission to the Holy Spirit.

If the church does not take preventive measures, the next millenium will see anarchy in many countries in our continent. Our aim should be to work for the establishment of God's kingdom in Africa, so that His will reaches us with the same intensity as in Heaven. The material in this book—some fruits of our symposium—offers food for thought for all of us who are or should be considering this challenge, to which the church clearly is called. My hope is that you will decide to take it up.

José B. Chipenda
General-Secretary
All Africa Conference of Churches

* * * * * *

After their independence, many African countries soon shared a common political characteristic: one-party regimes and, quite often, dictatorial governments in which political leaders tended to grasp power for life for their personal privilege and honour. During the last thirty years, real political participation by the African people has been minimal or nonexistent.

It goes without saying that in the quest for power and prestige, the ideology of tribal or ethnic groups is often manipulated in favour of a particular political party or leader. Many internal conflicts in Africa today are due to ethnic and even religious manipulation. Citizens are invited to believe that a particular tribe or religious group is against the progress and development of the whole nation or a threat to its security. Instead of creating national unity, such radical and fundamentalist ideologies divide peoples who have been living together for ages.

The victims of injuries in Africa are not only individuals but the family. Family structure, either restricted or extended, is one of the main values common to

African cultures. Because of internal conflicts, many families either have been broken up or dispersed. The social marginalisation of rural areas and the subsequent lack of employment creates an exodus, expecially of young people, from the country towards the big towns and cities, where industry and better possibilities are apparent, but where conditions of life are rough and tough for many, especially the least qualified workers.

Only in recent years has a new wind of democracy started to blow in Africa. As a result, many countries have moved towards multiparty politics and more democratic forms of government. Many other countries, however, are still far from being on the road to real democracy. Their constitutions need revision to facilitate a more pluralistic and democratic way of government. Both ruling and opposition political parties have to learn the real meaning of democracy and acquire more concern for the common good of their nations.

It is in this context that a group of church leaders met in Nyeri, Kenya, under the sponsorship of AMECEA, the All Africa Conference of Churches and the Nairobi Peace Initiative, to discuss and exchange, in an ecumenical spirit, ideas concerning their role in peacemaking and social change in Africa. The symposium participants were convinced that Africa is absolutely in need of men and women who, filled with the peace of Christ, act as peacemakers.

The work of peacemaking is entrusted to all of Christ's disciples, women no less than men. The ministry and message entrusted to the disciples of Christ can be summed up simply as "the gospel of peace" (see Ephesians 6:15, Ephesians 2:17, Acts 10:36). This peace characterises both the messenger and his work: peace is in the subject; it is also his work.

Making peace is an active role, an active ministry. It is not sitting idly by, waiting for something to happen or for events to take place. It is not just observing from the sidelines. It is not just talking about peace.

On the contrary, making peace is promoting the activities that will render peace possible, feasible and practicable. Making peace is removing the obstacles that prevent peace from being realised. Making peace is bringing people together—often those who consider themselves "opponents," "adversaries" or "enemies." Once they are together, they can better see that they share a common humanity and have similar needs, hopes, dreams and purposes in their life on this earth. Making peace is fostering mutual dialogue—speaking and listening to one another—with the aim of arriving at a common consensus and finding mutually acceptable solutions. Making peace is the commitment to refuse to give in to violence, whether violent thoughts, words or actions. Making peace is active nonviolence.

And what is "peace"? How shall we define this precious word? There is a definition of *peace* that is very old, very venerable and very much forgotten because too often we ignore history and pass over the wisdom of our fathers. It is the definition that Saint Thomas Aquinas gave to *peace* in his *Summa Theologica*.

Peace, said Thomas Aquinas, is the "tranquillity that flows from right order." When we put right order into the structures of our society, the tranquillity that results is peace. And so we see that the right ordering that brings peace is closely connected to justice. When we put right order into our relationships at every level, beginning with the family and continuing right up to the government and the church, the calmness that comes out of this right ordering is peace. When we put right order into the dealings between clan and clan, between tribe and tribe, and between political party and political party, the tranquillity that flows from that order is peace. Thus, the participants in the symposium were challenged to discuss and find ways by which they, as religious leaders, can rightly order their relationships and deal with one another so that peaceful tranquillity will be obtained for our continent.

Today, all of Africa is in flux. Change is all around us, some of it for the good and much of it, unfortunately, for the worse. Caught up in this fresh wind of change, Africa in the 1990s is experiencing a "second independence." This move towards multiparty competition, respect for a free press and the hope of protection and promotion of human rights, calls for "a new moral culture of responsibility and a new political and economic culture of accountability and transparency."

The political and social changes that we Africans are asking for are based on our concrete experiences: years of hopes never realised, aspirations frustrated and efforts misdirected. During the five days of the symposium, its participants discussed many aspects of social change in Africa and how they challenge us as religious leaders and as the church.

There is today more political maturity in Africa than at independence. The awareness of the importance of unity and solidarity among the nations that make up the continent is more valued, and African countries are trying to help one another solve their internal conflicts through arbitration and dialogue. In this context, the presence and work of the church is respected and appreciated by African governments. The voice of the church is listened to. Many African leaders, even those who are not Christians, recognise the moral authority of the church as the conscience of human society. The church continues to be the source of much hope because of its message of love, justice and peace.

The role of the church in peacemaking and social change is strengthened by the fact that the social and political crisis in Africa questions radically the message of the gospel. As one Rwandese Jesuit says, the injustice, the unrest, the racism and the resulting hatred indicates that the church has not succeeded in planting the message of the gospel in the hearts of the people. However, the churches have now, in spite of an initial timidity and hesitation, powerfully and courageously involved themselves in the political and social interactions of the continent.

The symposium papers reproduced here place on the church's shoulders a colossal task indeed. In the face of this heavy task, let us remember that those who set out on the open sea, trusting in the Word of Christ, are not surprised or shocked by the present manifold difficulties. They see these difficulties as a sign of life, as the tension of growth.

The pangs of childbirth are much better than the stability of the graveyard.

Peter Lwaminda
Secretary-General
Association of Member Episcopal
Conferences in Eastern Africa (AMECEA)

Introduction

Hizkias Assefa and George Wachira

The Nairobi Peace Initiative (NPI), the All Africa Conference of Churches (AACC) and the Association of Member Episcopal Conferences of Eastern Africa (AMECEA) held a symposium in Kenya from 18th to 23rd July 1993. The theme of the symposium, The Role of Religious Leaders in Peacemaking and Social Change in Africa, grew out of the organising institutions' observation of the African scene over many years. Their reasoning, in organising the symposium, went as follows:

Since the end of colonialism, many African societies have been dismayed by their experience of anomalies between the promises of independence and the actual accomplishments of the post-colonial state. In many ways, the ideals of justice, liberty, democracy and economic prosperity that inspired independence struggles in many African countries have not materialised. Wars of liberation were quickly succeeded by vicious civil wars or bitter strife between various factions of former independence movements. Where there has not been civil war, societies have been plagued by brutal repression, corruption, obsession with personal power, nepotism and tribalism.

The last fifteen years have been marked by economic stagnation and, in some instances, actual decline. Some African societies are poorer and more badly governed now than they were at independence. Nature also seems to have conspired against many African states. Drought, which no doubt is related to humans' environmental degradation and expansion of the continent's deserts, is becoming a recurrent phenomenon. The continent's tremendous population growth, combined with economic decline and lack of access to good education, has compounded these problems.

Africa is increasingly associated with hunger, abject poverty, war, dictatorship and the AIDS epidemic. The continent is being marginalised or ignored more and more by the world community.

Of course, external factors have contributed greatly to these crises as well. Although Africa became nominally independent from its former colonial masters, colonialism has been replaced by neo-colonialism—more devious but equally destructive. The continent became a theatre for cold war rivalry between superpowers who fanned and exploited African internal conflicts to serve their own political, military and economic interests. Unjust international economic structures that cause significant resource flows to the richer countries, structural adjustment programmes and the debt burden all have taken their toll, impoverishing and further marginalising Africa.

Given the enormity of the problems and the astuteness required to overcome them, Africa currently seems to suffer from a great leadership void. Some of the first-generation post-colonial African leaders who founded the Organisation of African Unity (OAU) provided a continental vision that inspired Africans struggling to define their place in the global community. The generation of African leaders that followed them failed to sustain the original dreams or create their own vision of the future of the continent. Political repression, highly authoritarian and hierarchical structures, massive emigration of intellectuals, lack of civil institutions and bad role models all have contributed to this leadership void.

In the last few years, however—in the wake of what some people have come to call the "second liberation" of Africa—some religious leaders, along with a few lay leaders, have played an active role that appears to be filling the leadership void in at least two areas: addressing the crises of governance facing many countries and dealing with some of the rampant conflicts vexing the continent. In South Africa, for example, churches were in the forefront of the national and international effort to end the apartheid system through nonviolent struggle. In Zambia, Madagascar and Benin, religious leaders have played important roles in the transition from single to multiparty democracy. Kenya and Zaire have witnessed similar struggles. Church leaders in Mozambique, Liberia and Sudan have actively tried to mediate peace between the fighting forces in their respective countries or organised grassroots peacemaking efforts.

The symposium organisers were intrigued by the question of whether such experiences are indicative of an emerging pattern and whether the involvement of religious leaders signals a ray of hope for filling the leadership void at national and continental levels. Aside from the fact that the church happened to be playing an active role in social change, in many parts of Africa—where most other civil institutions (including universities, trade unions, political parties and professional associations) either have been decimated or remain underdeveloped because of repressive political systems, perpetual wars or economic crises—it is also one of the few functioning institutions. Moreover, since religious organisations and their leaders operate from a certain moral base, they invite closer examination for the reason that they might be a source of strong ethical principles that could guide the continent's process of recovery. The organisers thought it might be important to document some of the churches' experiences and bring together the leaders who have been involved in their activities, as well as some selected African scholars, to look at these processes more systematically and critically. For the purposes of manageability, the organisers decided to focus on the experiences of eastern and southern Africa as the first step in this inquiry.

In addition, the convenors hoped that the symposium might generate some useful outcomes, perhaps helping the change processes already underway by enabling church leaders to draw insight and inspiration from each other, developing norms and visions informed by African indigenous culture and ethical values that could guide social change processes and generate ideas that could be useful for launching similar inquiries and symposiums in other regions of the continent.

Although in various instances Catholics and Protestants have worked for change independently, the convenors felt strongly that the symposium should be an ecumenical venture. By bringing together major Catholic and Protestant actors—such as the AACC and AMECEA—to co-sponsor the symposium, the organisers hoped to solidify and underline the African churches' unity of purpose and provide an example for other religious and secular institutions to address their common concerns jointly in a spirit of collaboration and unity. Given the formidable obstacles to change, it is important that churches eschew some of the unhealthy competitiveness in leadership that is often observed between the two groups and pool their intellectual and material resources to foster the evolution of a continental vision for the creation of just and humane societies in Africa. The different approaches and methodologies used by denomination-based initiatives no doubt could enrich each other tremendously.

Six case studies and four conceptual papers were prepared for the symposium. The six countries chosen for the case studies were Zambia, Madagascar, Kenya, South Africa, Zaire and Mozambique. In selecting these cases, the organisers chose two that illustrated the national-convention approach, which has been used mainly in francophone countries (Zaire and Madagascar), and two (Zambia and Kenya) that illustrated the constitutional-amendment approach, which has been used mostly by anglophone countries. Mozambique and South Africa were chosen to illustrate the additional component of the church's role in peacemaking in entrenched conflicts. Six people were asked to write case studies on these countries, focusing on the following points:

1. What exactly has been taking place under the auspices of the churches with regard to major social-change processes in the country under study?

What role did the actors play? What were their objectives? What motivations drove their actions? What is the basis upon which their initiatives were taken?

2. What has been the result of these initiatives or activities? What objectives were attained? Which objectives were unattained? What obstacles were encountered?

3. Reflections on lessons learned.

In order to develop some basis for evaluating and critiquing the case studies, the organisers requested the preparation of four conceptual papers* on the following themes:

1. Assessment of the African continent since independence: Why have crises proliferated in the continent? Are these crises prevalent at the elite level as well as at the grassroots of African societies? What is the future trend in the continent? Alternative visions and scenarios?

2. Perspectives from African history, traditions, cultural heritage and worldview to help understand the African predicament and give insights about possible future directions.

3. Theological imperatives that should guide involvement of religious actors in social-change processes in Africa.

4. Paradigm for peace and reconciliation that could serve peacemaking efforts in the continent. Although the proliferation of conflicts has made meaningful social-change processes very difficult and the resolution of these conflicts is a pre- or corequisite for effective change, do the philosophy and methodology of reconciliation provide insight into how other change processes outside the arena of open conflict ought to be conducted? If so, how?

The conceptual papers and case studies were presented at the symposium, which was held in Nyeri over the course of six days. Afterwards, the authors had the opportunity to revise their papers, and this book presents their work. The participants' conclusions and recommendations also are presented as Appendices I and II.

As will become evident to the reader, the case studies were written from different vantage points and approach the above questions differently. The

---

* Symposium participant Jesse Mugambi later developed some points from an informal discussion into a fifth paper, which is reproduced here as Chapter 3.

Zairean case study is written from the perspective of a Zairean pastor and scholar living abroad; the writer of the Kenyan case study has studied and worked closely with the church in Kenya but writes as an outside observer, even though she was involved in some of the recorded events; and the South African and Madagascan cases were written by church actors who not only had a very close view of what transpired, but also had a hand in the events (they both worked with the national council of churches in their respective countries, the former as head of a critical department and the latter as General-Secretary).

The Zambian and Mozambican cases were, however, written from somewhat personal perspectives by people who were centrally involved. In the Zambian case, the account—which focuses mostly on the Kaunda years—reflects the prevailing association between the writer and former President Kaunda. The writers of the Mozambican case were also personally involved, in this case as initiators and mediators in the peace process. Needless to say, each vantage point brings its own strengths and limitations with regard to objectivity or richness of detail.

Meeting the objectives of the symposium undoubtedly is an ongoing process. The organisers believe that to fully catalyse the generation of new visions and new directions towards a more hopeful and humane political, social and economic system in Africa—the larger motive for the symposium—will take continued systematic reflection and commitment. We view this book as a small first step towards this reflection process.

I

The Crisis of Neo-colonialism in Africa and the Contemporary Democratic Challenge

Kwesi Prah

The contemporary African crisis has deepened with time and assumed increasingly tragic proportions. Africa is the stepchild of the human family and holds the largest share of the wretched of the earth.

For centuries, as V. G. Kiernan points out in *The Lords of Humankind*, "an aura of servitude" has clung to the image of Africans. Centuries of Arab and European slavery and the social instability that it engendered, lack of technological advancement and general cultural recession in Africa have blinded humankind to the fact that the Egyptian civilisation of antiquity was essentially African, that *Homo sapiens*—humankind—by available evidence, has African origins, and that much of the history and socio-cultural development of humans as culture-creating beings, especially in the early stages, is, indeed, African history. Writing in 1967, one Western observer made the following remarks:

> It is only ten years since what has become known as the era of African independence began, with the advent of Kwame Nkrumah's Ghana. This emergence of a people so long enslaved and dominated by other nations aroused a warm, sometimes perhaps a conscience-stricken enthusiasm in the world generally. A new day seemed to have dawned for an Africa which, through its sufferings, would give much of value to the rest of the world. The new African leaders were listened to with respect, and their early attempts to establish governments and societies suited to their traditions and aspirations were watched with sympathetic admiration. The advanced countries regarded the assistance they gave to Africa not merely as a duty, but almost as a privilege. All this has drastically changed. A succession of coups [revealed] tribal divisions and corruption on a scale even pessimists had not foreseen. (Taylor, 1967)[1]

Today in Africa, potable water and decent sanitation are beyond the economic reach of the overwhelming majority of the African people, and a good number sleep hungry.

Health data indicate that Africans today have the poorest health and the highest death rate in the entire world. The pandemic AIDS has, since the 1980s, become the most dangerous and ominous threat to the health and well-being of Africans.

Unemployment and underemployment have become ubiquitous features of African societies. Most African countries are caught up in spiralling inflation. For those who are fortunate to find some employment, wages are invariably inadequate for keeping body and soul together, much less maintaining a family. Comparatively, Africans have the lowest incomes in the world. In real terms, their purchasing power has been in steady decline since the beginning of the independence era; migrant workers today have little or nothing to send home to the dependents they have left behind, while for decades, labour migration has shredded the fabric of family life and led to the proliferation of impoverished female-headed households in many parts of the continent. With little capital to attract labour and the steady decline of rural production, there has been a steady flow of migrants from rural areas to urban areas during the last decades. This trend has increased as the decline in rural commodity prices has accelerated. For the overwhelming proportion of the African citizenry, obtaining the minimum number of calories needed to sustain life poses a problem on a daily basis.

In urban areas, the masses of rural migrants end up in deplorable shanty towns which are to be found in all major African towns and cities. One of the most striking characteristics of African urban life is the enormous contrast between the living conditions of the elites and the masses. In the urban slums and shanty towns that house the majority of the population, people live cheek-to-jowl in structures pieced together from material as crude as cardboard and sheet metal to plastic and parts of packing cases.

In rural areas, land degradation, deforestation and destruction of wildlife are rampant. The pressures of population increase on available resources escalate by the day, while food production steadily declines throughout Africa and desertification rapidly encroaches on many parts of the continent. African economies are hardly growing; in most instances, they are stagnating or retrogressing. With the exception of a few countries, population growth rates are galloping at an ever-increasing pace, leading to deterioration in the quality of life.

The Neo-colonial Axis

The dreary scenario depicted above stands in sharp contrast with what Africans hoped for at the onset of the independence era. Indeed, there was a feeling of triumph and hope that Africa was emerging into the mainstream of the world community at independence. The end of colonialism was assumed to have ushered African countries into a period of national development and economic and political assertiveness on the international platform. Within a decade of Sudanese independence (gained in 1956), the euphoria had begun to subside. By the end of the 1960s, it was becoming clear that, in the words of René Dumont, "*Afrique noire est mal partie.*" Social and economic development was increasingly becoming a mirage.

Regarding the hopes of the African masses at the beginning of the independence period, Gideon Were (1983:2) has remarked quite rightly that

> to the masses it must have meant the end of hard times and uncertainties, and the beginning of the golden age. At last land, food, employment, social justice, liberty and happiness would become a reality. Bread and butter would no longer be a permanent source of anxiety and tension. No doubt educational and health facilities would now be improved radically in quality and quantity.

Both Were and Ajayi (1982) agree that independence meant different things to different social groups.[2] This was to be expected. The existential conditions of different socio-economic groups present correspondingly different life opportunities. Certainly the African elites have fared better than the masses.

Three decades later, a pervasive mood of gloom and foreboding has clouded the people's hope for betterment. Poverty, corruption, mismanagement, excessive human-rights abuses, dictatorship and militarism have helped to spawn war on an ever-growing scale throughout the continent.

In the post-independence era, Sudan, Chad, Djibouti, Niger, Mali, Uganda, Rwanda, Somalia, Angola, Mozambique, Ethiopia, Liberia and Sierra Leone have been or are caught up in full-blown wars. Senegal, Togo, South Africa, Mauritania, Kenya and Zaire are edging precariously towards possible armed conflict. The latter list is likely to enlarge as new tensions related to current change processes arise. Warlordism of various types has emerged in some parts of Africa. As Richard Gott put it in a recent issue of the *Guardian Weekly*, in many parts of Africa, "political control, in so far as it still exists, is maintained by gangs of armed men, answerable to no one but themselves." The various conflicts and tensions exacerbate the economic difficulties of African countries and prevent social and economic development by ruining their modest infrastructures.

Within the last decade, various factors have converged to create pressure throughout the continent for elected, representative and accountable government. But the process has, in most instances, been undermined by vote-rigging, vote-buying, media monopoly, manipulation and other unethical practices. One result of the many sham elections held in Africa in the last decade has been the ironical return to power, through the agency of the ballot box, of tinpot dictators seeking legitimacy for their continued rule.

Were (1983:2) observes that "it is within Africa's competence to banish hunger, poverty, ignorance, disease, insecurity and autocracy." Throughout the continent, overcoming these social ills is a fervent wish of many. But "[do] their leaders have the will, vision, courage and commitment to lead them across today's wasteland to the green pastures that lie on the other side?" The underpinnings of the answer to this question lie in the structure of African society and can be understood in conjunction with an appreciation of the historical heritage of the contemporary state in Africa.

Africans are not genetically greedier or more corrupt, nepotistic, tribalistic or chauvinistic than the rest of the human race. We are neither lazier nor less capable of creating and developing our cultures as total systems.[3] The reasons for our apparent inability therefore must be sought in the conditions that have created, permitted and supported the culture of underdevelopment, or what I call the "neo-colonial axis."

To attribute the African malaise solely to external factors, as some are apt to do, would certainly be erroneous. In other words, the blame for Africa's woes should not be attributed solely to the machinations of outsiders, as though Africans were incapable of escaping their unfavourable intentions, willful or otherwise. While such arguments are easily disputed, it is important to point out that the structure of the contemporary African state within which attitudes, values and policies are formed bears very strongly the marks of its colonial pedigree in economic, social, political and cultural senses.

In Renato Constantino's view,

> We see our present with as little understanding as we view our past because aspects of the past which could illumine the present have been concealed from us. This concealment has been effected by a systematic process of mis-education characterised by a thoroughgoing inculcation of colonial values and attitudes; a process which could not have been so effective had we not been denied access to the truth and to part of our written history. As a consequence, we have become a people without a sense of history. We accept the present as given, bereft of historicity. Because we have so little comprehension of our past, we have no appreciation of its meaningful interrelation with the present. (Meszaros, 1978:1)

Constantino's words were primarily directed to the Filipino experience, but they are quite relevant to the situation in Africa. Ngugi wa Thiong'o (1986:16) makes a similar observation when he points out that the most important area of colonial domination "was the mental universe of the colonised, the control, through culture, of how people perceived themselves and their relationship to the world. Economic and political control can never be complete or effective without mental control." Colonialism may reproduce the culture of the coloniser in the mind of the colonised, but because it is grafted onto a different root, an organic unity is never achieved. The colonised person is essentially a mimic, lacking the sort of autonomous creativity that the coloniser derives from his or her culture.

During the colonial era, Africans were treated as minors in the organisation and running of their societies. The prime object of colonialism was the exploitation and use of the colonial territory and its peoples primarily to boost the prosperity and interests of the mother country. While the colonisers rationalised this purpose as a benevolent and moral "civilizing mission" conceived as the "white man's burden," in practice it de-nationalised the colonised and endeavoured to mould the African into a person happy and even "proud" of being colonised—and therefore accessible to the wider economic and political intentions of the colonial power. In this, colonialism was successful to a considerable degree. As Lord Lugard (1923:618) the British proconsul, put it, the colonisers were "bringing to the dark places of the earth, the abode of barbarism and cruelty, the torch of culture and progress, while ministering to the material needs of our own civilisation."

When we consider the insensitive and cynical arrogance of colonial ideologues, this should be done with an appreciation of the acceleration and development of the systems of production and the advancing social relations that the establishment of Western society in Africa brought. The colonial economic system, geared towards exploitation and extraction of raw materials and agricultural produce, affected land tenure and the rural population either by expropriating the land of the African peasantry and creating large export-crop plantations or by subordinating peasant farming and petty-commodity production to the interests of the international market. Pre-capitalist rural producers, disengaged from their traditional production systems, were drawn mainly into mining or into the emergent plantation and other farming economies as wage earners. During the early years of colonialism, forced labour was common practice among all the colonial powers. It ranged from the cruel excesses of Leopold of Belgium's Congo Free State; Portuguese practices ranging from slavery to forced labour to free labour in Angola, Mozambique, Guinea-Bissau and Cape Verde; German exploitation and atrocities in Tanganyika, Togo and South-West Africa, where genocide against the Herero has haunted the German conscience to the present day; and British exploitation of forced labour, particularly when preoccupied with armed counterinsurgency operations, as a matter of policy. The suppression of the Nuer in the 1930s was the last stage of this period in British colonial history. The introduction of poll and hut taxes and passes during the early colonial era was calculated to force Africans into the labour market. In areas under settler colonialism, large-scale expropriation of land from Africans produced a mass of landless people who became a ready source of labour for the system. These processes inherently involved penetration of the cash nexus into societies that previously were monetised only to a limited extent. It created the growth and expansion of wage labour, previously relatively small in scale and limited to coastal ports and settlements where Western trade and influence were long established. The net effect of the emergence of colonial economics in terms of labour, however, was to alienate the African peasant from the means of production. (Prah, 1991:52)

The African peasant was drawn away from producing household and other social goods to produce for the international market. This process continued throughout the colonial period and has steadily undermined food production to the present day. Ironically, Africans now produce what they do not consume and consume what they do not produce. If wages under colonial (or neo-colonial) cash-crop production were commensurate with returns in terms of expended labour and time, the African producer would have been in a position to purchase his food and meet other needs. But international terms of trade have steadily deteriorated to the detriment of the African producer of cash crops and raw materials. This decline has continued throughout the post-independence period and is largely responsible for the increasing poverty of African societies.

Food aid to Africa is currently said to have contributed to the collapse of peasant producers' economic base. Starving Africa, in emergency situations, certainly needs food assistance, but its wider effects are often more than meets the eye. An article in a recent issue of *The Economist* (1993) points out that "all too often in Africa, outsiders give charity with one hand and deliver a slap with the other. Farmers are usually the victims. Many African farmers who are helped by Western aid agencies to improve their crops find that they cannot sell what they grow because the local markets are swamped by cheap Western imports." At the same time; trade barriers exclude many African products from Western markets; the rules of the international economic game are heavily biased against African interests.

The scorching effects of social impoverishment make people in public office, who are expected to be custodians of the public's wealth, prone to avariciousness. Increasingly, many people see public office as a chance to get rich as quickly as possible. Sadly, in many countries, public opinion has become so warped that those who do not get rich in office through corruption are regarded as deviant. Corruption has become the norm in almost all African countries. Probity, accountability and transparency in the conduct of public affairs may be popular slogans but are little practised in contemporary Africa.

The leaders who took the reins of power at independence displaced the earlier group of traditional rulers who had, in the later stages of colonialism, shared voice for African opinion and leadership with the Westernised and often professional elites created by colonialism as tools and intermediaries for the colonial affair. These elites served mainly as administrators, and as the culture of Western dominance established itself, they came to be regarded as links to Western power. Their influence was questioned in the post-World War II period by a new, Westernised mass of smallholders and small producers, clerks and petty bureaucrats, shopkeepers, teachers and other low-ranking officials. They demanded freedom from colonialism and staked their claim on the universal franchise. This marked the beginning of the ascendancy of a new lower-middle-class group as a critical social mass. This group saw popular enfranchisement as the immediate political goal of wider democratic institutionalisation in societies penetrated by colonial economics. Its members became the centre of a populist amalgam that drove the independence movement in co-operation with the lower strata of wage labourers in both rural and urban areas and with the wider peasantry.

In hindsight, the members of this broad coalition of social groups and interests benefited differently from the fruits of independence. In most of post-colonial Africa, the upper echelons of the native bureaucracy became the prime beneficiaries of the new order. With few material resources from the past, its members prospered on the privileges of office, with many using their positions for private benefit. Some petty merchants and entrepreneurs grew in influence in the post-independence period, but in most instances they were fairly weak in their ability to marshal and pool resources on a scale that could enable them to stand in clear competition with the operations of larger, overseas-based enterprises. The wider mass of working and labouring people have not, on the whole, seen much improvement in their quality of life. Although in areas such as health, and particularly in education, their offspring have benefited from the expansion of facilities (often poor in quality) throughout the continent, their numbers have grown phenomenally while their living conditions have deteriorated. The base of rural producers has also shrunk, and over the decades many have moved into wage employment, especially in the urban areas.

In country after country, as the independence train rolled on, the social and economic gap between the well-to-do and the poor increased. The elites who have served as a reference group for the wider mass of the society have tended to dispose themselves as largely Westernised and culturally alienated. Unfortunately, this Westernisation has excluded a sufficiently creative impulse to fundamentally transform African society and provide the prosperity all aspired to. If the wider society has been the victim of the malaise of contemporary Africa, the elites, often crudely imitative of Western values and approaches, have featured as the visible culprits. The cultural mimicry of this group had been the butt of ridicule by late 19th century and early 20th century African nationalists (including Pixley Seme, Omoniyi, Casely-Hayford, Attoh-Ahuma and Kobina-Sekyi), and the faithful reproduction of the culturally captive African continues even today.

The African elites inherited state structures that were principally unreformed in comparison with their colonial progenitors. This is particularly true of systems of production, distribution and exchange within African societies and of the way the local system relates to world centres of production and wealth. The colonial roots, character and form of societal organisation have been largely preserved. Herein lies the genesis of neo-colonialism as a historically derived form. Neo-colonial structures, abetted by local elites, provide the basic framework for the crises of African countries. The phenomenon of neo-colonialism underscores the limited sovereignty of African states and their dependence on centres of international economic and political power. As former Tanzanian President Julius Nyerere (1976:4) indicated, the reality of neo-colonialism

> quickly becomes obvious to a new African government which tries to act on economic matters in the interest of national development, and for the betterment of its own masses. For such a government immediately discovers that it inherited the power to make laws, to direct the civil service, to deal with foreign governments and so on, but it did not inherit effective power over economic developments in its own country. Indeed it often discovers that there is no such thing as a national economy at all. Instead, there exists in its land various economic activities which are owned by people outside its jurisdiction, which are directed at external needs, and which are run in the interests of external economic powers. If deliberate countervailing action is not taken, external economic forces determine the nature of the economy a country shall have, what investment shall be undertaken, and where, and what kind of development.[4]

Experience has demonstrated that African countries have had little scope for transforming their economies, whatever "deliberate countervailing action" they may have attempted. The neo-colonial relationship is reflected in all areas of social life in Africa. As a system, it is supervised by the local elites, but is ultimately dominated by the interests of the metropolitan powers of the world. Regarding "aid," Kwame Nkrumah, in *Africa Must Unite*, expressed the view that aid "must in fact come out of the trading profits made from forcing down the prices of primary products bought from the African countries and raising the cost of the finished goods they are obliged to take in exchange."

Neo-colonialism does not provide room for development that is emancipatory and affords scope for bettering the quality of life of the majority. As a developmental paradigm, more than a quarter of a century after independence, it has definitely failed to transform Africa in line with the aspirations proclaimed loudly at independence. Instead, it is a fetter on African emancipation. The map of the African continent is the most mosaic-like of all the world's continents, it consists of a patchwork of borders, two-thirds of which are straight lines hurriedly drawn without regard for the inclusion or exclusion of nationalities along historical and cultural lines. The continent is largely made up of unviable economic and political entities for whom, in a sense, independence means little beyond a national anthem and a flag.

The development of Africa will require transformation of the nature and structure of neo-colonialism as an economic, political, social and cultural phenomenon. Greater cultural selectivity and more autonomously derived processes of adaptation need to be encouraged, so that Africans build on their cultural heritage, borrowing selectively from outside, rather than picking only elements of their own cultural heritage and pasting them onto a borrowed cultural base.

Hurrah for Democracy

After decades of suppression of popular opinion by unrepresentative African governments, one-party rule and military dictatorships, the past few years have witnessed pressure for exercise of the popular franchise with a resurgence reminiscent of the period immediately preceding independence. In one country after another, Africans are demanding the right to elect their own rulers and representatives, and the right to reject the leaders they elect if their conduct negates the terms of their mandates. This rebirth of the voice of the masses in recent years has caught the older dominant groups by surprise, and many are resisting the demands to open up society. These demands have generated a great deal of public debate and demonstrations in countries where for a long period the only displays of mass opinion have been invariably orchestrated and fine-tuned by ruling regimes more interested in prescribing opinion than listening to it.

Citizens of African countries seem to have realised that effective development cannot exclude the organisation of society along democratic lines. However, a number of points need to be brought into focus in this respect. First, the concept of democracy and the current process seem to be too heavily informed by Western formulas with little or no relevance to the cultural basis of African societies. Second, Western powers that had supported many of the ruthless dictatorships in Africa until the end of the cold war recently seem to have revised their political prescriptions and are currently advancing the case for multiparty political systems in Africa. But multipartyism cannot in itself guarantee a democratic culture. A whole array of prerequisites are crucial to the success of such systems. Some of these are an open and free press, political tolerance, regularisation of the system, free association, and a transparent rule of law. It is the firm institutionalisation of these practices that enhances and enriches the culture of democracy. But it is most important that democratic political systems in Africa are properly adapted to the continent's culture and society.

In terms of historical timing, Africa's current democratic endeavour in the final decade of this century has set the pace for the establishment of new and responsive institutions. This is a time of dramatic change and flux. Several military and civilian one-party systems have crumbled and given way to multiparty democracy, which is more natural to the political aspirations of the African people at this point in time. In establishing the right conditions for democracy, Africa faces an enormous task. The growing conviction is that without it, real development cannot take place. Some arguments that must be put to final rest, however, are that Africa is not suited for democracy, or that Africans are not ready for democracy. Such views assume that democracy is essentially a Western form for which Africa is too "backward."

Democracy should be understood more profoundly as a historical process than as a specific form. It is essentially an institutionalised approach to decision-making geared towards the provision of choices or alternatives for the constituent members of a group in matters affecting their interests. It should also provide scope for the prevalence of consensual, collective or majoritarian opinion that respects and acknowledges minority interests. This formula clearly diverges from the narrow and limited contemporary formulations closely tied to Western liberal democracy. This latter narrow and particularistic form refers principally to democratic theory and practice as it figures in the selection and placement of the ruling party and government (or its sub-units) in the state. The extent and degree to which democratic practice guides social interaction and all types of decision-making is a measure of "democratisation" in a society. But what is perhaps crucial is the social unit in which the democratic right is ultimately vested and its comparative significance in relation to other clearly institutionalised, interest-articulating groups and structures in the society (Prah, 1993). If today "democracy" assumes universal adult franchise, we are reminded that it has not always been so. In a report that appeared some years ago in *Development Dialogue* (Third System Project, 1981:78), the authors wrote that

> democracy in its conventional sense (not that of people's power) was born in the political sphere and accommodated itself very well with, for instance, slavery. Even in the western formal democracies whose achievements, whatever their limits,

cannot be underestimated, democracy usually stops at the gates of the factory, the mine, the plantation, the school. People's power requires that it penetrates these spaces as well.

As I have elsewhere argued, in pre-capitalist Africa, structures such as lineage, clan, ward, ethnicity or their subsets were significant in making government and its selection processes routine. Many gerontocratic institutions such as age, sets were incorporated into the operational democratic principles historically relevant to pre-capitalist society—e.g. the *kgotla/khotla, pitso, leshotlo* and *phuthego* among the Sotho-Tswana-speaking peoples and, among the Akan of Ghana, *aberto*, or voting for purposes of election. The popular Western-inspired myth of arbitrary rule in pre-colonial Africa cannot stand up to the test of hard anthropological evidence (Third System Project, 1981:78).

Throughout the colonial period, the implantation of novel colonial institutions steadily undermined the significance of these older traditional ones. Today, while the effects of traditional institutions on the organisation of social life have been severely weakened, they have not been totally annihilated, especially among rural and more tradition-bound African communities.

There is neither anything inherently un-African about democracy nor anything undemocratic about Africans. Banning or throttling voices opposed to ruling regimes is not part and parcel of African societal make-up. Even though the search for democratic forms of organisation is now firmly on the political agenda of our times, ultimately democratic success depends partly on the extent to which institutional structures for democratic practice respond to sociological specificities. In Africa today, justification of the single-party state with the rationale that it represents a natural unit of the citizenry and reduces conflict does not hold up under close examination. The only way to achieve authoritarian single-party rule is to forcefully impose it; to pretend that it can be done otherwise is to falsify the reality of political life in Africa.

Few conceptual legacies from Western antiquity have been of such political consequence as the democratic system. Now, as the states of Africa and other continents are exploring this concept and its adaptability to their own historico-cultural conditions, it is worth remembering that even in the Western world, democracy remains a changing and deepening phenomenon. Europeans are still agonising over it more than two millenniums after their ancient example. Indeed, not all that long ago Nazi Germany, Mussolini's Italy, Franco's Spain or Salazar's Portugal could hardly have vied for the designation "democracy." And until recently, even those inveterate enemies of majority rule in South Africa claimed to be democrats. Meanwhile, "multipartyism" has become not only the latest addition to the many meanings the word *democracy* has acquired since the

5th century B.C., but also the yardstick with which recent developments in Africa are assessed.

But to view developments in the fledgling countries of Africa from an overly formalistic perspective is to leave out the indispensable will to be tolerant of the political outlook of others. The genuine commitment of the African people to conditions in which competing interests, opinions and priorities can contest equitably could hardly have been demonstrated more eloquently than with the enormous sacrifices ordinary people everywhere on the continent have made in pursuit of this end at various junctures. It is now time to take the process one step further, learning from the mistakes and weaknesses of the past and respecting African values and traditions in the process.

While the will for democratic dispensation undoubtedly exists everywhere in Africa, this in itself is not enough. There is, in addition, the need for adequate and appropriate institutions, established and respected procedures, accepted conventions and forms of social conduct through which democratic practice can be consistently implemented in the running of a country. An honest commitment to democracy in reality may not bring the desired results where vested interests, possibly legitimised by corrupted notions of "tradition," still control key instruments of the state. Practices such as one-party rule and queuing behind preferred election candidates (rather than voting by secret ballot) have been justified in the name of "tradition." Likewise, the best institutions and operational rules of democratic organisation will amount to little if politicians do not use them in good faith. While the field for the exercise of democracy needs to be kept level at all times, the ground also would need to be accepted and respected by all parties. This indeed is the only realistic way of consolidating the process of democratisation in Africa.

To do this, Africans should be fully aware of the need to consistently uphold the tenets of their constitutions, ensure that the underlying principles are well respected by all, and make a conscious effort, both in and out of their parliaments, to nurture and deepen the culture of tolerance and pluralism in all social transactions. Any tendency towards arbitrary and undemocratic rule should also be exposed. Societal understanding that no one party at all times has a monopoly on the truth must be implicit.

The Future

Africa's present social and economic crises have bred a mood of pessimism. Even though there does not as yet seem to be a light at the end of the tunnel, this mood of pessimism is not altogether justified. Africa is not doomed to failure and underdevelopment; in the broad sweep of time and, like the rest of humankind, it is on a march forward, although periods of stagnation and retrogression may occur. What is currently required is that Africans deduce the appropriate lessons from their past mistakes.

The central lesson from past experience is that the unity of the African people is basic and crucial to the progress, emancipation and redemptive development of the continent. The partitioning of Africa a century ago created grossly artificial units heedless of the continent's historical and cultural affinities. This led to distortion of the historical and cultural autonomy of Africans within the larger human family, creating new sets of identities legitimised by colonial powers. Colonial states were redesignated as "nation-states" as they passed on into independence. Ethnic loyalties and affinities were regarded as atavistic and brushed under the carpet in favour of the "unity" of these so-called nation-states, whose only historical validity lay in the intentions of the former colonial powers.

While ethnicity cannot in itself form the basis of modern social organisation, its reality and hold over African people cannot be denied. Acknowledging and providing this reality with a democratic form, however limited, that meets the demands of peace and collective prosperity in our times seems more sensible than denying its reality in the face of the numerous problems, from civil wars to "tribal" patronage, that prevail today. The acknowledgment of ethnolinguistic and cultural realities in Africa should be accompanied by acceptance of the fact that people have to relate in economic, political, cultural and social realms across borders. Such relations would enable Africans to lose some of the rigidity the present borders impose on people who from time immemorial have been linked. Africans need to be more African than Ghanaian, Senegalese, Sudanese, South African, Ethiopian or Kenyan, identities that are at most only a century old. This would mean developing democratic cross-border institutions that, while limiting the powers of the present states in some instances, provide a wider umbrella of African unity under which individual ethnic loyalties and affinities become minor drops in the wider ocean of Africanness or African nationhood.

Under the structure of a wider union of African states, no single ethnic group or cluster of groups can achieve dominance. The political significance of any one ethnic group pales when linked to scores of such groups. African unity therefore will provide a better perspective on ethnicity. In turn, a proper appreciation of the historical and cultural identity of Africans would offer a better premise for African development. The role of African languages is of specific importance in this respect.

African languages straddle borders in every single country in the continent. If these languages are to be developed as a way of reaching the masses in the overall development effort, interstate co-operation is necessary. Those languages that are proximate and mutually intelligible could, with scientific research, be unified as written forms. A united Africa, the moment it comes into being, would become a respectable force and voice in the councils of humanity, instead of the multiplicity of feeble, ineffectual voices with which Africans presently take part in the affairs of the human community.

Opposition to such interstate African institutions may possibly arise from entrenched local interests bound up with the post-colonial or neo-colonial state. The elites are most likely to resist the surrender of some existing state powers in favour of African unity. But if such interests are afforded wider scope in an enlarged, united Africa, this should go a long way towards offsetting the elites' perceived loss of social clout and influence. Kwame Nkrumah and Chiekh Anta Diop long advocated such approaches.

If African unity were undertaken in a carefully phased fashion (as with the European Community), progress in this direction would gradually be registered. All interstate co-operative ventures in Africa need to be supported. Free movement of African labour and capital accumulated by Africans needs to be encouraged. African entrepreneurs need to be helped to pool their resources instead of carrying on as ineffectual penny capitalists, unable to compete with large international financial interests. Such co-operation should not be restricted to purely economic endeavours.

A great deal of responsibility rests with civil society in Africa. Previously, during the heyday of military and one-party rule, state terror and repression had cowed civil society into silence, but today the climate is fast changing. Churches in Africa and their leaders are everywhere more consistently attesting that *Vox Populi, Vox Dei*. Women's organisations, free trade unions and a range of non-governmental organisations are standing up to be counted in the effort to bring greater democracy and development to the African masses. Civil society must maintain a watchdog position; it must refuse to be silenced any longer.

The churches in Africa have a crucial role to play in this crusade. They must, through their leadership, serve as the uncompromising conscience of society in the realm of democracy and human rights. This is surely in keeping with the tenets and foundations of Christian lore; if the church fails to speak on behalf of the voiceless, it will be difficult for it to maintain credibility in the eyes of its constituency. Here again, pan-African church efforts would strengthen issues of principle concerning democracy, human rights and development and vest them with greater authority.

Africa's prospects for the very near future may be dim, but its long-term prospects are good. In June 1987, the Beyond Hunger Project organised a workshop in Kericho, Kenya, for 19 participants, mainly African academics in a variety of disciplines. The participants, asked to come up with a vision of Africa's future, concluded that the present crisis is only a phase in the continent's evolution, a crisis that in due course will pass, giving "rise to higher achievements only if its leaders and its people dare to dream, to work imaginatively at their dreams and to strive to translate these dreams through research and action to concrete achievements" (Mabogunja, 1990).

Africans can only prosper under conditions of peace. Peace, however, will be elusive as long as the issues of rights, tolerance, democracy, justice and freedom at both the collective and individual levels are not addressed. But democracy, being more a principle than a specific form, is adaptable to historical and societal conditions. Africa has experienced the limits of "democracy" under neo-colonialism for more than a quarter of a century. Its peace and development requires the structural negation of neo-colonialism in all spheres of social life. Solutions that do not fly in the face of the culture of the African people but enlist that culture as the adaptable basis for democracy and economic and socio-cultural development must be sought.

Africa remains the most mineral-rich continent in the world. A good deal of its agricultural potential has gone to waste, but not irredeemably. One encouraging feature of contemporary Africa is the fact that many people have acquired education, skills and insight during the last few decades. These are bound to serve the continent well once favourable conditions obtain. With motivated and palpably beneficial application of human creativity, the African people will certainly rise to the challenge of democracy and development, the cry of the masses in our times.

Notes

1. The author makes other points worth noting in terms of the cynicism and lapse into stock European prejudice that they reveal: "Many in the world outside Africa, particularly in the developed nations, conclude that independence came all too soon, that (to use the all-too-popular phrase) 'the Africans are not ready to rule themselves'. More partisan critics allege that they will never be able to run their countries at all, in terms of Western efficiency."

2. Were (1983) draws attention to Ajayi's identification of four groups to whom independence meant different things. Ajayi (1982) outlines the following categories: the intellectuals, the traditional elite, the masses and the new political elite. While the attitudes attributed to these groups are credible, the selection appears to be rather idiosyncratic. I prefer a less overlapping socio-economic categorisation.

3. While Were makes well the point that there is nothing inherent in our make-up that predisposes us to such weaknesses, he is analytically unable to scrutinise the phenomenon. He writes, "Though corruption is an ancient and universal social evil, there is a clear distinction between the response of African leadership and the reaction of other nations to the same disease. It is this distinction and, in particular, the African leadership's attitude to corruption which makes the African situation at once desperate and potentially dangerous" (1983:9). This is a rather circuitous analysis. Were points collectively to poverty and lack of resources, poor leadership qualities, African traditions of gift giving, the disintegration of traditional morality and, in addition to these, the development in the colonial era of a desire to loot colonial governments as important causative factors. These factors are certainly relevant, but the attitudes and values, and the conditions that spawn them, are created and sustained by socio-cultural conditions.

4. See also K. Nkrumah, *Neo-Colonialism: The Last Stages of Imperialism* (London: Panaf Books, 1965).

References

Lugard, F.D. 1923. *The Dual Mandate in British Tropical Africa*. London: Frank Cass.

Mabogunja, A.L. 1990. "Foreword." In *Beyond Hunger in Africa*, edited by C. Achebe *et al*. Nairobi: East African Educational Publishers.

Meszaros, I. 1978. *Neo-colonial Identity and Counter-Consciousness*. London: Merlin Press.

Nkrumah, K. 1965. *Neo-Colonialism: The Last Stage of Imperialism*. London: Panaf Books.

Nyerere, J. K. 1976. "The Process of Liberation." Address to the Convocation of Ibadan University (Nigeria), 17 November, 1976.

"Overstuffing Africa." *The Economist* (May 8, 1993).

Prah, K.K. 1993. "Understanding Democracy and Governance in Africa, Past and Present: The Relevance of Anthropology." Paper prepared for the Democracy in Africa Reconsidered Project. Mimeo.

———. 1991. "The Notion of Cultural Blockage and Some Issues of Science and Technology Concerning the African Peasantry." In *Culture, Gender, Science and Technology in Africa*, edited by K. K. Prah. Windhoek: Harp Publications.

Taylor, D. 1967. *Africa: The Portrait of Power*. London: Robert Hale.

Thiong'o, Ngugi wa. 1986. *Decolonising the Mind: The Politics of Language in African Literature*. Nairobi: East African Educational Publishers.

Third System Project. 1981. "Alternatives for Survivors: A Report from the Third System Project." *Development Dialogue* 1:78.

Were, G. 1983. *Leadership and Underdevelopment in Africa*. Nairobi: Oxford University Press.

2

Good Governance for Development
Perspectives from the African Traditional Cultural Heritage

Timothy G. Kiogora

> Anyone who reflects on our traditional ways of speaking about morality is bound to be struck by the preoccupation with human welfare. What is morally good is what befits a human being; it is what is decent. What brings dignity, respect, contentment, prosperity, joy to [man] and his community. What is morally bad is what brings misery, misfortune and disgrace.
>
> *E. O. Iheoma*
> Nigeria

The Great Historic Alienation

To attempt to reconstruct life as it was at the village level[1] for many Africans is not, contrary to what some have come to believe, such a difficult task. Those of us who have grown up in the African rural milieu can relate easily to the simplicity, openness and creativity of village life. People were born and grew up in familiar surroundings and around kith and kin. "Strangers" from time to time were incorporated into the village structure through marriage and sheer human necessity. The rest of the world seemed to pass by as village talk was consumed with issues of subsistence, normal formation, continuity and the intricate communal obligations of life. Birth, childhood, adolescence, adulthood, parenthood and old age—even death and the spirit world—were some of the high-water marks in a person's earthly journey.[2] Life was good or bad depending on one's actions and ability to play fair with all significant others.

At the village level, a common general education was available for all and revolved around being a good person. This formal education was an absolute requirement. Another form of education was also available free of charge: how to make a living. Whereby village folk learned, as they went along with others, how to raise animals, among other things. This was informal education, and, again, it was required of all. Most social-ethical rules were built to protect these two types of education for life.

The village-level ethos is a living influence on modern Africa. In most rural areas, these approaches to life are still evident or in the subconscious minds of many. They even continue to influence urban dwellers (witness the very large "informal sector" in African city slums, a type of village).

Africa refuses to die. We live on, and the world seems to pass us by—except, of course, that this time we must be aware of the consequences. But few will dispute the fact that, for the most part, rural African folk live their lives at a different political, economic and even philosophical level than their governments have wished for them. They live without much money or political education and, happily, without insecurity and perennial worries of "economic collapse."[3] They raise their children (sometimes many) and remain suspicious of the true intentions of modern government's institutions, its schools included. Could this critical disarticulation of visions be at the root of Africa's lack of material and moral development? What has government to do with the meaning, purpose and direction of life for Africa's masses?

On colonial rule

African pre-colonial history may not have been free of conflict and the displacement of people during inter-ethnic wars, but clearly, the emergence of colonisation as a determined, organised European project in Africa produced a greater level of alienation than was hitherto known in the continent. Colonial rule in the 19th century superimposed a bureaucratic structure of foreign origins on Africa complete with religious, political, economic and legal ramifications for the daily lives of Africans. There was an immediate loss of communication between the old and new structures.

In East Africa, colonial administration, largely due to its pompous and heavy-handed nature, earned itself the nickname *serikali* (in Swahili, *siri* means "secret" and *kali* means "cruel"). Thus government was both secretive and cruel in its dealings with Africans. To this day, we still refer to government as *serikali* in East Africa, which in itself shows the continued distance between government and the governed. When people's rights are violated by those in power without concern or accountability, when taxes and fees are levied on poor people without a clear explanation, and when decrees must be obeyed without question, then we have *serikali*.

Disruption of routine village life, abuse of human rights and the resulting general despondency, quite apart from economic dependence on cash crops and external political and economic control, were the main legacies of colonial rule in Africa (Ake, 1981). Needless to say, the basic African cultural linkages to economics and political life were greatly eroded, although not entirely destroyed, by colonialism. Like loose, weak teeth, African cultural resources could not chew what Africa was being fed. We are now suffering from "indigestion" of all kinds.

On political independence

Looking back over the last thirty years or so of the so-called political independence of many former colonies of various European powers, the African record is mixed. On the one hand, it was necessary, even at the emotional level, for African countries to disengage from outright colonial administration from outside. On the other, it now appears that historically created economic dependencies are really hard to shake off (an economically dependent country is also necessarily politically dependent). Moreover, after the 1960s, the cold war standoff between the West and the East made Africa a superpower rivalry zone, clouding issues of human-rights abuses and the need for transition from colonial dependency to post-colonial economic "partnership."

The behaviour of the post-colonial state remained unclear as each state was firmly fettered to old colonial administrative and bureaucratic structures. To be sure, growth of confidence on the part of the new African leadership did occur, but no more than a rhetorical movement from an alienated to a more egalitarian community was evident.

It was not clear whether the post-colonial state was to return to a pre-colonial experience. Some have argued that "independence movements in Africa were not a return to a pre-colonial order, rather, they were a fresh chance for new things to happen" (Oduyoye, 1986:81). It now appears that this chance or opportunity has been squandered.

The cracks that appeared in post-colonial Africa in the first thirty years were really from within Africa: the loss of faith in African ideals and ideas and capabilities based on the resources available, Africa's inability or unwillingness to adapt to change and the global ethos while retaining her cultural and moral sensibilities and, hence, confusion in reading African minds. This was necessary because "every group is both producer and product of the ideas concerning it that exist in the minds of its members. These ideas are an integral part of the life of the group, since they embody the hopes and aspirations of its members, expressing their conception of the group's purpose, and the understanding about its process" (Lipson, 1960:52).

Africans under colonial rule naturally yearned for a new sense of community governed by African humanitarian principles; many expected the creation of a new Africa out of the old. Instead, those who assumed power seemed to disengage, as if through a curse, from these obvious aspirations. Military coups and political and civil unrest characterised the kind of resistance to oppression Africa witnessed for more than three decades. People were resisting their governments from within, sometimes with the full support of external powers who sought to further their own political interests. The point is that Africans *know* oppression when they experience it and have historically shown a capacity to resist it, passively or actively. A government they cannot overthrow is ignored, and that which can be overthrown is overthrown. But Africa's problems linger on.

Post-colonial Africa inherited at least five pervasive types of alienation: ethnic rivalry, political and economic disparities, religious differences, and gender-based inequalities. There is, of course, a critical connection between each of these forms of community breakdown, and these cannot be discussed easily in isolation. The post-colonial state's failure to transform itself into a nation resulted in the revival of ethnic consciousness, while political and economic monopolies by certain groups led to compounded tensions, often expressed in religious and gender terms. Although a full analysis of each of these is not possible in this chapter, the present conflictual situation on the continent is a multifaceted historical phenomenon. The question is, does Africa have the resources to resolve this impasse, and has anyone ever attempted to find a solution in the past?

Re-reading the African Text

It is not altogether true that Africa has not produced adventurous new thinking during the last three decades. Julius Nyerere's *ujamaa* (familyhood and personhood) and Kenneth Kaunda's humanism, among others, were serious attempts to deal with African problems after colonial rule. Both of these elders led post-colonial African countries (Tanzania and Zambia respectively) under very difficult circumstances. Each developed key ideas which he believed would capture the minds of Africans on the journey to a holistic society. Derided by their detractors for being naive and overoptimistic about solutions to African problems, both Nyerere and Kaunda have been relegated to the periphery of African thought. Yet they still have a special role to play in empowering Africa's vision of the good society. They believed, as we do here, that Africa does have a socio-ethical text that must be read and interpreted correctly—that is, contextually.

Both Nyerere and Kaunda analysed the possible content of this text. The interest here in what Nyerere and Kaunda suggested is in the context of the present changes in Africa. Indeed, as Kaunda said, "We must try to avoid becoming slaves of conventional terms such as socialism, democracy, capitalism and communism and so on for the world is changing every day" (Martin, 1972:103).

Nyerere's and Kaunda's visions

Both Nyerere and Kaunda saw African society through the village's highly humanised ethos, with the family being the most basic unit for humanising individuals and ushering them into true "development." For Nyerere, *ujamaa* was descriptive of a meaningful human dwelling, as opposed to *unyama* or "animal life." He elaborated on the concept of *ujamaa* when he said, "To build a nation in the true sense is to build the character of its people . . . of ourselves, to build an attitude of mind which will enable us to live together" (Nyerere, 1973:178).

Nyerere was concerned about human dignity, unity, freedom and equality among Africans. He was opposed to all forms of alienation between people. Structurally, he prescribed village-style living for Tanzanians under a special kind of socialism—which to be sure, was not a very wise politico-economic solution under the circumstances. He was right, however, in seeing all Tanzanians as offshoots of a quasi-extended-family structure, the "new nation-state." He wrote, "We are doing this by emphasizing certain characteristics of our traditional organization, and extending them so that they can embrace the possibilities of modern technology" (Nyerere, 1968:2).

Nyerere's insistence that Africa did have a traditional text was correct. He saw government as the larger community capable of caring compassionately for its own because, in the end, all people share a sense of continuity.

Kaunda does not depart from Nyerere's vision except in the fact that Zambian humanism lacked a rationalised structure comparable to the village-style formations in Tanzania. To Kaunda, humanism was a distinct style of life befitting national human beings. It was not a kind of atheism or loss of faith in the Creator. He wrote, "To a certain extent, we in Africa have always had a gift for enjoying man for himself. It is at the heart of our traditional culture" (Kaunda, 1966:22).

Although a more generalised philosopher than Nyerere, he also saw the African extended-family system as a source of clues to a new ideological formation:

> The extended family system constitutes a social security scheme which has the advantage of following the natural pattern of personal relationships rather than being the responsibility of an institution. (Kaunda, 1966:18).

According to Kaunda, the post-colonial state must learn to "read" the African traditional set-up in order to make inroads into development. He appeals for a people-centred government capable of utilizing all human resources creatively.

Both Nyerere and Kaunda are right in amplifying the centrality and necessity of principles of mutuality, acceptance and inclusiveness in an alienated post-colonial environment. At the conceptual or even mythical level, they are cautioning us to read what is written in the minds of Africans with indelible ink: a communal, compassionate lifestyle built around a sense of continuity.

As the world has suddenly discovered in the post-cold war period, no meaningful economic development can take place without mass political participation by all in shaping a country's future. But Nyerere and Kaunda discovered long ago that, in Africa, mass participation in political affairs strongly depends on deliberate appeal to African social ethics.

Today it is necessary to attempt a re-reading of the African text in the context of alienation, creating our quest for soulful myths anew, interpreting life in this continent as the search for a compassionate community that enables Africans to see each other in continuity (not discontinuity) and spread that vision to the global community. So far, this reading has been confused by the voices of others. Every society has a hidden text, and it is up to indigenous peoples to unravel the meanings of their texts in the context of the struggle for wholeness. Africans owe this task to themselves today.

Unfortunately for Nyerere and Kaunda, the confusion of language between the traditional text and the superimposed neo-colonial text ("socialism" and "capitalism") was inevitable. Attempting a second reading of the original text presents the opportunity to filter out any irrelevant baggage from modern concepts such as capitalism and democracy. Good leadership here involves a critical task of re-interpretation. But first we must reclaim the text and imbue it with our meanings, out of our past and present experiences.

If Africa opts for short-term economic gain without a strong socio-ethical foundation, our moral and political resources will remain even more underdeveloped. Since it is no longer fashionable to scramble for Africa in this post-cold war period, Africa has for once a new political space of immense creative proportions. It is in Africa's long-term interest not to be "needed" by the West, for now, at least. This is the essence of the need for a second liberation of Africa, and this time the movement is about freeing Africa from Africans who have failed in the first reading. They have opted, unconsciously, to be content with short-term gains and risked long-term underdevelopment for the whole continent.

When a former leader of Nigeria, General Olusegun Obasanjo, formed the African Leadership Forum,[4] his express aim was to address the issue of poor African leadership and seek ways of developing good leadership for the continent. Needless to say, Africa has not had meaningful leadership at the continental level due to a lack of clear goals for the future. Each national leader has been too preoccupied with domestic issues to be bothered by larger pan-Africanist ones. Moreover, leadership has in the past been seen as an activity confined to individuals and not as a conscious group process. We need, yet again, to emphasise the importance of new departures in such critical areas.

Coming of Age: "Re-membering" Ourselves

The image of Africa before us is that of a dismembered body. Cultural, political, economic and social dislocations have left the continent in disarray. The metaphor of "re-membering" is an appropriate one for carrying out the reconstruction of an Africa we desire. In this sense, to re-member means to put parts back where they matter, to bring about a wholeness. Each society lives according to a story remembered and carried on, even mythically, by her own people. Africans have a story about society, often forgotten, but still kept alive by millions of simple village folk.[5] It is dangerous for Africans to continue living as though they have no story to pass on for posterity, for behind the African story is the rationale for social morality and the good life. In Africa, the older a person is, so it is said, the wiser he or she becomes or, in traditional parlance, the more "educated." Africa has now come of age and ought to be able to re-member quite a bit!

The task of reconstructing a moral vision for good governance and development in Africa may be approached from two perspectives. First of all, modern government structures and age-old traditional elders' courts—such as the non-partisan traditional *njuri-ncheke* government of the Meru (Kenya) and other such structures throughout Africa—invite comparison. These traditional structures include the kingdoms and monarchies of southern and western African communities—some of which are far from being democratic institutions but have mechanisms for peacemaking and arbitration based on African values that could still be reconsidered. Is there an African political science, and what would be its content? This and other questions would form a historical-sociological approach.

The second approach, emphasised throughout this discussion, is the interpretive-metaphorical approach that is at the heart of both Nyerere's and Kaunda's philosophies. The main issue here is the precise meaning, in African socio-ethical idiom, of terms such as *government* and *development*. This is where we have failed thus far. The new must meet the old, so we need a new reading of the old to find the place where healthy grafting can be done. Every institution worthy of Africans' respect must be involved in this crucial exercise. Here, African schools would be crucial vehicles in fashioning a relevant humanities curriculum.

At the root of the interpretive-metaphorical approach are three terms that deserve careful analysis in light of the African search for a basis for democracy, government, human rights and prosperity: community, compassion and continuity. These, in their own right, sufficiently account for organised life in Africa and will inform a new vision for otherwise alienated communities. Thus, government, as the prime mover of the new Africa, must incorporate traditional metaphors otherwise subsumed under various African cultural practices.

Government is for community

There is absolutely no purpose and meaning in organising African peoples for anything less than community, which places the accent on what is to be achieved, not on the players. Africans understand the concept of community, narrow as it may have been. Community points to commonality of interests and destiny, emphasising togetherness through bonds of obligation. Communal rules are established so that there is harmony and justice and respect for people's rights. John S. Mbiti writes, "As in all societies of the world, social order and peace are recognised by African peoples as essential and sacred" (1969:267).

Community is the space created to facilitate dealing with the issues and obligations of the whole society. This space demands participation and reciprocity. Community is anti-individualistic and seeks the relative success of all. Most African governments have so far behaved like anti-community monsters, which is probably the main reason for the past failures to connect with the majority of African peoples. Therefore, the name and purpose of government is community; Nyerere says it is like *ujamaa* (extended family life), and he is correct. Hearing what other African communities mean by government—indeed, highlighting equivalent African terms for such an enterprise—is an absolute necessity.

To elevate the concept of community to the level of the state or nation is to empower Africans' ethical sensibilities and put in place a dependable point of reference for conflict resolution. There is nothing wrong with comparing notes with the Americans, whose democratic creed is government *of* the people, *for* the people and *by* the people. It is up to each African country to devise ways and means of defining patterns of leadership, representation, and arbitration in a communitarian government, but we need to add a second pillar to our construct:

if a communitarian government is *of* the people, it is *for* the people and must be a government of compassion.

Government is for compassion

Even a communitarian government may degenerate into an unresponsive structure controlled by the strong (mighty). The term *compassion*, as we use it in English, is derived from two Latin words: *com* ("together") and *pati* ("to suffer")—literally, "suffering together," "sharing in others' suffering" or, simply, "sharing."

Evidence of the emotive nature of this metaphor abounds in Africa. In every African communal setting, every event—birth, marriage and death from both natural causes and various calamities—are still public events involving more than those immediately concerned. Human beings are assumed to have a capacity to "feel" for others, and this feeling is what Kaunda meant by "humanism."

Why do African peoples, unique in the way they mourn the dead and deride misfortune, entertain acts of extreme human cruelty resulting in the deaths of so many? Why is Africa not outspoken on amnesty for wrongdoers? Africa needs to find a specific in-built mechanism with which to counter excesses of cruelty and gross human-rights violations.

A compassionate government is characterised by inclusiveness—acceptance of all including their limitations—and a capacity to "whisper together," the metaphor for arbitration. Implicit in African humanism is the individual's capacity to step down from his or her immediate interests and reconsider his or her position. The deal struck usually is mutually satisfying. All known African peoples detest a world of fixed prices, views and decrees; there is always room to manoeuvre! And this is the meaning of African compassion: where human beings are concerned, there is always space for the unknown, the unexpected. Thus, a compassionate government is an accommodating government, sensitive to people.

Government is for continuity

Finally, continuity is a useful interpretive concept upon which strong African governments could be founded. While there is nothing mystical about continuity, its meaning is well worth pondering in the African milieu. The issue is how to address conflicts created by "missing links" in a fast-moving world. The social, political and ecological problems caused by such a world would have significant capacity to weaken the best of communitarian governments.

Retired people in the African milieu, especially those who have held key leadership positions, must find a place in a communitarian government. At the same time, intentional education for those being groomed to take up leadership should be explicitly spelled out. Africa is weak in both bequeathing (so that a generation hands over) and in succession (so that prepared people take over leadership). This is catastrophic for our future as a continent. Political continuity ought not to be continuity by default, as it is in today's Africa.

The past and its relationship with the present has always been of great importance to Africans. Some have even said that Africans do not have a sense of the long-term, but an enduring sense of a powerful past.[6] It is true that somehow the presence of the departed is felt by many Africans, especially during stressful periods in life. Solutions to the struggles of life usually are found in what those who have gone before have done. But that is not all.

A government for continuity is sensitive to the general ecology of all living organisms and seeks to understand why, in Africa, the universe is regarded as a collection of forces that must be approached carefully. Indiscriminate abuse of land and water certainly will displease our ancestors, but now we also know our very lives are under siege. Human beings, Africans have long believed, share the universe with "significant others." This concept of cohabitation could be the most original African contribution to the continent's modern political, social and ecological crises.

The usefulness and the relatedness of all human beings and creatures—indeed the sacred nature of life—is the substance of African traditional religions.[7] With awe are we to approach life. And, it might be said, with awe are we in Africa to approach the great issues of good governance and development for the next century.

Conclusion

Within the above tripartite framework of community, compassion and continuity, developing a new language in Africa, for instance, with which to speak of human rights, will be possible. The crucial human-rights principles here are three: political, economic and civil rights as stated by Howard (1970).

Political participation in a communitarian (not communist!) governmental structure, provision of economic means of livelihood for all, and protection of all under the law is a possibility and, indeed, a basic right. Good governance for development, built on concepts of community, compassion and continuity and capable of addressing the current crises, is a real possibility for Africa.

Notes

1. A village is usually a few or several households with a common subsistence structure. Most important, a highly developed community interdependency is the rule. However, some African communities were nomadic, and for them the village was a very loose-knit structure. Still, the sense of community was always there.
2. For a study on the "rites of being," see Mbiti (1969).
3. Rhoda Howard (1970) predicts that Africans will move back to rural areas in search of a basic subsistence in the years to come.
4. This body promises to be the first serious elders' council for Africa and includes prominent elder statesmen such as Julius Nyerere and Kenneth Kaunda, who understand Africa's predicaments
5. The theme of "re-membering" a story with which we hang on to life is of interest to various modern scholars. See especially Hauerwas (1981) and Dykstra (1981), although both write only from a Christian perspective.
6. John S. Mbiti, for example, does not think much of Africa's sense of a distant future. He insists that Africa is primarily fixed on the past. See Mbiti (1969).
7. African languages have no name for religion. Africans just live with some critical assumption that all life is sacred. See Mbiti (1969).

References

Ake, C. 1981. *A Political Economy of Africa*. New York: Longman.

Dykstra, C. 1981. *Vision and Character*. New Jersey: Paulist Press.

Hauerwas, S. 1981. *A Community of Character*. Notre Dame (Indiana): University of Notre Dame Press.

Howard, R. 1970. *Human Rights in Commonwealth Africa*. New Jersey: Rowman and Littlefield.

Iheoma, E. O. 1985. "Moral Education in Nigeria: Problems and Prospects." *Journal of Moral Education* 14 (3).

Kaunda, K. 1966. *A Humanist in Africa*. London: Longmans, Green and Co.

Lipson, L. 1960. *The Great Issues of Politics*. Englewood Cliffs (NJ): Prentice-Hall.

Martin, A. 1972. *Minding Their Own Business: Zambia's Struggle Against Western Control*. London: Hutchinson.

Mbiti, J. S. 1969. *African Religions and Philosophy*. Nairobi: East African Educational Publishers.

Nyerere, J. 1973. *Freedom and Unity*. Dar es Salaam: Oxford University Press.

———.1968. *Freedom and Socialism*. Dar es Salaam: Oxford University Press.

Oduyoye, M. 1986. *Hearing and Knowing*. New York: Orbis Press.

3

Churches and the Reconstruction of Society for Democracy
Some Insights from the African Heritage

Jesse N.K. Mugambi

The end of the cold war has helped Africans to appreciate more seriously that democracy cannot be imported or imposed, but must evolve within the cultural context of the continent's citizens. The constitutions the colonial powers approved for decolonisation and the launching of African republics were endorsed as "democratic," but they did not lead to the welfare state they seemed to promise. Whereas the former colonial powers, on the basis of the agreements signed during decolonisation, continued to reap huge profits from their investments in the continent, the peoples of Africa, on average, have become increasingly impoverished and exploited. Africa emerged from the cold war more indebted than ever before, as though its hidden purpose had been to turn Africa into a perpetual debtor, at the mercy of powerful bilateral and multilateral creditors. The people's capacity to influence public affairs in their respective countries too has been increasingly eroded, and their disillusionment and frustration overflowed into the clamour for constitutional conventions and reforms in the 1990s.

During the cold war, each African country was expected to follow the sociopolitical model prescribed by the ideological bloc of which it was a satellite. Each bloc claimed to be democratic, even though neither was primarily interested in democracy in Africa. Ironically, "democracy" seems to have been considered a necessity in the metropolis but a luxury in Africa. Thus, dictatorships and military regimes were tolerated and sometimes encouraged by both blocs, as long as their African satellites did not stray from their influence. In international forums, the non-aligned lobby defined its stance in the context of the two ideological blocs

---

Note: This chapter is a revised transcription of the author's oral response to two of the symposium's concept papers: "Good Governance for Development" by T.G. Kiogora (Chapter 2 in this volume) and "The Search for a Modern Black African Democracy" by Tshiyembe Mwayila (not available in English and hence not reproduced in this volume).

and was unable to forge its own ideological identity. Thus, each of its members was directly or indirectly associated with either of the two blocs.

The "new world order" brings with it multilateral and bilateral conditions that force African nations to undergo "democratisation" as a precondition for development assistance. These new conditions confirm that during the cold war the ideological blocs, far from considering democracy a priority for Africa, used "democracy" as a tool for synchronising African economies with the global market. Economic synchronisation, rather than globalisation, is the primary objective of the current democratisation campaign. Although "democratisation" has been associated with multiparty politics, general elections and a liberalised press, there has been inconsistency in the imposition of the prescribed conditions. In eastern Africa, for example, it appears that both multiparty and non-party political systems are acceptable, provided that the national economy in question is sufficiently open to allow commodities from other parts of the world to be dumped in its markets as a means of furthering "economic liberalisation."

If the people of every culture must evolve their own social institutions, taking into account their social heritage, there are four main foundations on which we might formulate democratic practices relevant to Africa: (1) the principle of plurality and appreciation of unity in diversity; (2) the principle of freedom, in which both the individual and the community are recognised by others; (3) the principle of collectivity, under which Africa could subsume its multiplicity of ethnic identities; and (4) the principle of conciliar consultation and management of social institutions, in which we must take seriously the role of the council of elders (Mwayila, 1993).

If *democracy* is defined as a socio-political system in which the ordinary citizens of a country effectively participate (as individuals and as groups) in decision-making on all matters affecting their sorrows, joys and hopes, the range of possibilities for structuring society to ensure such effective participation is obviously wide. That people should participate in shaping their destiny may have universal appeal, but in view of human beings' natural endowment for creativity, the form of that participation can be organised in an infinite number of ways. The Westminster model that Kenya and other nations have followed—the product of a particular cultural history, which has incorporated much Graeco-Roman social thought—is one such way, but it is not the only one. The communitarian emphasis in traditional African social engineering, for instance, has a different intellectual pedigree, which, in its cultural habitat, has been effective in ensuring the participation of individuals and groups in decisions dear to them.

Both the North Atlantic and the traditional African models have strengths and weaknesses that a critical analysis would reveal. The challenge, as Africa prepares for the 21st century, is to discern models of democracy that are compatible with the cultural heritage of African peoples without having to replicate models that nations in other parts of the world have evolved for themselves. Social realities are so central to the evolution of democracy in Africa that any process of democratisation that ignores or belittles them is destined to fail. The notion of democracy that has been imposed on Africa has tended to champion the values of individuality, self-centredness and discontinuity. As Kiogora (1996) emphasises, a process that takes Africa's social realities seriously will have to incorporate the elements of community, compassion and continuity.

This challenge has serious implications for contemporary social engineering in Africa. For example, when we say that democracy must be for community, it seems to me that one of the problems we have is that our sense of community as Africans is not congruent with the community talked about in government institutions. When a person in a rural area thinks of himself or herself as a member of a community, that community is not the type of community that the state's ministry of community development or ministry of social services has in mind. Civil servants are employees of the state, with a history discontinuous with that of the rural populace and the traditional African sense of community present in its daily life.

Community and Democracy

The ordinary rural African associates "community" with the immediate family, the extended family, the clan, the network of relationships, and the interaction between people and the natural environment. In contrast, the civil servant associates "community" with government policies, plans, budgets, programmes and projects. It is an object to be served (or manipulated) for objectives that may or may not be openly declared. Many Africans regard civil servants as secretive officers charged with the duty of harassing ordinary citizens without clear explanation. The question in practical terms is, how do we bridge this gap? How do we bring about a synthesis?

The dilemma is that state government has become an indispensable reality of the 20th century. Abolition of state government without a viable alternative is a recipe for social chaos. At the same time, a return to traditional forms of government does not seem practicable because of the influence the North Atlantic has had on many Africans, especially young people, through schooling, advertising and propaganda. Decolonisation bequeathed North Atlantic forms of government to Africa and made it impossible for traditional African social institutions to serve as the foundations of governance. State government, as a "secretive" institution alienated from the traditional community, was not designed to be "transparent" and "accountable." Moreover, state government already wields both constitutional and executive powers that its beneficiaries would not voluntarily abandon in favour of traditionalism.

If we were to try to do away with state government (or *siri-kali*)[1], so that we can revert to the community that people know, we would not be likely to succeed. *Siri-kali* is already in place, and the traditional community does not wield the power. Likewise, if we were to try to deal with community only as it is defined by the *siri-kali*, we would not get anywhere either. (It could be argued that one of the disappointments of governance in Africa during the last thirty years has been that state government has been unable to come to terms with the traditional African sense of community.) The challenge, therefore, is to cultivate a synthesis between the two understandings of "community." Can the church play a role in bridging this gap, facilitating the creative evolution of such a synthesis? If the church were to accept the challenge and the responsibility, how would it go about this task? These are questions that churches and church-related agencies ought to take very seriously.

Democracy and Statehood

Political theory commonly suggests that the state is a creation of society (Mwayila, 1993). Although this may be the case in the social history of North Atlantic nations, it is certainly not so in the history of Africa since 1884. Africans did not participate in the creation of the states to which they belong and did not openly debate to ratify the constitutions bequeathed to them during the process of decolonisation. Thus, the African situation stands mainstream political theory on its head; elsewhere, nationalist consciousness led to the creation of states, but African states have laboured for thirty years to create African nationalist consciousness in their citizens. The state in Africa is in crisis because it endeavours to forge national consciousness where there are hardly any sentimental or historical roots to back the effort. In the North Atlantic countries, nationalist sentiments are often backed by ethnic pride and history, whereas since 1884 in Africa, colonial powers drew state boundaries at random, dividing ethnic communities—even extended families—with an arbitrariness that defies all reason. A cardinal principle of decolonisation (because the colonial powers wished to maintain their spheres of influence intact) was that these boundaries were not to be altered. This principle cannot be said to have been based on democratic considerations.

If African peoples never participated in the creation of the states of which they found themselves citizens, it should not be surprising that they have found it difficult to sustain Westminster-style democracy in their midst. The African social reality is that we did not create the states to which we belong. If present African societies are a creation of the state, the question again is, how do the agents of reconciliation bring about social consciousness so that our societies can own the states to which they belong? Today, *siri-kali* is viewed as someone else's business because, thirty years after independence, it is seen as an extension of the colonial state. The state, far from being a facilitator of democracy, remains an obstacle. How do we bridge this gap and remedy the contradiction?

Culture and Democracy

Finally, our talk of Africa as a cultural bloc or as a unity is itself problematic. At the beginning of Europe's interaction with our continent, Europeans did not see Africa as a cultural bloc. V. Y. Mudimbe recently published a book with a telling title, *The Invention of Africa* (1988). Indeed, Africa is not a cultural bloc that has always existed; it has been constructed. Unfortunately—or fortunately—we cannot wish it away. How do we reconstruct Africa (Mugambi, 1995) so that it serves the cultural needs of African peoples?

To make a few other observations, I would like to use the analogy of an African hut. All over Africa, the most dominant geometric figure or symbol is the circle. I cannot explain why, but it seems practical, especially during discussions, to sit in a circle. When you are seated in a circle, you have no acoustic problems because everyone is the same distance from everyone else. When you are in a circle, you can see everyone else and there is equality. The circular African hut is much more than just a building that happens to take a specific shape. It has a centre pole that helps it stand. Without the centre pole, you cannot have the rafters, and without rafters, there can be no roof. It is the centre pole that gives the hut its identity. When constructing the hut, you start with the centre pole because it gives you a radius on which the outside poles, and hence the walls, are constructed. If we take this hut to represent African culture, I see a culture with five major outside poles, or pillars, that define the circumference.

The first pillar is politics. I define politics simply as the distribution and management of social influence. If there are only two people, there is no politics, but if there are three people, politics comes in. When there is a decision to be made, two will gang together, and the third will be alienated. How decisions are made among crowds is what politics is all about. To say that there is a distinction between the church and the state insofar as politics is concerned is not realistic. You may talk of church politics or secular politics, but you cannot do away with politics in any aspect of society.

Economics, which is simply the distribution and management of resources, is the second pillar. The way resources are shared and managed is what economics is about.

Thirdly, you have the pillar of ethics, which is the system of values. Ethics defines what is good and what is bad, what is right and how people should relate to one another, and how individuals should relate to the community.

The fourth pillar is what I call aesthetics, which is our sense of beauty and proportion. If Africans were in charge of the Miss Universe beauty contest, the vital statistics would be very different. But since this contest is managed by people who have another set of values by which they determine what constitutes a beautiful woman, the chances of an African winning a Miss Universe contest are very scanty.

The fifth pillar is metaphysics, which, simply put, is the worldview. When all things are put together, a summary emerges by which our view of the world and community is articulated. Religion is the instrument used for this purpose.

If we look at culture from the perspective of the African hut, the question is, what has happened to our cultures? It seems to me that we have not been able to assert ourselves, perhaps because we have not viewed culture from this holistic perspective. We seem to think of culture merely in terms of aesthetics. If we are now to think of cultural foundations for the social reconstruction of Africa, how do we go about it?

Social Reconstruction

At every one of the pillars discussed above, we should ask ourselves what we can derive from our African experience and heritage in order to build a new social structure within which we can live. Each one of us, challenged in this way, may be able to think originally and creatively. In the realm of politics, I would refer to the writings of Ali Mazrui, especially his book *The Africans: A Triple Heritage* (1986). When you compare African political values with the political values emerging from the cultures of the North Atlantic nations, you see a radical difference.

In economics we have, for example, a work by Goran Hyden, *No Shortcuts to Progress* (1983), which clearly distinguishes between what the author calls the "economy of the market" and the "economy of affection." He says that African economies are based on forces of affection, and transactions thus depend very much on who you know and the prevailing relationship. I am not quoting him here because I agree with him. Quite to the contrary, when he wrote the book, he was addressing himself to the "problem" of how, somehow, Africans can be incorporated into the market economy. He laments that Africans have refused to be incorporated by remaining tied to the economy of affection. Instead of going to the shop that offers the lowest price, Africans buy from people they know. But somehow this economy has helped us survive. This is only one example. I am sure that if we look at African economies, we might find other principles derived from our heritage.

In the realm of aesthetics, I want to refer to a theme dramatised in Okot p'Bitek's poems "Song of Lawino" and "Song of Ocol" (1971), which are metaphorical. Lawino is a woman who has not gone through formal education and is married to the son of a chief. Her husband, Ocol, has been to Cambridge. When he comes home, he says he does not want anything to do with what he sees as the primitivity of his people's culture. He says he is going to destroy all the round huts and all the social institutions in order to replace them with his newly acquired culture from England. At the end of the day, Ocol is very frustrated.

Okot p'Bitek uses the metaphor of the pumpkin. He says, "Let no one uproot the pumpkin from the old homestead." In traditional African culture, when you move from one piece of land to another, you do not uproot all the food plants because you will need some food while still adjusting to the new homestead. Ocol and his like in us are cursed because we have uprooted the pumpkin.

In metaphysics, I am sure there are other examples, but allow me to refer to some of my own writings. Not long ago, I published a book, *The African Heritage and Contemporary Christianity* (1989), in which I reflect with my students on how we might make sense out of the beliefs and values we have received in Christianity through the missionary enterprise and how these relate to our African religious experience. There is also a small book, *God, Humanity and Nature in Relation to Justice and Peace* (Mugambi, 1987), in which I emphasize that the African community is not merely a community of individuals, but one that extends to cover the unborn, the young, the old, the dead, animals, plants and spirits. If we profess this worldview, the kind of economics and politics that we practise will be different.

How we move from here depends very much on our worldview. How we construct our politics depends very much on everything else. As we have seen, the pillars are linked together to form a whole.

I have one final remark that is a challenge for us all. It has been stated that Africans are the most unsophisticated lot among humanity because they do not have temples. But if you have a worldview in which God, humanity and nature are integrated, in which the whole world is your temple, what do you need a temple for?

Note

1. *"Siri-kali,"* the source of *serikali*, the Swahili word for "government," means "tough or bitter secret." See also Chapter 2.

References

Hyden, G. 1983. *No Shortcuts to Progress.* London: Heinemann.

Kiogora, T.G. 1996. "Good Governance for Development: Perspectives from the African Traditional Cultural Heritage." In *Peacemaking and Democratisation in Africa: Theoretical Perspective and Church Initiatives,* edited by H. Assefa and G. Wachira (Nairobi: East African Educational Publishers).

Mazrui, A. 1986. *The Africans: A Triple Heritage.* London: BBC Books.

Mudimbe, V. Y. 1988. *The Invention of Africa.* Bloomington: Indiana University Press.

Mugambi, J. N. K. 1995. *From Liberation to Reconstruction: African Christian Theology after the Cold War.* Nairobi: East African Educational Publishers.

———. 1989. *African Heritage and Contemporary Christianity.* Nairobi: Longman.

———. 1987. *God, Humanity and Nature in Relation to Justice and Peace.* Geneva: World Council of Churches.

Mwayila, T. 1993. "The Search for a Modern Black African Democracy." Paper presented to the Symposium on the Role of Religious Leaders in Peacemaking and Social Change in Africa, Nyeri, Kenya, 18-23 July, 1993.

p'Bitek, Okot. 1971. *Song of Lawino and Song of Ocol.* Nairobi: East African Educational Publishers.

4

Peace and Reconciliation As a Paradigm
A Philosophy of Peace and Its Implications for Conflict, Governance and Economic Growth in Africa

Hizkias Assefa

We all can agree that there is a great need for peace in the continent of Africa. But before we can begin discussing how to bring peace, we are confounded by a very basic problem of agreement on the meaning of peace, even though we regularly use the term in many contexts of our daily lives.

The term *peace* features prominently in the daily news, in discussions at global forums and in religious worship. It is used in everyday greetings in many cultures. "Peace Be Unto You" is a common greeting for Jews and Christians. Muslims say "*Asalaam Aleikum*," which means the same thing. However, with the amount of bloodshed within and between these groups, it does not seem possible that "peace" connotes the same thing for all of them. In the 1980s, the MX missile, one of the most destructive nuclear bombs ever invented, was nicknamed "The Peacekeeper." A commonly used adage in international diplomacy is, "In order to make peace, prepare for war."

Are these senseless contradictions? Do all these references to peace mean the same thing, or does the word mean different things to different people? Could the lack of consensus and clarity about the concept be one of the reasons why there is absence of peace in the world?

Various Conceptions of Peace

Some people have understood "peace" to be the absence of violence. By this, people normally mean the absence of overt physical harm to people and property that emanates from wars, riots, murders and vandalism, among others.

Note: The author would like to express deep appreciation for the comments and editorial assistance he received from Gretchen Van Evera, Harold Miller and George Wachira.

This conception of peace holds that the maintenance of law and order and the pursuit of stability and a relatively safe social and political order are primary objectives of peace. In this understanding, the presence of a relatively small amount of visible (overt) violence in society provides an indicator of successful peace and peacemaking. Police forces, courts and prison systems are usually the instruments used to bring about and enforce this type of peace in the domestic arena. Internationally, the equivalent concepts include balances of power, nuclear deterrence and hierarchical power structures in which the bigger and more powerful states become the arbiters or policemen of global affairs. This approach to peace has been characterised as negative peace since its focus is on the absence of violent conflict and war.

One major shortcoming of this conception is that, in its preoccupation with controlling overt violence, it may condone or perpetrate another kind of more covert violence that has come to be called structural violence. Structural violence has been defined as social and personal violence arising from unjust, repressive and oppressive national or international political and social structures (Galtung, 1969). According to this view, a system that generates repression, abject poverty, malnutrition and starvation for some members of a society while other members enjoy opulence and unbridled power inflicts covert violence with the ability to destroy life as much as overt violence, except that it does it in more subtle ways. In other words, it is not only the gun that kills. Lack of access to the basic means of life and dignity does the same thing (Wehr, 1979:14).

For others, peace is a condition of tranquillity in which there is no disagreement or dispute, in which conflicts are banished and people, individually and collectively, live in calm and serenity. A major shortcoming of this conception is its failure to recognise conflict as a fact of life. Instead of acknowledging its existence and learning to use appropriate mechanisms to deal with it, this notion of peace can lead people into the misguided perception that by avoiding conflict, it will go away.

For still others, peace goes beyond a preoccupation with the absence of conflict or violence. It is seen as the transformation of conflictual and destructive interactions into more co-operative and constructive relationships. This understanding, which will be advanced in the rest of this discussion, equates peace with conflict transformation and resolution. In this view, peace is not simply a state of general tranquillity or an imposed order that suppresses discord but is, rather, a network of relationships full of energy and differences. Structures are available through which personal and social differences can be identified and worked out in ways satisfactory to all involved parties, as well as to the society at large. Sometimes in this process, the *status quo* may be disturbed or long-standing structures shaken, but this definition maintains that peace is achieved only when the root causes of the differences or conflictual relationships are explored and resolved.

From this perspective, peace and peacemaking are not just techniques deployed to patch up differences when conflicts erupt, but are larger concepts with applications even in situations that are not visibly conflictual. Peace is a philosophy and, in fact, a paradigm with its own values and precepts, which provide a framework within which to discern, understand, analyse and regulate all human relationships in order to create an integrated, holistic and humane social order. What, then, are the values and principles underlying this definition of peace?

Values and Principles

The following is a brief summation of some of the most important values and principles:

1. *Conflicts cannot be resolved or peace made unless the root causes of the conflicts are identified and dealt with.* For conflicts to be resolved, peacemakers must look beyond surface issues and address the substantive and emotional issues as well as the parties' needs and interests that are at the root of the conflicts. In other words, lasting peace between conflicting parties is possible only when deeper needs are accommodated and satisfied.

2. *It is not possible to resolve conflicts and attain peace unless attention is given to the justice and fairness of the process as well as to the outcome of the settlement.* In other words, peace without justice is a rather meaningless concept, although this is not to suggest that the pursuit of justice and the pursuit of peace are one and the same thing.[1] In this context, the search for justice requires concern for the impact settlement of the dispute might have on parties not represented in the peacemaking process. In other words, this definition of peace disavows dispute settlement that favours the interests of the parties in conflict at the expense of the interests and well-being of unrepresented parties and society in general.

3. *People's deeper needs are not totally incompatible.* Parties in conflict can discover a commonality of interests and objectives that can lead to mutually acceptable solutions to their problems. Often the help of third parties, whose perceptions have not been distorted by the conflict, may be necessary in such explorations. If parties operate on the level of human needs, it is possible to arrive at creative solutions satisfactory to all the contestants. As Mahatma Gandhi put it, "There

is enough in the world for everybody's need but not enough for everyone's greed."

4. *Conflict resolution, and therefore peacemaking, involves a restructuring of relationships.* The process is a transition from an order based on coercion to one based on voluntarism; from a relationship characterised by hierarchy to one marked by equality, participation, respect, mutual enrichment and growth (Burton, 1986:333-344).

A close examination of the values and principles of peace and peacemaking makes it clear that most of them are at the core of what may be considered mature human attitudes, behaviours and relationships. A brief digression into what is meant by mature human behaviour may help to explain this point.

Mature human behaviour

Broadly speaking, the human personality is presumed to evolve through three stages: childhood, adolescence and adulthood (maturity). Each of these stages is typically associated with general attitudes and characteristic behaviours. *Childhood* is identified with dependency emanating from the child's inability to do things and a heavy reliance on others for the satisfaction of needs. *Adolescence*, in contrast, is characterised by a struggle to reject dependency and assert the need for independence and autonomy. It is a stage preoccupied with the pursuit of self (and often selfish) interest without much regard for others. It relies primarily on the individual's power and ability to realise his or her perceived self-interest. *Adulthood* is the stage in which the individual is expected to attain his or her full human potential as a mature person. This stage is characterised by interdependence, which develops out of a broader concept of the self and self-interest that is capable of accommodating others. The sense of interdependence is derived from the realisation that life is a process that requires people to co-ordinate their efforts and work together because individuals can succeed only if others also succeed, and vice-versa. In this context, interdependence is the individual's willingness to renounce part of his or her autonomy, power and independence in order to accommodate others' needs and interests and enhance the common good in a mutually enriching manner. At this stage, individuals opt to co-operate, give and take, and be mutually dependent without sacrificing their own needs, deep values and identity. Here human and social relationships are marked by equality, respect and mutuality. It is possible to say that healthy human development entails evolution from dependence to independence and, eventually, to interdependence.

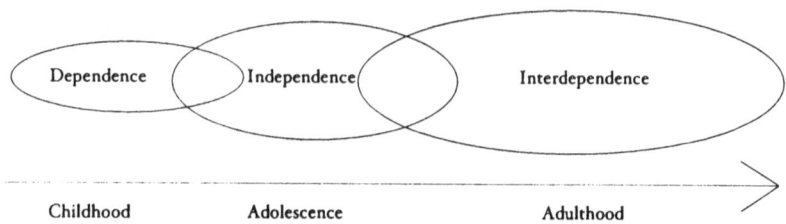

It is in this sense that the conflict-resolution values and principles enumerated above are central to mature, interdependent relationships. This evolution applies not only to interpersonal, but also to institutional relationships including those of small groups, organisations, societies and states.

From this analysis it becomes apparent that the peace and peacemaking values, attitudes and approaches have relevance to a vast array of social relationships ranging from those between two people all the way to global institutional relationships. The scope of peace, however, becomes even wider on examination of the concept of reconciliation.

Reconciliation and Conflict Resolution

The field of conflict resolution has been treated as a social science discipline. Much of the literature in this discipline, however, does not deal with the concept of reconciliation, although intermittent references to it are found in various writings.

Reconciliation's meaning or relationship to the social science understanding of peace and peacemaking is not clear. Most discussion of reconciliation is found in theological literature. We therefore turn to this literature to see if it might be possible to get a better grasp of the concept as well as examine its relationship to the working definition of peace adopted in the previous section.[2]

Dimensions of reconciliation

The concept of reconciliation is a very important theme in Christian theology. The term *reconciliation* is derived from the Latin root word *conciliatus*, which means "to come together," or "to assemble." According to John Nelson (1969:16), it implies "walking together."

Reconciliation refers to the act by which people who have been apart and split off from one another begin to stroll or march together again. Essentially, it means the restoration of broken relationships or the coming together of those who have been alienated and separated from each other by conflict to create a community again. Reconciliation is conflict resolution, but it has greater dimensions and more profound implications.

The Bible discusses reconciliation in many contexts. In the Old and New Testaments, it is possible to discern four dimensions (Burkhardt, 1974): reconciliation with God, reconciliation with the self, reconciliation with neighbours and the human community, and reconciliation with nature.

In Christian thought the first dimension, reconciliation with God, means creating harmony by mending the conflicts that separate individuals from God. This is done through:

1. the individual's recognition of his or her role in alienating God;

2. confession and repentance of misdeeds and request for forgiveness; and,

3. a decision to turn away from the misdeeds and rectify them if possible.

After these steps have been taken, it is God's forgiveness and mercy towards the individual that establishes reconciliation in this first spiritual dimension.

In the second dimension in this scheme, reconciliation with the self, internal conflict with the self is minimised through reconciliation with God.[3] Renunciation of "sinful selfishness" and the feeling of being forgiven past wrongs in order to start afresh are expected to generate tranquillity, peace and harmony within the individual. This reconciliation with the self could be seen as a consequence of, or spillover from, the first kind of reconciliation.[4]

The third dimension, which involves reconciliation with neighbours and the human community at large, means that the forgiveness and mercy that the individual has experienced in being reconciled with God must now be transferred to, or shared with, other human beings; the forgiven individual becomes the forgiver and becomes reconciled with his or her fellow human beings. Again, this dimension of reconciliation could be viewed as a spillover from reconciliation with God. The privilege of being forgiven and reconciled with God creates the obligation to forgive and be reconciled with others.[5]

Here, the Bible takes an even more interesting perspective regarding the relationship between the first and third dimensions of reconciliation. It makes reconciliation with neighbours a prerequisite for reconciliation with God. Matthew 5:23-25 (RSV) contains a clear prescription: "So if you are offering your gift at the altar [as a gesture of seeking reconciliation with God], and there remember that your brother has something against you, leave your gift there before the altar and *Go,* first be reconciled to your brother and then come and offer your gift" (emphasis added). The implication is that God will not accept gestures of reconciliation from an individual as long as he or she carries a grudge or knows that others have grievances against him or her.[6] This same conditionality is repeated in the most important Christian prayer, The Lord's Prayer, which says, "And forgive us our trespasses [debts], as we also have forgiven our trespassers [debtors]" (Matthew 6:12).[7] It is interesting to note that the verse does not say, "Forgive us so that we *can* forgive others," but "Forgive us as we *have* forgiven others."

It also can be argued that the third dimension of reconciliation is a spillover from the second as well. The individual's reconciliation with the self, which results from renouncing sin, selfishness and greed, can also generate an attitude of benevolence and compassion towards others. It can make the individual sensitive to the needs and interests of neighbours and cause him or her to seek and foster relationships of justice, respect, mercy and love.[8] The inverse situation, in which peace with others could result in peace with the self, is also postulated in the theological literature.[9]

The fourth dimension of reconciliation, reconciliation with nature, develops from a recognition that humans cannot be fully reconciled with God while living in a conflictual, disrespectful and abusive relationship with God's creation. Abusing the non-human creation, including the earth and its environment, also profanes the individual's relationship with the creator.[10] This kind of reconciliation, therefore, calls for a relationship of respect and care for nature and ecological systems.

This relationship is further reaffirmed by examining the association between the earth and human beings envisaged in Genesis 2:7, which says,

> The Lord God formed a man's body from a lump of the soil and breathed into it the breath of life. And man became a living person.

Further, Genesis 2:8 and 2:15 say,

> Now the Lord God planted a garden ... [and] took the man and put him in the Garden of Eden to work it and take care of it.

These verses establish that spirit and matter comprise the human being and that the material component is the earth. Thus, being reconciled with the self implies being reconciled not only with the spiritual self, but also with the material self—the earth. In other words, individuals cannot be in an abusive and conflictual relationship with the earth and its environment while claiming to be reconciled and at peace with themselves. According to this understanding, conflictual attitudes towards the earth or activities that harm the planet and its ecology are tantamount not only to harming the self, but also the other beings who share the earth's materiality. Moreover, the kind of relationship envisaged in Genesis 2:15 between the earth (represented by the garden) and humankind is that of custodianship and mutual nurture instead of plunder or selfish and irresponsible exploitation.[11] In fact, the concept of the Jubilee elucidated in Leviticus 25 reinforces this view by articulating the need for balance, harmony and mutual care between people and their environment.[12]

The four dimensions of this theological notion of reconciliation can be illustrated graphically as a series of highly interrelated circles with the arrows indicating the direction of linkages.

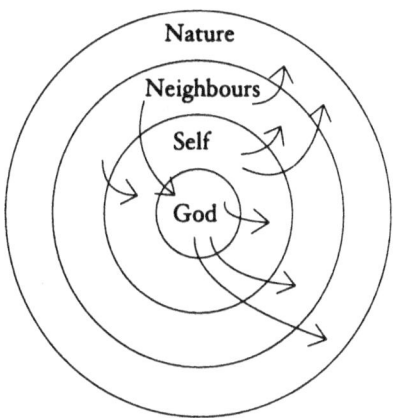

Alternatively, the four dimensions of reconciliation could be presented as follows, using social science terminology:

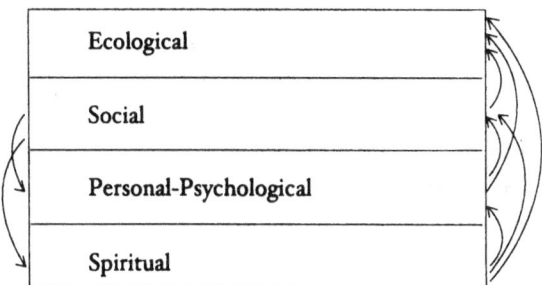

Implications

What are the implications of this analysis of reconciliation? What does this analysis tell us about the scope of peace and peacemaking processes? Do the concepts of peace and reconciliation have any relevance to domains of life and human interaction other than conflict?

Understanding of peace and peacemaking

A major significance of this analysis of reconciliation is its demonstration that peace is a vast concept encompassing many aspects of life. The social science discussion of the scope of peace is primarily restricted to interpersonal and social relations, while in this analysis of reconciliation, the scope extends from the very intimate and deep spiritual level to the personal-psychological, to the social, and all the way to the ecological level. From this perspective, peace integrates the individual, society and nature. It thus becomes a comprehensive paradigm from which to discern life and relationships in general, instead of being simply a technique for dealing with social disputes. The concept of reconciliation underscores the notion of interdependence discussed in the social science context of conflict resolution. But here interdependence is not simply a result of utilitarian pragmatism, but is rooted in a notion of deep spiritual and material interconnectedness that links human beings and nature to a common foundation. Thus, the concept of reconciliation not only expands the scope of peace, but it also provides a comprehensive and rather elegant framework for discussing it.

A second implication of this analysis is its demonstration of the highly interrelated nature of the various dimensions of reconciliation. Spiritual reconciliation spills over to the personal, from the personal to the social, and from the spiritual and the social to the ecological. Inner peace and outer peace are interrelated—that is, a person's ability to make peace with others is enhanced by that individual's ability to be at peace with himself or herself. A person cannot be at peace with others while torn by inner conflict. In turn, a person's ability to create peace within the self is a function of his or her peace at the spiritual and social levels. This paradigm, therefore, calls for a special methodology of peacemaking that can address its multiple dimensions.

A third important implication of this analysis is its demonstration of the very large spiritual dimension of peace and peacemaking. Indeed, according to the analysis, the spiritual dimension is at the centre of the whole process. This is not meant to suggest that unless peace is established in the spiritual dimension there can be no peace at the social level. There is no doubt, however, that a peacemaking process that enables the parties to reflect on the spiritual implications of their behaviour, especially their hatred, contempt, callousness or self-centredness, and on their destructive actions in general, is likely to lead to a more conducive atmosphere for the quest of just and lasting solutions to their disputes. In typical peace negotiations, the parties in conflict come to the table armed with very self-centred cost-benefit calculations, ready to deny or defend their wrongdoings, determined to attribute total blame for the conflict to their opponents, and intent on extracting maximum concessions from their adversaries. In contrast, bringing the spiritual dimension into the peacemaking process can create access to the more deep-seated, affective base of the parties' behaviour, enabling them to examine critically their own attitudes and actions. This, in turn, may encourage them to accept responsibility, confess their wrongdoings, be flexible with their demands, grant and ask for forgiveness when the need arises, and seek mutually beneficial solutions.[13]

Implications for churches

A very important conclusion that emerges from this analysis of reconciliation is that peacemaking and reconciliation are mandates and not merely options for the Christian church. Often churches have been inclined to perceive their primary duty as the fostering of reconciliation between God and human beings or, at most, effecting reconciliation with the self as a by-product of reconciling the individual with God. Thus, much church energy has been preoccupied with sharpening concepts and tools to facilitate such reconciliation with God by enabling people to renounce sin and seek God's forgiveness. As noted earlier, however, in situations of social conflict it is not possible to be reconciled with God before people are reconciled with each other. God will not accept people's offerings unless they are first reconciled with their brothers and sisters (Matthew 5:23-25 and 1 John 4:20), and will not forgive their trespasses unless they have forgiven those who have trespassed against them (Matthew 18:23-35; 16:12-15).

Thus, in conflict situations (in which people have grievances against each other or have inflicted harm upon each other), the church's attempt to bridge the gap between God and people is futile unless it also becomes a bridge between people by acting as an agent of social reconciliation. The church is shirking its responsibility if it does not recognise the social aspect of spiritual reconciliation and its obligation to be a peacemaker between people.

The church can fulfil this reconciliatory obligation in various ways, particularly in societies with ongoing conflicts, where it can cultivate or prepare the ground for social reconciliation.

Likewise, as the church engages in the task of reconciling God and human beings, it needs also to challenge its congregations to examine the implications of such reconciliation for relationships with other human beings and with nature. The repentance that the individual must experience to be reconciled with God must include self-criticism and examination of attitudes towards other people (neighbours, ethnic groups, nations, etc.) and nature. Instead of always pointing to what others have done to us, the spirit of repentance and self-examination should enable us to identify behaviour in ourselves that incites others to behave the way they do towards us. The church could spread the message of self-reflection and self-criticism at the individual, group, community and national levels through its pastoral and prophetic activities.

Of course, in addition to preparing the groundwork for peace, the church also needs to engage directly in building bridges between people separated by conflict, in reconciling adversaries, and in creating community between former enemies.[14] In order to be a credible actor, however, the church needs to begin with itself and lead by example. It must recognise and confess the role it has played in contributing to injustice and conflict, both within its own ranks and in society in general. It needs to find mechanisms with which to foster the spirit of confession within its congregations and call them into a community of repentance and forgiveness. It must promote reconciliation among the various Christian denominations since an unreconciled church can hardly be a credible reconciler of others.

Governance

Since independence, most African states have been under the control of oppressive military or single-party dictatorships. The last five years, which have come to be called Africa's "second liberation," have witnessed the abolition of many such regimes and their replacement by multiparty political systems. Many African countries are in the process of conducting competitive political campaigns and elections. Does the peace-and-reconciliation paradigm have any significance for the current democratisation processes in the continent? Does it inform, offer critique or provide insights? Does it provide any criteria by which to evaluate these processes, or does it suggest any alternatives?

The decades of political repression across the continent have not only shattered the hopes of many Africans regarding the promises of independence, but have also led to the angry dismantling of repressive governments with the hope of replacing them with others that can guarantee freedom and participation. Many would-be reformers view multiparty politics as a ready alternative to the oppressive systems of the past. Some have even erroneously viewed multiparty politics as the only path towards democratisation. A careful review of multiparty experiments in African countries and many others raises questions that merit careful consideration before the rest of the continent plunges wholeheartedly into the system.

First of all, the multiparty system is premised on very special social and philosophical assumptions reflecting the economic, cultural and historical setting in which it developed. It assumes that society would be better off if individuals and groups compete to sell their views in the marketplace of ideas, and that the views bought (supported) by the majority (as evidenced by their votes) therefore reflect the public will. It is presumed that such a process gives everyone a chance to contribute to and participate in governance and political decision-making. However, many underlying assumptions in this claim need to be fulfilled in order for the multiparty system to work as envisaged. One critical assumption is that everyone has equal access to the marketplace of ideas and has equal capacity to sell his or her views and opinions. As can be seen in many Western countries (and already in Africa), having access to and selling ideas in a competitive multiparty situation requires complex organisational capability and abundant material and human resources. Ordinary citizens are usually restricted in their ability to sell their ideas due to a lack of access to these means. Therefore, it is usually individuals with wealth, connections and strong organisations who can put their views forward and exercise their influence.

In principle, just as demand is intended to stimulate production in the free-market economy, under a multiparty political system, the opinions and preferences of ordinary citizens are intended to become the stimulus for government decisions and public policy. Political parties are intended to identify and channel these ideas so that they become the input for social decision-making. In reality, just as the market logic becomes distorted in the free-enterprise system when production begins to drive demand,[15] similar distortion occurs when politicians, party leaders and influential individuals become opinion makers and begin to sell their ideas to the public. This practice has often entailed a great deal of media manipulation, distortion, bribery and corruption carried out by politicians who desire citizens to buy (support) their ideas.

Let alone in less literate societies like those of Africa (where the capacity of ordinary citizens to critically examine the ideas being sold to them by sophisticated politicians and sensational media is quite limited), much manipulation and sleight of hand takes place in more literate societies like the United States. Increasingly, massive sloganeering, slick media sound bites and professional image-making are becoming common features of political campaigns and mass persuasion to the extent that the ability of the electorate to make meaningful choices or influence public policy effectively is increasingly doubtful. Citizens' alienation from the so-called democratic governments is evidenced by the electorate's steadily declining participation rate in national elections.

From limited observation in Africa, most multiparty elections have been more about throwing out or bringing into office certain political personalities than about meaningful input from the ordinary citizen into government decision-making. As a result of such elections, representatives of one or more ethnic groups may have simply replaced other ethnic groups that had been in power, while elites representing a certain political persuasion will have replaced other elites with different orientations. Ordinary citizens remain marginalised and alienated from their governments; what transpires in government or opposition-party circles often remains very remote from their lives, concerns and priorities.

Another major assumption of the multiparty system is that competition provides the best approach to decision-making. Although there are recognised benefits to competitive decision-making processes, it has also been shown that competitiveness encourages hostility, redundancy and waste, and that co-operative decision-making processes produce psychologically healthier social environments and can generate outputs qualitatively equal to those of competitive processes (Cohen, 1986).

The most serious problem with the multiparty system has to do with its high degree of win-lose orientation in election contests. One party wins, and the other loses. The winner gloats in triumph, while the vanquished lick their wounds. Losers must accept their loss and wait for their turn in the next round of elections to try again to defeat the opponent. This approach works in societies characterised by a strong measure of social consensus in which the issues of contention are relatively marginal.

For example, in the United States, there has been a very large degree of consensus among the people and between the two main political parties on the general orientation of the society, the economy and the state. Therefore, most of the time, the distinctions between the Democratic and Republican party platforms are matters of degree or variations on the theme rather than radical differences on how to structure society. Under such circumstances, the victory of one party over the other is not such a serious blow to the adherents of the losing party, nor does it present a dangerous threat to their security, well-being and continued political activity. Thus, party leaders and supporters can rather readily accept defeat and wait for their turn in the next round.

Many African societies, however, have deep cleavages based on factors such as ethnicity and religion; social harmony also may be precarious and consensus minimal on many basic issues of governance such as the nature of the state, the nature of the economy, where state power should reside, criteria for access to political and economic systems, and the mechanisms for the control of power and accountability, among others. Under these conditions, multiparty competition tends to exacerbate rifts rather than provide resolution of outstanding social and political issues. It can aggravate tension, for in such circumstances winning power is very lucrative, while the price of losing power can be very severe. In the absence of consensus on many critical social issues, and with a shortage of institutions committed to fostering, protecting and enforcing such consensus, the winner, once in power, is in a position to define issues, norms and institutions to his or her own advantage. In particular, when ethnicity is an important factor in party affiliation, losing an election might mean exclusion from power for an entire ethnic group, followed by discrimination and even repression. This can therefore foster the mentality, among the competing parties, that they must win at all costs; in ethnically or politically polarised situations, the loser may not survive until the next electoral contest. Although people in multiparty systems tend to recognise the maxim "winning is not everything," in deeply divided societies, winning may be the *only* thing.

In fact, in societies that have experienced civil war or political violence, multiparty processes such as political campaigns and elections become alternate avenues for conducting war, except that in these circumstances the ammunition is words, manipulation and subtle intimidation instead of bullets. Otherwise, the prevailing mentality between the competing parties is similar to that of a war—characterised by deep animosity, contempt, desire for revenge and intransigence. The outcome of elections, although less deadly than war, can still have similar psychological consequences for the participants: anguish and fear on the side of the losers and triumphalism and reprisal on the side of the victors. Moreover, the results tend to be suspect and challenged by the loser, no matter how proper election procedures may have been. In such circumstances, instead of resolving contentious social issues, elections may create a new cycle of uncertainty, fear, resentment, tension and even open hostility.

The Angolan elections of 1992 illustrate this point. After the ceasefire was signed, people thought that multiparty elections would settle the major issue of the war: control of the government. Although the electorate spoke and the Union for the Total Independence of Angola (UNITA) lost, the latter did not feel that its concerns, aspirations and interests were being addressed by its adversaries who had been voted into office. UNITA therefore decided to continue the armed conflict. Since Angolan society has been torn apart for generations, it has not been able to forge a solid consensus on basic issues of governance and has not established enough confidence in the political system to make all citizens' groups feel that their interests can largely be taken care of, even if they do not control political power. In the absence of consensus and a common vision, the question of who controls power becomes a life-and-death issue, and the win-lose character of multiparty elections only exacerbates the battle.

Similar attempts are underway in a number of African countries to organise competitive elections aimed at "settling" major controversial issues underlying their civil wars.[16] These countries, however, have had little experience of social consensus on many vital national issues, or whatever consensus that had existed has been shattered by protracted armed conflict. Therefore, the losing parties are not likely to derive much comfort from being told that the majority has voted against them. They will likely find ways of challenging the process or seek separation, as UNITA did in Angola and as the white right-wing minority in South Africa has suggested on many occasions. Alternatively, the losing groups may simply continue their armed struggle until their concerns have been accommodated. Instead of resolving the issues they were intended to settle, elections results in Burundi, Ethiopia and Kenya have created many new tensions.

Given the history of deep ethnic, religious, ideological and even racial cleavages that exist in a number of African societies, whether originating from inside or outside, a question arises about what kind of political decision-making processes might best promote meaningful participation and, at the same time, foster more community harmony and less disruption.

To begin with, it must be remembered that the repression and social disruption that many African countries are experiencing is not simply a post-independence phenomenon. Three hundred years of dehumanising slavery and more than a hundred years of degrading colonialism have preceded the thirty years of post-independence malgovernance, repression and internal wars. Each experience has left its own deep wounds. The fact that many African societies and cultures have survived these centuries of pain, abuse, rupture and intentional destruction is an amazing testimony to these cultures' stamina and resilience. The power behind their endurance is a subject worth deeper examination since in it may lie clues for understanding Africa and shaping its future. Given this long history of external and internal brutalisation, what kind of political or social decision-making processes could repair the damage that has been inflicted?

Reconciliation politics

Initial suggestions for a political system that might avert the negative consequences of multiparty politics in deeply divided societies can be drawn from the peace-and-reconciliation paradigm. These suggestions begin to form what can be called "reconciliation politics," which proposes that before deeply torn African societies are subjected to the divisive assault of multiparty competition, their community spirit must first be restored and nurtured back to health. What is needed at this point is a political system that emphasises healing and wholeness instead of more upheaval and disruption. What would be characteristic of this kind of politics?

Such politics would encourage consensus building and a quest for common ground. It would emphasise inclusion rather than exclusion. Unlike the win-lose approach of multiparty elections, reconciliation politics would use processes in which there are no total losers or winners; instead, everyone would win something together. Decisions would be made, not by the verdict of a majority, but by a process of what is known in the field of conflict resolution as "interest negotiation." This is a process in which parties engage in give-and-take interactions until a solution is reached that can accommodate everybody's interests and needs. In this process of continuous interest negotiation among individuals or groups, the role of high-level leaders is that of an interest mediator and their tools are principles that derive from the peace-and-reconciliation paradigm.

The politics of reconciliation suggests that in deeply divided societies, social healing should take precedence over elections. As multiparty campaigns and elections are likely to re-open wounds and further reinforce mutual resentments, incompatibilities, fears and suspicions, this kind of politics would suggest delaying multiparty elections until the social wounds of the past are for the most part healed. The process of healing and construction of consensus might take somewhat longer than organising elections, but the politics of reconciliation opts for long-term effectiveness rather than short-term "efficiency," which may not ultimately meet the needs of the society.

Some African countries have experimented with national conventions as a starting point towards democratisation. In some instances, these have worked better than in others. If done well, national conventions could be useful instruments for reconciliation and healing: if they were inclusive; if all perspectives and shades of opinion were solicited, presented and discussed; and if, through such intensive and at times delicate consultation, a common vision were to emerge about the nature and direction of the society that everyone can identify with, an important first step towards healing will have been taken. Obviously, these processes are very complex and time-consuming and require tremendous sensitivity and skilled guidance. But, if conducted correctly, they could create a more harmonious and viable society than can be achieved through multiparty elections in societies that do not have a general consensus on vital issues.

Reconciliation politics is a politics of co-operation. Unlike competition, which has a narrow definition of self-interest, co-operation sees the self in a relational context and includes others (those on whom we depend and those who depend on us) who enable us to become what we are in the definition of our self-interest. Co-operation therefore means arranging our relationships in such a way that our benefit becomes the benefit of others, and theirs ours. By helping others, at the same time we also help ourselves. Interestingly, the rewards of such relationships are greater than when we operate on the basis of the notion of helping ourselves to the exclusion of or at the expense of others. This notion of co-operation and reconciliation politics illuminates the often misunderstood New Testament notion, which holds that people receive best not by taking but by giving:

> Give, and you will get. A good measure pressed down, shaken together and running over, will be poured into your lap. For the measure you use, it will be measured for you. (Luke 6:29-35)

While this maxim could be dismissed on first impression as paradoxical and even illogical, closer observation reveals that it holds water in many domains of human relationships. We get respect when we give it to others instead of when we simply demand it. We get love and affection when we give it. We get more fulfilment when we help others be fulfilled. We attain security by ensuring that others feel secure rather than by threatening them with our mighty defences. Interestingly, even in politics, individuals get more power when they share it with others instead of just amassing it for their own sake. Those who are empowered by being allowed to share power in turn empower those who empowered them, while those from whom power is taken away try to weaken the snatchers by attempting to claim their power back. Surprisingly, even in conflicts over material resources that appear mutually exclusive (i.e., when there is a perception of scarcity that contributes to a feeling that if one person gets something, others have to lose it), it becomes apparent that much of the conflict revolves around status, recognition and respect, which are achieved and augmented not just by demanding them from others, but by giving them to those from whom they are expected. Once these needs have been met, even apparently mutually incompatible material issues can be handled in a much more accommodating and amicable manner. This is what co-operation and the politics of reconciliation are all about.

As this analysis shows, the concepts of co-operation and the politics of reconciliation are not simply naive or fuzzy-minded idealistic notions. Not only are they desirable ends in themselves, they can also be justified on pragmatic and utilitarian grounds as much as, if not more than, competitive politics. In short, the qualitative and quantitative benefits that accrue both to the individual and society from pursuing co-operative politics are quite high.

The kind of politics of consensus suggested here seems to be more consistent with many African traditions, which emphasise community rather than individualism and competition. Interestingly, implementation of this type of politics does not require sophisticated party structures, expensive campaigns, international observers and the like. Rather, it is possible to use existing traditional consultative structures that are already accessible to ordinary citizens, peasants and poor people in the form of chiefs, traditional elders, village mediators and religious institutions. The arbitrary and oppressive facets of these institutions could be identified and the public could be educated about these defects. Mechanisms could then be developed to correct these defects while maintaining the positive aspects of these institutions. In this way, it may be possible to move towards the creation of a much more rooted, participatory and harmonious society than can currently be attained from a quickly organised, competitive multiparty political system or newly grafted political institutions that have little connection with the societies they are intended to serve.

In short, the peace-and-reconciliation paradigm offers an alternative understanding of governance. From this perspective, governance is about encouraging and rewarding co-operation. It is about building institutions that foster the development of mature, empathetic and mutually enriching social relationships as opposed to being a process that takes the Hobbesian[17] dog-eat-dog view of human nature as immutable and is content just to manage it so that it does not get out of control. The argument is not that there is no room at all for competitive politics in Africa, but that in deeply divided societies, healing of past wounds, common vision for the society and consensus on vital issues must precede the wrenching and divisive processes of multiparty campaigns and elections of the kind recently witnessed in many African countries.

Statehood

The peace-and-reconciliation paradigm also has implications for the process of state building that has been underway in Africa since independence; the last four decades have witnessed the transition of almost all African countries from colonial dependencies to independent states. The model these countries have followed has been that of the sovereign nation-state with all the autonomy and independence of action assumed under international law. Just like the promises of freedom and participation, however, the creation of sovereign nationhood and the exercise of national independence have eluded many African states. The reasons for this frustration have been partly structural and partly conceptual. The current global political economy is structured in such a way that many former colonies are only nominally free. They are still bound by neo-colonial ties, making them subservient to more powerful states in the North in economic and political matters.

At the conceptual level, the pursuit of total independence or autonomy is by itself an illusive goal. The compelling model of all living systems in this universe is interdependence. To aspire to total independence (not to influence others or be influenced by them) is to aspire to an existence outside the circuit of life. In interstate relations, despite the model of the independent sovereign nation-state that many have clung to tenaciously, it is becoming clear that the welfare and security of one state cannot be meaningfully considered in isolation from the welfare and security of other states. It is becoming apparent that even the manner in which a state governs its citizens and succeeds or fails in promoting economic well-being and social harmony within its boundaries has a push-pull effect on its own as well as on neighbouring populations. Instability and disruption in one society is easily transmitted across national boundaries. Concern about the environment and ecological systems is forcing us to transcend notions of individual sovereignty and look at Planet Earth as one entity. It seems that the competitive pursuit of selfish state interest at the expense of other states is becoming the path to self-destruction. In such an increasingly economically, politically, culturally and ecologically intertwined and interdependent world, the pursuit of total independence becomes an absurdity; independence, unless it is a transitional stage in the movement towards more interdependence, is not a sustainable and meaningful concept.

If, as was discussed earlier, the development of maturity in personal and organisational life is marked by an evolution from dependency to independence and then towards interdependence, this suggests that African countries should look at their independence as a transitional phase on the way to more interdependence rather than as an end state. They must envisage themselves as part of a greater entity and move towards building relationships with their neighbours and other states. The way to overcome the existing limitations and frustrations of their sovereignty and independence is not by intensifying their individual and competitive struggle to fortify or defend that sovereignty—which would always be limited and inadequate anyway, since they suffer from many disadvantages and constraints. Instead, they should be prepared to seek the sovereignty of a larger commonwealth by formulating mutually enriching, collaborative structures with others. This means that they should be prepared to relinquish some of their individual sovereignty for purposes of developing common approaches to common problems and predicaments, while at the same time developing greater viability and capability as collective actors in the international arena.

This paradigm, therefore, calls for a strengthened consciousness of the commonalities that tie African states together as interdependent entities. It suggests a fresh and invigorated look at regionalism and pan-Africanism as the next promising steps in the development of African states. Here again the values, principles, methodologies and tools that emerge from the peace-and-reconciliation paradigm are valuable assets in this evolutionary process.

Although the process of human development discussed earlier suggests an evolution through the stages of dependence, independence and interdependence, this process does not necessarily suggest that African societies must develop strong, independent states before moving towards interdependent relationships. The experience of the United States of America is instructive in this regard; the original thirteen states that formed the American union came together before any of them had developed deeply entrenched notions of independence and separate identity that later would have hindered the establishment of collaborative behaviour and institutions. European countries—although the various states have attempted to perfect the notion of the sovereign nation-state over the centuries—are now beginning to unlearn their attitudes of fierce independence, emphasising instead their interconnectedness in the interest of building more interdependent relationships. In the African situation, a case can be made that now is the time to make the transition to more interdependent relationships, before each state continues to entrench its independence by building more and more autarchic institutions, which later will stand in the way of a smooth transition towards collective consciousness and identity.

The call for more interdependence or the acknowledgment of larger sovereignty does not emanate from a simplistic notion that bigger is better. The creation of bigger entities and the formation of larger faceless bureaucracies that marginalise or destroy the individual units that constitute the collectivity would be contrary to the values of dignity, responsible freedom and mutuality that are at the core of the peace-and-reconciliation paradigm discussed here. Instead, the suggestion of more interdependence comes from the concern that the creation of a more beneficial human community should not be undermined by arbitrary institutions that tend to artificially and detrimentally compartmentalise people's identities and affinities. As there are ties that bind people as members of a nation-state, there are also ties—sometimes of equal and even more importance—that bind them as members of a region, a continent or, ultimately, the human family. The suggestion of a move towards interdependence is not meant to obliterate the idea of the nation-state altogether but, rather, to give expression to the consciousness that the nation-state is not the ultimate identity for human beings, as the traditional concept of the sovereign nation-state seems to have suggested and encouraged. Just as a healthy nation-state augments the commonality between its citizens without squelching individuality and diversity, an interdependent commonwealth should not destroy the units that form it but promote their common ties and enhance their ability to form mutually rewarding relationships. From this perspective, then, even regionalism and pan-Africanism are not end states but stepping stones towards larger consciousness of a greater identity that encompasses the whole human community in global citizenship.

Modernisation and economic growth

Does the peace-and-reconciliation paradigm have any insights to offer in the area of modernisation and economic growth in Africa?

Since independence, the creation of modern societies capable of achieving high standards of living for their citizens has been a major preoccupation for African countries. So far, however, their efforts have generally yielded dismal results. By many of the accepted measures of material prosperity, a number of African societies are economically poorer today than they were thirty years ago. Not only has poverty become more endemic, but the very efforts to modernise and promote economic growth have also generated numerous negative side effects, among them community disruption, cultural alienation and disconnectedness; wide-spread misery and degradation, especially of the least fortunate; and intensified psychological and social conflict.

Many reasons have been advanced for the failure of economic growth and the resultant inability to raise the standard of living. One identified factor has been the socialist-inspired, highly centralised and authoritarian model of economic growth that was followed in many African countries. With the current breakdown of socialism as a major ideology, there is now a shift from this model towards the market-economy system as the solution to African poverty. One newspaper describes this new consciousness as

> the reluctant awareness in Africa that the free market reforms are the cornerstone of future economic growth.... Africa [has been] in the process of a double transition in the 1990s—the switch from one-party politics to pluralism and a move towards the free market after years of heavy state-run economics. (Tadesse, 1993:10)

However, when we look more closely at the experiences of African states as well as those of the "rich" Western societies that they are trying to emulate, many serious issues arise regarding the free-market model of development.

In the free-market growth model, the major engine for economic growth is presumed to be production, while the spur for production is deemed to be consumption. Thus, in the context of poor countries, economic growth is believed to be stimulated by building up the production and consumption capacities of these societies. To the extent that there are a lot of unmet basic human needs in many of these poor societies, those needs could generate the demand to spur production if the productive capacity could be developed. As long as the analysis is restricted to production geared towards meeting basic human needs (which would determine what is to be produced), the logic of this development approach is sound.

This logic becomes distorted, however, as the economy begins to produce goods and services that are not aimed at meeting basic needs. In this case, instead of demand determining what is to be produced, production begins to determine demand. Through advertising and promotions, producers begin to manipulate people's desires and create wants in consumers' minds to buy the goods the producers have already decided to produce.[18] These mechanisms inculcate perceptions that equate happiness and satisfaction with consumption of such products. At the same time, the economic system must nurture continual discontent and a restless yearning for more and more consumption in order for the production system to continue producing and generating growth. This process fosters new habits of mind that unleash an insatiable desire for more goods in the illusory expectation that greater satisfaction will come with more consumption. According to Wachtel, for citizens of growth-oriented societies, enough "is always just over the horizon, and like the horizon it recedes as we approach it.... Wanting more remains a constant, regardless of what we have" (1989:17).

Commenting on the impact of this form of development on some of the richest societies of the world, Wachtel writes,

> It is ironic that the very kind of thinking which produces all our riches also renders them unable to satisfy us. Our restless desire for more and more has been a major dynamic for economic growth, but it has made the achievement of that growth largely a hollow victory.... [It is] a treadmill—one which, we are increasingly recognising, can damage our health and shorten our lives. (1989:17)

In addition to the "psychological poverty" bred by this approach to growth, many have pointed to its destructive environmental consequences. The inculcation of the notion that material consumption is the source of satisfaction, that more is better, has encouraged selfish and irresponsible exploitation of natural resources, pollution, waste[19] and plunder of the earth's non-renewable assets, thereby destroying the planet's ecological systems and threatening life. In the words of Wachtel, "The siren call of growth has us enthraled. But like the sirens of antiquity, it calls us to a disastrous course" (1989:6).

There is another distorted facet of this notion of economic growth. Once basic needs have been met, and sometimes even while the economy is still at the stage of trying to meet them, the consumption pattern moves towards what economists have called "positional" goods and services (Hirsch, 1976). The enjoyment of these goods and services depends upon others not having them. For example, many kinds of luxury goods such as Mercedes-Benz cars generate satisfaction because they are exclusive. They lose value as generators of pleasure when they become more widely accessible. Envy, or what has been known as "keeping up with the Joneses," becomes the motivation for others to work hard to buy luxury cars. But as more and more people acquire Mercedes-Benzes, the cars begin to lose their attractiveness, and it becomes time for those who can afford the car to search for something else that others cannot easily buy. Thus, enormous amounts of resources could be wasted in positional consumption aimed at either titillating the covetousness of others, fuelling a futile race to catch up, or, worse, creating the need for protection from the consequences of the envious behaviour of others (such as resentment and crime) that such consumption has provoked.

For less developed African societies, the currently emulated economic-growth model seems to raise many problems. First of all, the promised results are not easily attainable. Despite what the prophets of development have claimed, the path out of social poverty to prosperity seems unclear, and the human and social toll appears quite high.[20]

Even when economic growth is attainable, many in the so-called rich countries have lamented the psychological and spiritual crises that have arisen from the strong materialistic orientation of this notion of growth, as well as the loss of community, isolation, meaninglessness and sense of emotional exploitation that have accompanied it. The drive for economic performance seems to capitalise on and nurture unhealthy and sometimes destructive human motivations such as greed, envy and insatiable discontent. It also creates the illusion that economic growth and material prosperity will ensure happiness, provide security and solve every human problem or cure all social ills.

The emergence of such social problems does not even wait until a society is totally modern or rich. When we see the experiences of somewhat more affluent, urbanised ("modernised") centres in Africa, we can observe that they already suffer from the psychological, spiritual and social crises present in the already prosperous societies. In these poorer countries, however, the human consequences are more severe since the crises occur in a context of degrading poverty. In richer countries, the negative repercussions of economic growth can be softened or disguised by the material wealth of the society.

The plight of poor countries aspiring to emulate and catch up with the already prosperous countries is very agonising. This is because the pursuit of "modernisation" and "economic growth" has caused them to abandon some of the elements of their traditional worldview (i.e., spiritual values, security derived from ties with people, sense of rootedness, etc.), which earlier provided a sense of community and meaning. Many of these values were abandoned largely because they were thought to be inconsistent with the goals of modernisation. Unfortunately, the goals of modernisation and economic growth have not come much closer to being achieved. The emulated societies do not wait for their followers to catch up because their own dynamics of growth make them pursue even more advanced stages of production and more and more positional consumption that will always be beyond the reach of the poorer emulating societies. For these poor countries, the goals of modernisation and economic growth become receding targets. Hence these societies are caught in a tragic situation—they have given up much of what they were, but are unable to attain what they aspire to. No doubt this frustration will be a constant source of disruption, conflict and disillusionment at both the individual and societal levels.[21]

Talking of the general direction being taken by poor countries to extricate themselves from poverty, Lutz and Lux give a prophetic warning:

> Increasing mass production has destroyed the traditional local economy, markets have grown in scope and size.... Yet such an "evolution" will move people even more into the background. Interpersonal relations will give way even more to relations between things. We do not know who produces what. The market is silent; it does not care and neither can we. All we do know and care about is the nature of the commodity and its price. People become means, and commodities become new ends. Human . . . values give way to pecuniary calculation and materialism. With this continuance human welfare would be at a low point. . . . We have to keep in mind that marketisation and materialism are two sides of the same coin. Both cater to the desire for things or the lust for power, rather than to the need for interpersonal relationships. And society becomes increasingly atomistic. (1988:315)

The values and principles of the peace-and-reconciliation paradigm discussed in this paper suggest a model of economic development that is more human centred. One of the fundamental premises of the paradigm, after all, is harmony and integration between the various dimensions of life and nature (i.e., integration between the spiritual, psychological, intellectual, material and social dimensions of the human being on the one hand, and harmony between the individual, society and nature on the other). From this perspective, then development implies growth on all these counts. Approaches to economic prosperity at the expense of spiritual growth and community are inconsistent with this paradigm. All of these concerns must go hand in hand.

As indicated earlier, the modern preoccupation with the generation of material prosperity tends to subordinate human beings and the whole of nature to the economic production process. (According to Korten, the value orientation of the prevalent development model is one that "assumes that the labourer exists to serve the economy, rather than the reverse" [1990:43].) The peace-and-reconciliation paradigm suggests a model that subordinates the economic system to the service of humankind and nature. This might be represented diagrammatically as a shift from the order depicted in the upper diagram to that in the lower one.[22]

Justice

Another of the core values of the peace-and-reconciliation paradigm is justice. From this perspective, economic growth and prosperity must therefore be associated with strong values of justice and equitable distribution within and between societies. The imperatives of justice also imply that people must nurture and rehabilitate the earth in equal proportion to their use and exploitation. There has to be a balance between the demands on the ecology from economic activity and the regenerative capacity of the earth. Nature, according to this paradigm, is not just an input in the production process, but an end in its own right.

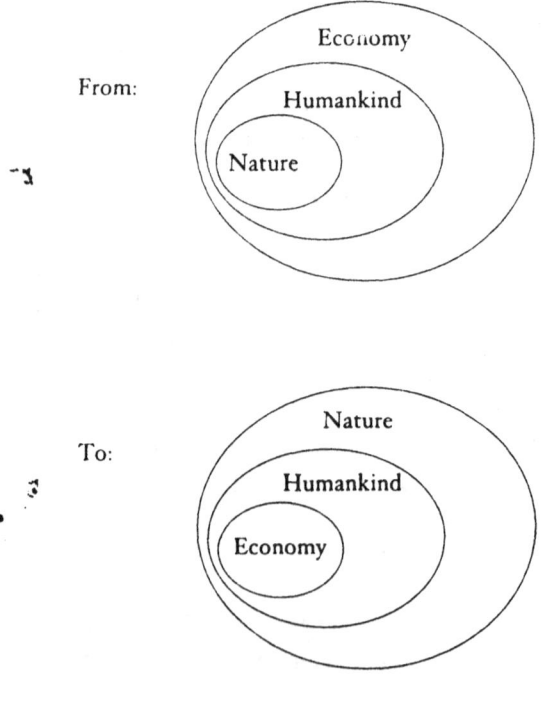

According to the paradigm, the success of economic growth should not be measured simply by the amount of material consumed in a society. The major drive of the production process must be meeting human needs instead of the exploitation of greed. This implies that priorities in the allocation of the earth's limited resources must be towards production to meet "essential instead of non-essential consumption," to focus on the "irreducible needs of society's marginals" instead of on the "wasteful wants of society's overconsumers" (ANGOC, IRED Asia and PCD Forum, 1993:5).[23] The extent to which an economic system fosters the ability of human beings to develop humane relationships with others and nature at large is another yardstick by which the system must be evaluated.

Conclusion

This attempt to construct a holistic general framework for looking at the crises the African continent faces with the hope of providing pointers on how to begin developing appropriate responses has synthesised insights from different intellectual disciplines and used them to analyse four areas of vital significance for the continent: conflict resolution, governance, statehood and economic development. However, these areas of application are not intended to be exhaustive. The framework developed here could be applied to analyse ethnicity and inter-ethnic relations, human rights, the role of the media in society, church-state relations, humanitarianism, management of organisations and people, family relations, and other issues. Each of these areas deserves very careful analysis, obviously too extensive to be presented here.

Despite its name, the peace-and-reconciliation paradigm is not about stopping conflict when it erupts. It is about individual and social transformation. It is about change from immature relationships to mature ones, from dependence or independence to interdependence, from destructive competition to energising co-operation, from hierarchy and coercion to equality and voluntarism, from pursuit of selfish interest to mutuality, and from an economic model that focuses simply on material prosperity to a model that integrates material development with social cohesion and psychological and spiritual growth. In other words, the paradigm is not simply about controlling or solving conflict; it is about fostering harmony by promoting a change process aimed at building a just and humane social order. It is about constructing national and continental visions that could point to ways out of the crises besieging African societies.

The paradigm indicates not only end objectives, but also identifies approaches to be utilised in bringing about the desired changes. These processes entail dialogue instead of coercion, accepting responsibility instead of only assigning it to others, receiving by giving instead of by taking, negotiation instead of win-lose decisions, focusing on needs instead of wants and positions, and cooperation instead of competition. Consistent with these processes, the paradigm also suggests roles for actors leading the kinds of change and transformation processes indicated here. Some of these roles are those of bridge builders, consensus seekers, mediators, reconcilers, healers, catalysts for the creation of humane relationships and a compassionate social order and, most important of all, leadership by example.

Of course, the insights and guidelines developed for each area examined here need further analysis and development and then translation into concrete and practical steps and procedures. The work of the Nairobi Peace Initiative has, to a large extent, involved the development of concrete steps and procedures to operationalise the paradigm in the area of handling conflicts in Africa. Similar efforts need to be undertaken in areas such as governance, economic development and state building. The analysis presented here perhaps can serve as a beginning point.

Notes

1. Although justice is an ingredient of peace, the pursuit of peace goes beyond the pursuit of justice. Peace is pursuing justice while at the same time maintaining a positive relationship of respect and mutuality with the person from whom justice is sought.

2. Because of the author's familiarity with the discipline, this discussion is based on Christian theology. Such insights, however, are not restricted to Christianity. It is very likely that systematic examination of the theology of other religions by those more familiar with them would provide similar insights.

    Please read the biblical texts contained in the footnotes. They constitute an important part of the analysis in this and subsequent sections.

3. See Romans 7:15-25, in which Paul laments the inner conflict and contradictory tendencies between people's intentions and their actions and indicates how reconciliation with Christ reconciles these inner conflicts as well.

4. The Psalms have various illustrations of the relationship between spiritual reconciliation and reconciliation with the self. Psalm 32:1-2 says, "What happiness for those whose guilt has been forgiven. . . . What relief for those who have confessed their sins and God has cleared their record." Another illustration is Psalm 37:11: "But all who humble themselves before the Lord shall be given every blessing and shall have wonderful peace." John 14:27 is illustrative of the peace that emanates from spiritual reconciliation: "I am leaving you with a gift—peace of mind and heart. And the peace I give isn't fragile like the peace the world gives. So do not be troubled or afraid." (Quotations from Living Bible.)

5. In the Sermon on the Mount, Jesus tells a parable that underlines this relationship between the first and third dimensions of reconciliation. He tells a story of a servant who owed his master money and was compassionately forgiven from payment because he was unable to pay. But the servant refused to grant the same forgiveness to another unfortunate person who owed him money and was unable to pay. When the master heard what the servant did, he retracted his forgiveness and recovered every cent he was owed. At the end, Jesus says, "So shall my heavenly Father do to you if you refuse to truly forgive your brothers." See Matthew 18:23-35.(Living Bible)

6. The apostle John raises the same question squarely when he says, "If anyone says, 'I love God,' and hates his brother, he is a liar; for he who does not love his brother whom he has seen, cannot love God whom he has not seen" (1 John 4:20) (RSV). Burkhardt (1974:20) argues that most sins against God are not offenses directly against Him but against other human beings. By the same token, reconciliation with God presupposes mending offences against other human beings that were the causes of the conflict with God in the first place.

7. Matthew 6:14-15 (NIV) reiterates, "For if you forgive men when they sin against you, your heavenly Father will also forgive you. But if you do not forgive men their sins, your Father will not forgive your sins."

8. Psalm 34:11-15 illustrates this point.

9. In Philippians 4:8-9 (Living Bible), Paul writes, "Fix your thoughts on what is true and good and right. Think about things that are pure and lovely, and dwell on the fine, good things in others. Think about all you can praise God for and be glad about. Keep putting into practice all you learned from me and saw me doing, and the God of peace will be with you."

10. Psalm 24:1 (RSV) says, "The earth is the Lord's." In Leviticus 25:23-24 (Living Bible), the Lord says, "And remember, the Land is mine.... You are merely my tenants and sharecroppers."

11. Some point to Genesis 1:28, where it is written, "God blessed them and said to them, 'Be fruitful and multiply, and fill the earth and subdue it'," as a licence to exploit the earth in whatever way human beings see fit. Many have indicated, however, that "subdue" does not mean that God has given humans unrestricted power to do with the earth whatever they will. Since the earth is the Lord's (Psalm 24:1), human beings could only be stewards to manage what is God's (Burkhardt 1974:29). See Forrester Church, who argues that "in the first chapter of Genesis, humankind was created in the image of God. We were given dominion over the earth, charged to fill the earth and to subdue it. But in the second chapter, which reflects a different strand of the ancient traditions brought together in the Bible, we are placed here not to subdue the earth, but 'to dress and to keep it'" (1988:62).

12. One example of this idea is the restoration and conservation of the earth as articulated in Leviticus: "When you come into the land that I am going to give you, you must let the land rest before the Lord every seventh year.... Don't sow your crops and don't prune your vineyards during that entire year. Don't even reap for yourself the volunteer crops that come up, and don't gather the grapes for yourself; for it is a year of rest for the land. Any crops that do grow that year shall be free to all.... Cattle and wild animals alike shall be allowed to graze there" (Leviticus 25:1-7, Living Bible).

13. Negotiation and mediation approaches usually are very rational processes. But people's conflict behaviour might also be based on less rational emotional considerations and thus may not be changed simply by rational negotiation processes and agreements arising from such negotiations. Cognitive decisions or commitments do not necessarily translate into feelings and actions. The gap between the cognitive and the affective, between intent and action, is very reminiscent of the contradiction and schizophrenia that Paul describes in Romans 7:15-24 (NIV): "I do not understand what I do.... For what I want to do I do not do, but what I hate to do.... For I have

the desire to do what is good, but I cannot carry it out.... For in my inner being I delight in God's law, but I see another law at work in the members of my body, waging war against the law of my mind and making me a prisoner of the law of sin at work within my members. What a wretched man I am! Who will rescue me.... Thanks be to God [I am rescued], through Jesus Christ our Lord!" Therefore, providing a spiritual environment in which such contradictions are identified and the emotional and spiritual problems at the root of these anomalies are worked out would no doubt bring to the individuals caught in this contradiction the freedom and reconciliation that Paul refers to in Romans 7:25.

14. For an outstanding example of how churches and ecumenical bodies helped in providing direct peacemaking and reconciliation assistance in a major conflict situation, as well as transferable lessons from that experience. See H. Assefa, *Mediation of Civil Wars: Approaches and Strategies – The Sudan Conflict* (Boulder [Colorado]: Westview Press, 1987).

15. See discussion of this concept in the next section's analysis of the free-market approach to economic growth and prosperity.

16. At the time of writing, these were Liberia, Somalia and Mozambique.

17. Thomas Hobbes, a 17th-century English philosopher, felt that if human beings were left to themselves, they would lead a life he described as "solitary, poor, nasty, brutish, and short." In his view, the role of government is to ensure that the "natural" tendency of human beings to destroy each other is checked.

18. Paul Wachtel (1989:6, 148) calls these advertisements "billboards stirring envy and insatiable desire." He indicates that more than US$ 100 billion a year is spent on advertising and sales promotions in the United States alone.

19. Examples of this waste are planned obsolescence and regular changes of style built into the production process. These can influence consumption behaviour by creating the desire for new styles while the old are still utilisable.

20. Examples of this human toll are the massive layoffs and cuts in social services for the most disadvantaged that structural adjustment programmes have imposed on African societies, ostensibly to stimulate their economies for future prosperity. For a more detailed analysis of SAPs and the contradiction between promise and reality, see D. Korten (1990:53-59).

21. In one capital city ravaged by civil war, the author observed manifestations of this frustration among the youths who were involved as combatants. From their demeanour and attitude, it appeared that they were desperately trying to imitate images of the "good life" drummed into their heads by Western movies and television. But they also appeared to be painfully and angrily aware of their own poverty and the "backwardness" of their society; worse, who and what they were (their nationality, race and colour) seemed to stand in the way of their even coming close to their fantasies. They seemed to dislike who they were but couldn't become who they aspired to be. Such self-contempt might be an underlying factor behind their inclination to engage in excessive violence and brutality (the "Rambo" syndrome), mowing down everyone who reminds them of aspects of themselves that they hate.

22. This diagram was developed in a discussion the author had with Father Nazamajo, Director of the Songhai Centre, Porto-Novo, Benin.

23. Currently, 20 per cent of the earth's population earns 80 per cent of global income and consumes 75 to 80 per cent of the earth's resources (ANGOC and PCD Forum, 1993:5).

References

ANGOC, IRED Asia and PCD Forum. 1993. *Economy, Ecology and Spirituality: Toward a Theory and Practice of Sustainability.* New York: The People-Centered Development Forum.

Assefa, H. 1987. *Mediation of Civil Wars: Approaches and Strategies—The Sudan Conflict.* Boulder (Colorado): Westview Press.

Brown, S.J., and K.M. Schraub (eds). 1992. *Resolving Third World Conflict: Challenges for a New Era.* Washington, D.C.: United States Institute of Peace Press.

Burkhardt, W. 1974. *Towards Reconciliation.* Washington, D.C.: Catholic University Press.

Burton, J.W. 1987. *Resolving Deep-rooted Conflict: A Handbook.* Lanham (Maryland): University Press of America.

———. 1986. "Generic Theory: The Basis of Conflict Resolution." *Negotiation Journal* 2(October):333-344.

Church, F. 1988. *The Seven Deadly Virtues.* San Francisco: Harper and Row.

Cohen, A. 1986. *No Contest: The Case Against Competition—Why We Lose in Our Race To Win.* Boston: Houghton Mifflin

Curle, A. 1990. *Tools for Transformation: A Personal Study.* Stroud (U.K.): Hawthorn Press.

Galtung, J. 1969. "Violence, Peace and Peace Research." *Journal of Peace Research* 3.

Hirsch, F. 1976. *Social Limits to Growth.* Cambridge (Massachussetts): Harvard University Press.

Korten, D.C. 1990. *Getting to the 21st Century: Voluntary Action and the Global Agenda.* West Hartford (Connecticut): Kumarian Press.

Lutz, M.A., and K. Lux. 1988. *Humanistic Economics: The New Challenge.* New York: Bootstrap Press.

Mitchell, C.R., and K. Webb (eds). 1988. *New Approaches to International Mediation.* Westport (Connecticut): Greenwood Press.

Nelson, J.O. 1969. *Dare to Reconcile: Seven Settings for Creative Community.* New York: Friendship Press.

Tadesse, T. 1993. "OAU Out To Build New Image at Talks." *Daily Nation* (Nairobi) May 24:10.

Wachtel, P. 1989. *The Poverty of Affluence: A Psychological Portrait of the American Way of Life.* Philadelphia: New Society Publishers.

Wehr, P. 1979. *Conflict Regulation.* Boulder (Colorado): Westview Press.

5

Religious Leaders, Peacemaking and Social Change
Some Theological Perspectives

Laurenti Magesa

Attitudes and events of the past always form a part of the present in human life. For better or worse, consciously or otherwise, the past moulds and impels us. Therefore, individually and collectively, we are to some extent what we have been. Whether one's view of life and history is linear, cyclical or an ever-expanding spiral, a bit of the present is in the past, and the future lies in both.

This applies to the life of the church and its leaders as well. If today church leaders feel that God is calling them to respond in a certain way, their history—past and present—has something to do with it. And certainly the future—the realisation of the reign of God on earth in anticipation of eternal life in heaven—is at stake; depending on the response to the call, that future could be secured or squandered.

Christian leaders are called to be responsive to the circumstances of the people they lead. The prophecy to which church leaders are now called comes in the face of appalling conditions in Africa. At the same time, this call can be interpreted as God's criticism of attitudes that have prevailed among church leaders. This is why church leaders, as they become more and more actively engaged in the struggle for change in Africa as the conscience of the body politic, must guard against the sins of pride and self-righteousness. By all scriptural accounts, a true prophet should never be self-righteous. Genuine prophets are invariably acutely conscious of their own involvement in social sin, be it by acts of commission or omission. In other words, they are aware that they, as much as anyone else, cannot be entirely free of blame and responsibility for the prevailing state of affairs.

Consider, by way of example, some well-known biblical figures: from the Old Testament, Isaiah walking naked for three years (Isaiah 20:3); Ezekiel's strange actions (Ezekiel 4:4, 12:6); Jeremiah's entire life (Jeremiah 16); and Hosea's miserable marriage—all of these are symbols, devices to put God's message across. But they are also admissions of the prophets' complicity in national misdeeds. Taking up the prophetic vocation is thus not an instantaneous absolution of guilt. It is, among other things, the beginning of a process of disengagement from wrongdoing.

If African church leaders are to keep things in proper perspective at this period in the continent's history, they will do well to remember to listen to what God is saying to them even as they proclaim the demands of God to others. The apostle Paul's case is quite vivid in this respect, although we seldom regard him as a prophet. To be sure, he may not have been one in the manner of those Old Testament personalities we have just mentioned. (The circumstances prevailing in his time hardly called for that kind of prophet.) However, if prophecy means, above all, proclamation of the message of God, Paul of Tarsus is clearly a major New Testament prophet. And no one is more alive to his past than he. The book of Acts contains several accounts of his persecution of the church. Among these is his own version in his speech before King Agrippa:

> As for me, I once thought it was my duty to use every means to oppose the name of Jesus the Nazarene. This I did in Jerusalem; I myself threw many of the saints into prison, acting on authority from the chief priests, and when they were sentenced to death I cast my vote against them. I often went round the synagogues inflicting penalties, trying in this way to force them to renounce their faith; my fury against them was so extreme that I even pursued them into foreign cities. (Acts 26:9-11)

Paul makes the very point that I am trying to emphasise—we must be aware of our own pasts so as to be able to participate with a clear vision in the process of changing the present and shaping the future. Nicolai Berdyaev, a contemporary prophet in his own right, has written in a similar vein. Referring to conditions in Bolshevik Russia in the first part of the 20th century, he warns,

> Christians who condemn Communists for their godlessness and anti-religious persecution cannot lay the blame solely upon these godless Communists; they must assign part of the blame to themselves, and that a considerable part. They must also be penitents. Have Christians done very much for the realization of Christian justice in social life? Have they striven to realize the brotherhood of mankind without that hatred and violence of which they accuse the Communists? The sins of Christians, the sins of the historic churches, have been very great, and these sins bring with them their just punishment. (Pobee, 1993:3)

In seeking to outline the shape of the future from the vantage point of the present, we need to understand how we got to *this* present. Clearly, we have to consider, however briefly, church-state relations, which have contributed to the emergence of the situation that now calls for a courageous prophetic stand by church leaders, what I have called "a process of disengagement from wrongdoing." In sub-Saharan Africa, this process will involve restructuring church leaders' thirty years of theologically dubious association with prevailing socio-political and economic ideologies.

Ambiguous Alliances Between Church and State

Relationships between the church and civil leaders for the last three decades in sub-Saharan Africa have hardly been divine. Historically, the 16th and the 19th centuries were characterised by ambiguous alliances between preachers of the gospel on the one hand and slave traders and colonial metropolises on the other. Similarly, the church's identity was compromised in post-independence Africa due to its leaders' attitudes and behaviour towards the African state. Following are some of the major traits that have marked this compromise.[1]

Collusion with and dependence on post-independence governments

During the struggle for independence in the 1950s and 1960s, African religious leaders generally allied themselves with political activists. This was understandable because both had the same goal, even if their motives sometimes differed. Shortly after independence it became apparent that, despite their rhetoric, many politicians were only interested in assuming the political and economic power of the colonialists before them. On the contrary, most African church leaders at that time genuinely supported the independence struggle from deep theological conviction. They were veritably concerned about the instrumentalisation of African people by colonialism. They viewed colonialism as another form of slavery and a desecration of the image of God in the human being. Like the political leaders, they wanted colonialism ended.

Various churches and individual church leaders offered considerable moral (and sometimes material) support to African political activists. Notable examples of the church's contribution to the struggle for independence can be cited in the cases of Tanzania and Zambia and, later, in Mozambique and Zimbabwe, among many others. Besides theological justification, the church had other reasons to back the independence movement. In several countries, the emerging political leaders were prominent Christian laymen. Not only did they expect the church to support them, but also the church felt obliged to do so (Hastings, 1979:5-34, 86-107; Sivalon, 1992: 9-30). Moreover, having correctly read the impending death of classical colonialism, the church wanted to be on the right side of the emerging independent African states.

Soon after independence, signs indicated that the African political leaders now in power were no match for the internal and external contradictions they had inherited. With very few exceptions, they turned their countries into virtual dictatorships. The new presidents and prime ministers quickly began forcing policies down their people's throats. Above all, they amassed wealth for themselves and their relatives and friends. Corruption at every level of government grew and became entrenched. Of course, many governments were soon overthrown by the military. But the dances to welcome the military "salvation" councils soon turned into dirges. In Ghana, in Nigeria, in Zaire, in Uganda, in the Central African Republic, military regimes took over governments and, in many cases, became more oppressive than the previous civilian governments.

Unfortunately, the church in many countries failed to make a clean break with the corrupt and oppressive civilian and military regimes. It hesitated to comment on government policies, even when there was adequate theological basis for doing so. Meanwhile, the regimes in question interpreted the church's hesitation as support, or at least compliance, and, like the Roman Emperor Constantine, they cleverly used the church to further their own political and economic ends.

Post-independence government leaders used different methods to keep church leaders allied with them or simply silent. As the situation required, they threatened, cajoled and promised. Some governments went as far as peddling the falsehood that a basic human right such as freedom of worship was a favour from the state to the church, and therefore criticising government behaviour amounted to ingratitude! Only a few official church voices protested such distortion. Was it out of fear of losing its considerable real estate holdings and other privileges peripheral to the gospel that the church remained silent? Whatever the reason, it was a neglect of the church's prophetic responsibility.

Near monopoly of intellectual culture and identification with the civil elite

Among the notable achievements of Christian missionary activity in Africa was the introduction and gradual consolidation of formal education. Almost as soon as they set foot in Africa, European missionaries made education one of their top priorities. Mission stations at first were set up as centres for catechetical instruction, but it was not long before the elementary teaching of the three Rs became a regular feature of mission work across Africa. Individual missionaries did outstanding work in translating the Bible into indigenous languages, boosting their use in the process. In this respect, the work of Johann Ludwig Krapf and Johann Rebmann of the English Church Missionary

Society (CMS) to promote Swahili on the East African coast deserves mention.

Of course, the intent and motivation of some of these schools and centres and the education they provided may be questionable. Did, for example, the missionaries see the education they offered as a liberating instrument for Africans? Or was it intended to prepare pupils to be responsible citizens within their own environment and culture? On the one hand, what A. E. Afigbo says about Nigeria seems pertinent to the rest of Africa. According to him, mission schools had other predominant interests:

> They were more concerned with raising pious low-grade teachers and mission hands, and with using schools in effecting the mass conversion of children and, may be, their parents. (Afigbo, 1978:178)

On the other hand, we know that formal education produced some revolutionary thinkers who led Africa's struggle for political independence. But if this happened, it was largely in spite of, rather than because of, the intentions of the "educators."

Missionary education in government schools often imparted elitist attitudes that continually resurface and dominate. The most obvious flaw in this education was the deliberate denial and denigration of Africans' cultural values and humanity. As a result, while still under missionary control, African religious leaders exhibited an extreme form of submissiveness. As soon as this situation changed, though, they teamed up with governing and other elites, alienating themselves from the general populace.

The elitism in the lifestyle and general demeanour of many African church leaders has been rarely questioned until recently. In poorer regions of the world such as Africa, elitist aspirations breed corruption of all sorts. Thus, instances of nepotism or patronage, financial malfeasance or manipulation of the faithful in the church were not uncommon. Church leadership in this period was, as Walbert Buhlmann describes it, very much like that of mediaeval Europe:

> No wonder, then that many native priests perpetuate this frame of mind, directing their devoted obedience upwards and dominating downwards. They demand respect and will not take any criticism, especially when, owing to the old seminary regime, they have been educated to a lord's life and in some countries have been the first to enjoy the advantages of a European education. (1978:249)

Raymond Mosha, a theologian from Tanzania, has observed that, because of "their formal education and standard of living," it has become customary for church leaders in Tanzania "to associate with the wealthy and the powerful" and solicit favours from them. In the minds of the people, Mosha points out, church ministers are bracketed together with government officers and party officials as "important or powerful people" and are treated as such. Mosha's conclusion that, in a situation like this, "spiritual leadership ... [becomes so] constrained by social and worldly power" that the "Church leaders involved begin to lose their prophetic imagination, courage and prophetic authority" (Mosha, 1991:28-29) is therefore easy to understand. Consequently, prophetic ministry is reduced to a minimum or, in extreme cases, disappears altogether.

Abuse of ecclesiastical power and support of authoritarian regimes

The debate on more responsive democratic leadership in church and government is relatively new in this region. It did not feature very much in African theological thought of the late 1960s and early 1970s. Styles of leadership in the church were predominantly domineering, with some leaders espousing a rather benevolent type of ecclesiastical authority. In other words, the theological understanding of divine inspiration was limited to leaders and excluded the rest of the faithful. Consequently, except for sustaining the church financially, the laity remained marginalised. Those who bore the brunt of this marginalisation were women, the youth and the poor—i.e. those already marginalised in secular society.

The abuse of ecclesiastical power was not only confined to leaders of churches with strong hierarchical traditions—hardly any Christian denomination can escape this criticism—but what did this abuse of power consist of in the day-to-day life of the church? Because of church leaders' monopoly of intellectual culture and their alliance with the civil elite, for example, they took little interest in the grassroots in administering the church. The privilege of education became, perhaps inadvertently, an instrument of mind control for the faithful. Although obedience to authority is, in the scriptures, an evangelical virtue (Galatians 2:11-14), it was turned into an ideology of submission by church leaders.

So, after independence, the style of the church's leaders hampered the African church's march towards what Chukwudum B. Okolo calls "adult status." As the late Cardinal Joseph Malula describes them, the leaders

> conceived and thought out everything by themselves; they chewed ideas over and broke them down to give them, then, to the consumer. The local people had nothing to do, but swallow. Hence the passivity. (Okolo, 1991:67)

But the author of the letter to the Hebrews speaks of mature Christians "with minds trained by practice to distinguish between good and bad." Such people are capable of consuming the solid food of personal Christian discernment (Hebrews 5:12-14). Christian leadership styles that do not empower the faithful are therefore oppressive (Kanyandago, 1989:112-122). It is in this respect that we have the essential ingredient of authoritarianism and totalitarian systems.

Who decides who should be included or excluded from the decision-making process on matters affecting individual lives? It will only be the few "enlightened" ones. And it is but a short step from here for leaders to claim divine justification for what are actually improper styles of leadership. In the absence of a sustained theological critique, the church, in many parts of the continent, has tended to operate with little critical reflection, making it an easy ally of dictatorial civil rulers. Fortunately, only a few individual church leaders, rather than churches as institutions, came out publicly in support of corrupt regimes. Nevertheless, from independence until very recently, the church and its leaders did not consistently speak out against the injustice and oppression perpetrated by the civil powers in so many African states:

> How shall we explain this silence and uninvolvement, this blindness and unbelief? For some of us, the reason lies in a life that is not confronted by the suffering and struggle of the poor, and therefore the choice of a convenient God who does not challenge us to take part in a movement for change. For others, however, the reason lies in a choice of privilege and power, and a conscious defence of the status quo. In many cases, it includes taking part in attacks against movements for change, in repression and the killing of the poor. (CIIR 1989:15)

Saint Paul speaks of three enduring spiritual gifts: faith, hope and love. He correctly identifies love as the greatest of the three (I Corinthians 13:13), for in the last analysis, everything is, or ought to be, in the service of love. Yet love must be founded on hope. Active hope works to bring about concrete change in the world in anticipation of the final coming of God's reign. For the church in particular, hope both vivifies it and holds out the promise that no matter how low the church may fall, the Holy Spirit will lift it up and set it on God's own path of loving justice. Without hope, life itself, in both the physical and the spiritual senses, loses meaning and value.

Recent events and attitudes indicate an active awareness of this reality among a significant number of church leaders. The Holy Spirit appears to be agitating the church and its leaders to arise from culpable indolence. After thirty-odd years of silence and ambiguous association with "the prince of this world" (John 12:13), some church leaders at last are heeding their vocation to stand up for the hopes and aspirations of the "little ones" of the world (Matthew 18:6). They now seem to be ready, even at great cost to themselves, to speak up for the voiceless. Whereas not long ago they identified themselves with the wealthy and powerful, they are now learning to attend to the concerns of those unjustly marginalised by the former. In spiritual terminology, no expression adequately describes this situation except the word *conversion*. The 1984 Nobel Peace Prize laureate, Archbishop Mpilo Desmond Tutu of Cape Town, South Africa, observed the emergence of this conversion in the church and said,

> We are helping to make a song and dance about human rights.... It is beginning to happen. Consider the role played by the Churches of Kenya in the face of a hostile regime, or the witness of the Roman Catholic bishops in Malawi. A similar stand has been taken in Zaire. When an honest broker was needed in Benin to facilitate the transitional process, the political parties looked to the Church. This constitutes a new opportunity for the Church to regain its integrity and to promote the cause of justice and peace on this continent in a manner that has not been done since the beginning of the African independence process. The Church is not true to itself if it keeps silent when people are exploited or abused. To violate the rights of the people is to violate God whose image dwells in them. To neglect or abuse people is to neglect or abuse Christ himself. Whatever we do to others, we do to him. It is as simple as that. (1993)

Christian conversion is always a *kairos*, a unique moment that must be seized and utilised when it presents itself. What is happening now in many places in Africa is a *kairos* to which the church has begun to respond by awakening from its spiritual torpor (Romans 13:11). However, Christians should not take this privileged moment of their transformation for granted. For the cause of justice and peace to succeed, certain values need to be enhanced and taboos observed. The church's present commitment to peace and justice is not yet on a firm footing. If this commitment is derailed, not only will Africa's socio-political condition worsen (Matthew 12:43-45), but the church itself will be grievously damaged.

The church's role in this process of change, inculcating values in the political process, is one that will outlast its direct involvement and put the continent firmly on the road to just socio-political practices. These values are theological imperatives for Christians. But even though they arise from Christian convictions (and perhaps for this reason), they are deeply human and potentially acceptable by all people genuinely concerned about the welfare of humanity.

Important Theological and Practical Imperatives

What is the role of the church in a disenchanted, dispossessed continent? The majority of Africa's population has not experienced any significant positive change, even with independence. They have practically lost faith and hope in their politicians, and many are looking to the church for inspiration and leadership. A significant number of church leaders has been impelled by faith to take up the challenge. If these, in general, are the facts, some questions need to be asked: What principles should guide church leaders in fulfilling the challenge? How will they be different from the "politicians"? Without a clear understanding of their calling at this time, church leaders could fail the people, just as the politicians have done. It is therefore essential that church leaders construct a framework, informed by their Christian faith, in which to situate the ministry they are now challenged to exercise.

Three pillars should structure the Christian response to the current socio-political situation in Africa:

1. the people, whose integral sovereignty is the expression of the sovereignty of God;
2. popular participation in the socio-political process as the method for effecting the sovereignty of the people, and so of God; and,
3. loving justice as the indication of the reality of God's reign among us.

These pillars should make up the subject, the means and the goal of what has been referred to in theology as "realized eschatology." Church leaders' involvement in the political process must establish and consolidate these pillars. If they genuinely do this, their direct involvement in political processes will be only temporary, as it should be. Nevertheless, once these pillars are consolidated, the strength of the church also will ensure that it is not then relegated to the sidelines, or compromised into a conspiracy of silence, whenever the state reneges and tramples on the rights of its people. As envisaged here, the stronger these pillars are, the firmer the foundation for an ongoing prophetic role for the church in society.

The sovereignty of the people as the sovereignty of God

The real significance of this first pillar is that it effectively puts an end (at least conceptually) to the privatisation of faith and religion that is re-emerging with disconcerting strength as right-wing Christian movements spread throughout the continent. These movements are centrally concerned with life in heaven and distance themselves from the affairs of life on earth.

But life in this world *does* matter. Even though we are not *of* the world, we still are *in* the world (John 17:14), and it is in this world that we all should work out our salvation "in fear and trembling" (Philippians 2:12). It is this same world that God so loved "that he gave his only son, so that everyone who believes in him may not be lost but may have eternal life" (John 3:16). Ultimately, life in the world is not only about the mystery of humankind's creation as "little less than God" (Psalm 8:5), but also about the much deeper mystery of its redemption through God's incarnation in Jesus Christ. Through these mysteries, God wishes to reveal his primacy in the primacy of human beings. This is what sovereignty of the people means. Psalm 8 could not be clearer:

> Yahweh, our Lord
> how great your name throughout the earth!
> Above the heavens is your majesty chanted
> by the mouths of children, babies in arms.
> You set your stronghold firm against your foes
> to subdue enemies and rebels.
> I look up at your heavens, made by your fingers,
> at the moon and stars you set in place—
> ah, what are human beings that you should spare a thought for them.
> Humanity that you should care for it?
> Yet you have made humankind little less than God,
> you have crowned them with glory and splendour,
> made it lord over the works of your hands,
> set all things under its feet. . . .

All this indicates that church leaders have a responsibility to ensure that personal and societal dignity is an integral part of the ethic of nations. Human dignity can best be ensured through respect and enforcing the rights of the individual. Liberties or rights are God-given solely on the criteria of the recipients' humanity, regardless of race, class, status, faith or any other physical, psychological or spiritual characteristic. This last point on rights and liberties is especially important with regard to faith and spirituality because in many countries dangerous rifts are springing up between Islam and Christianity. No church leader can afford to ignore these developments.

Human rights are "natural" and "moral" rights in the sense that, as already pointed out, they are God-given. In concrete terms, church leaders must attend to some of the following as they participate in the process of shaping the life of the continent at this juncture of its history:

1. Take the United Nations Universal Declaration of Human Rights as a basis upon which to build an ethic of human dignity. From a Christian point of view, much more is required in human relationships than is laid down in the charter, but the conscientisation that religious leaders need to emphasise in the secular sphere could revolve around it.

2. Work against all forms of discrimination, whether racial, ethnic, gender or class. Discrimination denies or diminishes a person's or society's humanity, rights and dignity and is an offence against God.
3. Promote interaction and understanding among members of different ethnic and religious groups and African countries. Tribalism and religious intolerance threaten to become the bane of the continent. Can the church be a credible witness to the rest of the world on the universality of God's love?
4. Learn to listen and avoid dogmatism. As John Pobee has noted, "truth . . . from the human perspective is never so final that it may not be revised" (1993:5). The example needed from religious leaders is to discern truth from whatever quarter and integrate it into the life-styles of our nations.

Mass participation in the socio-political process: towards realisation of the primacy of the people

This pillar represents more than a democratic ideal. Underlying it is the ethic of human equality, which presupposes the equal worth of every person regardless of individual characteristics. Physical differences between individuals, differences in intellectual acumen and even divergent aspirations must all be recognised and appreciated, of course. Society's cohesiveness, and human dignity itself, will be severely strained if the social contract is not structured to cater adequately for the physical, intellectual and moral inequalities of each and all of its members. (Guerry, 1961:64-68; Mutiso and Rohio, 1975:43)

Human interdependence and supplementation of individuals' qualities and capabilities is the reason and justification for interaction in society. Personal qualities, outside the context of relationships, really are of little or no consequence:

> So that in the realm of truth, goodness and beauty (for example), two men with unequal statements will need mutual co-operation in order to realize their existential ends individually as well as collectively. (Akoi, 1970:181)

In this context, Jesus' pronouncement that we only save our life by losing it in the service of our fellow human beings (Matthew 16:25) becomes understandable. Relationships, fostered primarily by an inner conviction of mutuality, reciprocity and service, should be the basis for participation in the socio-political process. Relationships enhance confidence and individuals' sense of personal worth as children of God along with everyone else.

This pillar also touches on the economic order, among other things. At the risk of sounding "socialist," which is no longer fashionable, it is important to emphasise what is essentially a theological view of socio-economic organisation, leading to fuller and more meaningful participation in decision-making. If a social or economic order systematically allows some to exercise control over others (in the sense of concentrating resources necessary for biological, psychological and spiritual survival in a few hands), then those excluded from this control inevitably have their dignity as human beings reduced: first, because it becomes very difficult for them to sustain their lives and, second (and perhaps more significantly), because their equal participation in the social contract is curtailed or eliminated. "Participation" as a slave or client to a master or patron is not real participation and, from the Christian point of view, is not in line with human dignity.

In abject poverty, disease and ignorance there is no dignity. These can be effectively combated only when resources and intellect are put at the service of human beings. Economic or technical advances are only important insofar as they serve the human dignity of all. The Second Vatican Council correctly insists that what people do "to obtain greater justice, wider brotherhood, and a more humane ordering of social relationships has greater worth than technical advances" (*Gaudium et Spes*). In the process of true, integral human progress, the high ideal of the dignity of individual people and groups supersedes the right to individual acquisition of wealth.

During this time of so-called transition to market economies in Africa, religious leaders are in danger of forgetting that sharing and co-operation, beyond being central to African culture, are also principal Christian virtues. The market economy, as advocated by the North in this post-cold war period, is really an euphemism for capitalism. We must not confuse capitalism with democracy. The structural adjustment programmes (SAPs) being urged upon Africa and the entire South as part of the democratisation packet are often deadly. They are neither conducive to democracy nor, for that matter, to integral development and human dignity. Due to SAPs, Africa sinks further and further into an oppressive and explosive situation:

> While capital hemorrhages from the South, the poor suffer from the remedy prescribed by the International Monetary Fund (IMF) which has taken on the role of global debt policeman. The IMF mission is to ensure that countries pay back their debts. They do this through "structural adjustment programs." Countries are told to cut their budget deficits and increase exports, even if it means cutting down the remains of their forests, encouraging highly pollutive strip-mining, or exporting their teachers to work as housemaids overseas so the government can tax the money sent back to their families. Southern governments have some leeway in where budget cuts should be made, but military budgets are seldom reduced for

fear of a military backlash, and taxes on the rich are rejected by wealthy legislators. As a result, the heaviest burden of "adjustment" falls on the poor. Money in the budget to provide immunizations and medicines to fight preventable diseases, to promote child nutrition, clean water, education, and to build basic infrastructure for development is shifted out of social service programs in order to pay the debt. Even worse, governments lack the political will to tax the wealthy, and they typically impose sales taxes which hit the poor the hardest. The debt is indeed being paid on the backs of the poor. (MSSC, 1992)

This situation becomes worse each day because the people are denied their right to participate in decision-making processes. The first level of action should be for religious leaders to empower people to speak up in matters concerning them. This could be done in various ways:

1. Education at all levels can play a big role in liberating people from fear and nonchalance. The church therefore should increase its investment in education. It is fundamental that students be well informed on poverty in their society and its causes. We can then hope that they themselves will be resourceful enough to come up with solutions to the problems.

2. We must not underestimate the power of the word of God in effecting change. Religious leaders have to reflect on how they use their homilies and sermons, catechetical instructions, informal contacts with people and so on. Do they use the word of God to bring about a false sense of peace or to free people from the shackles of fear, superstition and the violence quietly inflicted upon them? The word of God is still a prophetic "double-edged sword" (Hebrews 4:12-13), not an instrument of domestication. All church leaders therefore must be aware of their potential to effect change.

3. Similarly, we must not underestimate the power of example. According to Pope Paul VI, people today trust those who teach by example rather than with mere words (1975). The church would be defeating its own witness if it urged popular participation in civil affairs while eliminating it from ecclesiastical affairs. This is a very serious point because it concerns the major denominations of the church. These churches need to engage in earnest soul-searching lest their urging for political reform load burdens on others that they themselves do not move a finger to lift. (Luke 11:46)

Loving justice as the concretisation of God's presence among us

The theme of loving–or righteous–justice (*dikaiosune* in Greek and, *tsedeq* or *tsedequah* in Hebrew) is perhaps the most important in the scriptures. Its significance in Christian life cannot therefore be lost on us. For what is the goal on earth of the faith of the Christian except loving justice? What is the concrete sign of realised eschatology but the practice of loving justice? It is impossible to resist quoting at length the Seventy-second Psalm which speaks graphically of this theme and its opposite, oppression (Hebrew: *ashaq, daka* and *tok*). The king in the psalm is, of course, the national ruler. But the good national ruler (president, prime minister) stands on earth in the place of God himself, hence God's expectation of national and international order:

> Give the king your justice, O God
> and your righteousness to a King's son.
> May he judge thy people with righteousness,
> and thy poor with justice!
> Let the mountains bear prosperity for the people,
> and the hills, in righteousness!
> May he defend the cause of the poor of the people,
> give deliverance to the needy,
> and crush the oppressor!
> May he live while the sun endures,
> and as long as the moon,
> throughout all generations!
> May he be like rain that falls on the mown grass,
> like showers that water the earth!
> In his days may righteousness flourish,
> and peace abound, till the moon be no more!
> ....
> For he delivers the needy when they call,
> the poor and those who have no helper.
> He has pity on the weak and the needy,
> and saves the life of the needy.
> From oppression and violence he redeems their life;
> and precious is their blood in his sight
> ....
> May there be abundance of grain in the land;
> on the tops of the mountains may it wave;
> may its fruit be like Lebanon;
> and may people blossom forth from the cities
> like the grass of the field!
> May his name endure for ever,
> his fame continue as long as the sun!
> May people bless themselves by him,
> all nations call him blessed! (trans. Tamez, 1982:21)

The scriptures, however, do not speak of "dry" justice, as the psalm shows. Psalm 72 aptly juxtaposes, in a singe breath, "justice" and "righteousness," "deliverance" and "pity." Charity born of mercy is an essential part of justice, and vice-versa. Shakespeare's *The Merchant of Venice* is quite clear (and profoundly theological) in this respect (in Portia's plea to Shylock):

> The quality of mercy is not strain'd;
> it droppeth as the gentle rain from heaven
> Upon the place beneath: it is twice bless'd;
> It blesseth him that gives and him that takes:
> 'Tis mightiest in the mightiest; it becomes
> The throned monarch better than his crown;
> His sceptre shows the force of temporal power,
> The attribute to awe and majesty,
> wherein doth sit the dread and fear of beings;
> But mercy is above this scepter'd sway,—
> It is enthroned in the heart of kings,
> It is an attribute to God himself;
> When mercy (or love) seasons justice. (Act IV, Scene I)

Several of Paul's letters, in their turn, give clear instructions on the need for the same merciful love in the concrete form of almsgiving by and for "the saints": "If any of the saints are in need," Paul writes to the Romans, "you must share with them; and you should make hospitality your special care" (Roman, 12:13). The Corinthian church he instructs,

> Now about collection made for the saints:
> you are to do as I told the Churches in Galatia
> to do. Every Sunday, each one of you must put
> aside what they can afford, so that collections
> need not be made after I have come. When I am
> with you, I will send your offering to Jerusalem
> by the hand of whoever you give letters of reference
> to; if it seems worthwhile for me to go too, they can
> travel with me. (I Corinthians 16:1-4)

Among the most important things that James, Peter and John impressed upon Paul was that he ought to "remember to help the poor" (Galatians 2:10). It seems that this recognition had been an aspect of Paul's conversion since even without their counsel he was already "anxious" to do so (Galatians 2:10). Thus, in his ministerial duties he sets a high priority on this task and on occasion has to excuse himself and postpone a visit to the church at Rome because

> first . . . I must take a present of money to
> the saints in Jerusalem, since Macedonia
> and Achaia have decided to send a generous
> contribution to the poor among the saints
> at Jerusalem. A generous contribution as it
> should be, since it is really repaying a debt:
> the pagans who share the spiritual possessions
> of these poor people have a duty to help them
> with temporal possessions. So when I have done
> this and officially handed over what has been
> raised, I shall set out for Spain and visit you
> on the way. (Romans 15:25-28)

The details of what the early doctors of the church have to say about justice and charity are not cruicial to this discussion. Suffice it to note that their theological exposition of the centrality of loving justice has not been equalled to this day. In fact, a serious practical error has crept into Christian pastoral practice worldwide. It stems from justice.

The kind of "charity," "kindness" or "love" that prevails in situations of structural injustice is pseudocharity and is antithetical to human dignity. It only cushions the most destructive effects of the injustice, and so perpetuates them. Such charity cannot restore justice. Since charity and justice are interdependent virtues, charity is authentically virtuous if it furthers justice. The reverse is also the case. True charity liberates, making individuals and peoples take charge of their integral growth (Freire, 1970:29).

The reform or change the North is now advocating throughout Africa may have the effect of co-opting the African political, economic and intellectual elite into an unjust international economic structure and condemning the rural and urban poor as objects of charity. The most serious concern is that the church may itself be used by the wealthy merely as an agent of charity. There is no Christian joy in distributing charity food in Somalia, Sudan, Liberia, Kenya, Tanzania or Mozambique. The first task for the church is to address itself to the causes of such situations.

The African church's dependence on the wealthy churches of the North has often compromised its mission. Instead of criticising the churches of the North's complicity in the structures that cause the misery of the South, the African church has often been content with charity. It is not fair for Africa to continue to give the Northern churches the impression that through charity the North is fulfilling the demands of the gospel while international structures prejudicial to the economic freedom of the South remain intact.

With regard to justice, the church ought to seriously consider and implement a number of things:

1. On the domestic scene, the church has done much for integral human development in Africa. Yet the gap in life-style between church leaders and the general populace is still embarrassingly wide and growing. Some years ago, there was talk in the African church of a moratorium on charity from the North to make church leaders aware of this disparity. Perhaps it is time to reconsider the moratorium issue. This time around, we need to be clear that the call for a moratorium is not motivated by a desire for isolationism. It will, however, logically imply a lowered standard of living for church leaders. It is justified in that it aims for justice and dignity for all.

2. On the issue of human rights, the church should first create a continental, ecumenical human-rights-monitoring organisation. Such an organisation would command more respect and visibility and help the church in its prophetic mission. The creation of a sort of ombudsman should follow. Before making any official statement, proposal or complaint, church leaders need to be thoroughly informed about the facts. The ombudsman, or a similar office, would serve this purpose.

3. The African Recovery Unit at United Nations headquarters in New York makes what may be a startling revelation for some:

The lack of significant debt relief has meant that Africa's debt servicing continued to soar throughout the 1980s, growing five-fold between 1983 and 1990 and accounting for 30 per cent of the continent's export earnings—themselves hard-hit by commodity price declines.

This is an extraordinary burden for the world's poorest continent. Africa spends four times more on debt servicing than it does for all the health services it provides to its 600 million people. Mozambique alone loses more children to malnutrition and easily preventable or curable diseases than do all the struggling countries of the former Soviet Union. Indeed, less than one-third of Africa's debt service bill would fund the additional annual cost of programmes required to meet the key social-sector goals set by the World Summit for children in 1990. (ARU, 1993)

No wonder, then, that Africa's debt crisis has been called the "silent killer." It is an urgent moral issue. Could not the church use its international connections to urge creditor governments and institutions in the North to cancel, reduce or reschedule Africa's debt payments?

Specific Considerations

More than thirty years of authoritarian and repressive rule in African countries has catapulted the church and its leaders to the centre of calls for social change in Africa. Within the key issues church leaders need to address theologically, however, there are narrower, more specific and immediate questions that deserve brief mention:

Multipartyism

Many church leaders have distinguished themselves by advocating multipartyism in the last three years or so. Kenya and Malawi offer two outstanding examples. In practically every African country, the single-party system has been exploited unscrupulously for selfish ends. Because of this, religious leaders may fall into the trap of identifying multiparty systems with democracy, thus lowering their guard against injustice and oppression that may be perpetrated in the name of multipartyism. This must not happen.

Democracy in Africa should not be approached primarily as an idea or as a comparison between types of parties or political organisations. Democracy in Africa ought to refer to, and be about, the majority of the people's conditions of existence and how they can improve themselves. In concrete terms, democracy in Africa is that process that enables people to devise ways and means of resurrecting themselves from the tomb of subservience, exploitation, fear, poverty and illness. If the multiparty system does this best, well and good. But all energies should not be invested in issues of democracy that are really theoretical and secondary. To confront the sin of injustice that is in all of us (and thus in every system) is the primary mission of religious leaders in Africa (Miranda, 1977:1-6). Loving justice should be concretised in structures that enhance equality and human dignity.

Religious pluralism

Western Christianity contemptuously ignored what African spirituality could have taught it about religious tolerance. Now, after centuries of cruelty and indignity inflicted upon people in the name of God and religion, Western theological scholarship (and, to some extent, the official church itself) is awakening to religious tolerance as in accordance with God's law of love (Buhlmann, 1982; Dickson, 1991; Hick and Knitter, 1987; Hillman, 1989; Knitter,

1985). Religious intolerance is immoral. But religion is nothing if it is not about morality, and

> morality's keystone and inescapable conclusion is that no end, no matter how sublime or divine or eternal, justifies causing-or indifferently allowing-an innocent person to suffer. Infinite retribution in another life does not compensate for even a small injustice in this life. And if the god of [a certain] theology proclaims that it does compensate, then he is an immoral god and in conscience we are obliged to rebel against him. (Miranda, 1977)

Certain approaches to Christian evangelism in the past, and the advent of Christian and Muslim fundamentalism today, have caused and are causing a lot of suffering. One of the greatest challenges Christian religious leaders face in the foreseeable future is, first, dealing with fundamentalism in their own denominations and, then, relating to Islam. Nigeria, Sudan and Tanzania are countries where intolerance has erupted into open conflict between Islam and Christianity, with considerable loss of life and property. The conditions that caused the conflict in Nigeria, for example, exist in other countries as well. All so-called Muslim countries in Africa have elements of deep-seated religious intolerance dating back to previous centuries. If there is no change in attitude and development of a wise, understanding and accepting religious pluralism, it is only a matter of time before there is an explosion. While it is quite legitimate and necessary to defend one's religion when it is unfairly under attack, Christianity must take care to eschew the triumphalism that characterised such defence in the past. Triumphalism does not differ much in actual practice from levelling an attack on other religions.

Mediation of conflicts

In the context of the change now taking place on the continent, Christian religious leaders have a role to play in reducing or eliminating the root causes of simmering or open violence and effecting true peace. One way of effecting true peace is by becoming agents of conflict resolution through the mechanisms of "good offices, inquiry, mediation (and) arbitration" (Assefa, 1987:3-4). This is a *kairos*, an opportune moment provided by God, and the church must not let it pass.

Marvin C. Ott enumerates the characteristics and skills of the successful mediator in conflict situations:

1. Impartiality regarding the issues in the dispute.
2. Independence from all parties to the conflict.
3. The respect of and acceptability to all protagonists.

4. The knowledge and skill to deal with the issues.
5. Possession of the required physical resources.
6. International support for the mediator.
7. Leverage—i.e., the possibility for the mediator to put pressure on one or both parties to accept a proposed settlement. (Assefa, 1987:26)

Paul Wehr identifies the mediator's skills as, among other things, clarity, empathy, the ability to listen, a sense of timing, communication, imagination and crisis management (Assefa, 1987:26).

The fact that religious leaders are approached and accepted as mediators shows that, because of their spiritual disposition, they are believed to possess the characteristics and skills in question. As peacemaking is a permanent ministry of the church—"Blessed are the peacemakers, for they shall be called the children of God" (Matthew 5:9). Christian religious leaders have a responsibility to sharpen and deepen their skills. They should, as Peter advises all of us,

> have (an) answer ready for people who ask you
> the reason for the hope that you all have. But
> give it with courtesy and respect and with a
> clear conscience, so that those who slander you
> when you are living a good life in Christ may be
> proved wrong in the accusations that they bring.
> And if it is the will of God that you should suffer,
> it is better to suffer for doing right than for
> doing wrong. (I Peter 3:15-17)

Advocacy for the marginalised

The church ought to be specifically concerned about the enduring injustice against specific groups of people in Africa, especially women and the youth. Since the church is itself caught up in this structural injustice, its leaders have tended to shy away from the issue. All the church's efforts at peacemaking and social change on the continent will come to naught if it does not clean up its own house first. It has been said, correctly, that "everyone who ventures to speak to people about justice must first be just in their eyes" (Synod, 1971). The church has to listen to the ever-growing grievances of its womenfolk, make true peace with this half of the human population, which is cruelly used, and thus unleash social change of revolutionary proportions. We must empathise and acknowledge that women account for more than half of the South's population. They participate in the development process in a myriad of ways, but their contribution to economic and social change continues to be inadequately recognized and greatly undervalued, because male-dominated cultures have given them an inferior position in society, and custom, taboo, and the sexual division of labour keep them subordinate to men. (Henriot, 1992:24)

The church must face its own gender divide with openness and honesty. The issue is simply equal participation by all members of the congregation in the life of the church as the body of Christ. "Theological" reasons that have continuously been adduced to prevent this do not withstand critical examination.

A similar case must be put for the vast majority of Africa's youth. Their population and place is as significant as that of women. What future do the youth have? The church faces a crisis if it remains, for all intents and purposes, a gerontocracy in its planning and praxis.

Conclusion

Throughout the ages, the church has been an agent of social change, for better and for worse. Africa can cite numerous examples on both sides of the ledger. There have been positive, well-timed initiatives, but there have also been missed and misused opportunities. Either because of negligence, fear or prejudice, the church has failed to seize the *kairos*, the unique moments God has provided it to effect change (*metanoia*) in the deepest, most comprehensive sense of the term. But such unique moments always recur, if only we stay alert and read the signs of the times.

By available evidence, it seems God is calling the church to be a visible agent for peace and justice in Africa. The call is for the church to act now for the sake of the future of the continent. Some members of the church have hesitated to accept this call, but many Christian leaders have begun to take on the role of Moses, encouraged by God's promise: "I shall help you to speak and tell you what to say" (Exodus 4:12). Of course, there is homework to be done in order to appreciate the signs of the times. Ultimately, however, our help is in the name and gospel of Jesus. The discussion in this chapter has described the call and the conditions necessitating it and proposed a possible response.

Note

1. Sociologist of religion Otto Maduro, historian Anna Maria Bidegain, and theologian Pablo Richard, to whom I am indebted for inspiration in writing this section, also mention these features of church-state relationships in many countries of Latin America for the last 500 years.

References

Afigbo, A.E. 1978. "Essay" in *Christianity in Independent Africa* edited by E. Fashiole-Luke *et al.* London: Rex Collins.

Akoi, P. 1970. *Religion in African Social Heritage.* Rome: Pontifical Urban University.

ARU (African Recovery Unit). 1993. *African Debt Crisis: A Continuing Impediment to Development.* New York: United Nations Department of Public Information.

Assefa, H. 1987. *Mediation of Civil Wars: Approaches and Strategies—The Sudan Conflict.* Boulder (Colorado): Westview Press.

Buhlmann, W. 1982. *The Chosen Peoples.* Slough (England): St. Paul Publications.

———. 1978. *The Coming of the Third Church: An Analysis of the Present and Future of the Church.* Maryknoll (N.Y.): Orbis Books.

CIIR (Catholic Institute for International Relations). 1989. *The Road To Damascus: Kairos and Conversion.* London: Catholic Institute for International Relations.

Dickson, K.A. 1991. *Uncompleted Mission: Christianity and Exclusivism.* Maryknoll (N.Y.): Orbis Books.

Fashiole-Luke, E., *et al* (eds.) 1978. *Christianity in Independent Africa.* London: Rex Collings.

Freire, P. 1970. *Pedagogy of the Oppressed.* New York: Herder and Herder.

Gaudium et Spes (No. 35).

Guerry, E. 1961. *The Social Teaching of the Church.* London: St. Paul Publications.

Hastings, A. 1979. *A History of African Christianity 1950-1975.* London: Cambridge University Press.

Henriot, P.J. 1992. "Integral Development Guidelines for Africa from the Church's Social Teaching." *African Christian Studies* 8(3).

Hick, J., and P. F. Knitter (eds.) 1987. *The Myth of Christian Uniqueness.* Maryknoll (N.Y.): Orbis Books.

Hillman, E. 1989. *Many Paths: A Catholic Approach to Religious Pluralism.* Maryknoll (N.Y.): Orbis Books.

Kanyandago, P. 1989. "A Biblical Reflection on the Exercise of Pastoral Authority in African Churches," in *Jesus in African Christianity: Experimentation and Diversity in African Christology,* Edited by J.N.K. Mugambi and L. Magesa. Nairobi: Nairobi Peace Initiative.

Knitter, P.F. 1985. *No Other Name? A Critical Survey of Christian Attitudes Toward the World Religions.* Maryknoll (N.Y.): Orbis Books.

Maduro, O., A. M. Bidegain and P. Richard. 1992. Notes taken by the author on their talks about five hundred years of church identity and understanding in Latin America, Maryknoll, New York, July.

Magesa, L. (ed.). 1991. *The Prophetic Role of the Church in Tanzania Today: Symposium of Five Papers.*

Miranda, J.P. 1977. *Being and the Messiah: The Message of St. John.* Maryknoll (N.Y.): Orbis Books.

MSSR (Missionary Society of St. Columban). 1992. *Beyond Debt.* (Newsletter of the Campaign on Debt and Development Alternatives, Washington, D.C.) (July).

Mutiso, G.M., and S.W. Rohio (eds). 1975. *Readings in African Political Thought.* London: Heinemann.

Nairobi Peace Initiative. 1993. "Symposium on the Role of Religious Leaders in Peacemaking and Social Change in Africa: Concept Paper." Nairobi. Photocopy.

Nyerere, J.K. 1973. *Freedom and Development* [Uhuru na Maendeleo]. Dar es Salaam: Oxford University Press.

Okolo, C.B. 1991. *The Liberating Role of the Church in Africa Today.* Eldoret (Kenya): AMECEA Gaba Publications.

Paul VI, Pope. 1975. *Evangelii Nuntiandi* (apostolic exhortation no. 45).

Pobee, J.S. 1993. "Doing Theology in a Global Village." *Ministerial Formation* 61 (April):5.

Sivalon, J.C. 1992. *Kanisa Katoliki na Siasa ya Tanzania Bara 1953 hadi 1985.* Peramiho (Tanzania): Benedictine Publications *Ndanda.*

Synod. 1971. *Justice In the Word.*

Tamez, E. 1982. *Bible of the Oppressed.* Maryknoll (N.Y.): Orbis Books.

The Jerusalem Bible (Standard Edition).

Tutu, D. 1993. "The Church in Africa and Human Rights." *African News Bulletin* 231.

6

The Churches' Involvement in the Democratisation Process in Kenya

Agnes C. Abuom

As in many other societies, Kenyans' desire for democratic governance has been driven by a vision of a new society in which all people have the possibility of influencing government decisions and living in dignity, conscious of each individual's worth. People's desire and need to participate and chart out their common future has always journeyed with humanity in the evolution process from time immemorial.

Often, however, the people's desire for democratic governance is antithetical to their rulers' wishes, resulting in a conflict of interests between the state and its citizens. This conflict has been dramatically played out in many countries—and Kenya has been no exception—with each side standing steadfastly by its interests in a no-retreat, no-surrender posture. On the one hand, the state has instituted, maintained and depended, for its existence and survival, on structures that in turn depend on the state for their justification. These structures—the armed forces, the judiciary, etc.—have been used with a great deal of "success" by the state through manipulation, coercion and arm-twisting.

On the other hand, the people have not just resigned themselves to the machinations of their rulers, but have relentlessly resisted dictatorship and cruelty. State propaganda, bribery and the use of influential institutions have not broken their resolve to be free. Among the critical institutions that the state has used to perpetuate oppression is the church. The people also have turned to the church in their quest for democracy and self-dignity, giving it a paradoxical role in the "second liberation" of Africa that began in the late 1980s.

The church's role in the struggle for democracy must be considered in the context of the church-state relationship, especially in light of the fact that, in Kenya, the church and the state have had very cordial relations, especially in the area of development programmes. The various churches have been active in the areas of human rights, peacemaking, civic education and development. The churches also have taken a variety of positions on major social, political and economic issues. The nature, scope and significance of church-state and church-citizens' relationships are critical insofar as social change is concerned. Church-state relationships during the last decade have helped inform the role of the church in social change and democratisation. In the case of Kenya, three main groupings among the churches illustrate the parameters of these relationships.

The first grouping comprises (most) churches that fall under the umbrella of the National Council of Churches of Kenya (NCCK) or the Catholic church. These churches individually and collectively have articulated certain positions regarding church-state relations through pastoral letters and/or press releases. The second grouping includes churches under the umbrella of the Evangelical Fellowship of Kenya (EFK). This group of churches also has occasionally commented on the church-state relationship. And a third grouping comprises the mainstream of independent churches, which do not articulate positions collectively but have a following at the local/grassroots level.

The objectives and motivations that have driven the three church groupings in state or public affairs are not necessarily shared or commonly known by their members. Although these groups' objectives and motivations may have been noble, they largely remain the domain of church leaders. Churches that have been systematically engaged in socio-economic development projects have been more articulate on social change and democratisation given that, in the course of implementing their development projects, they come into direct contact with the institutions and powers of the state and can therefore appreciate how they impact upon the people. However, the church's theological and philosophical conceptual frameworks have been poorly articulated within its involvement in social-change processes. Consequently, it has only managed to provide knee-jerk comments on questions of governance and has been caught up in the various conflicts that beset the nation. The democratisation process taking place in the social, political and economic spheres is a critical challenge to the church and its leadership to re-examine itself as an institution.

To focus on the role of the church in democratisation in Kenya does not imply that other civic organisations have not played a part. On the contrary, student organisations and professional associations such as the Law Society of Kenya have played a central role. The church, however, is the only formal organisation in Kenya besides the ruling party (the Kenya African National Union, or KANU) with a mass following and the capacity to attract loyalty. Furthermore, the church in Kenya has been in the forefront of social change for a long time.

Historical Background

Kenya as we know it today was carved out and moulded by the British Government during the European scramble for Africa. It was then given a British administrative structure that had absolutely nothing in common with traditional models and systems of administration. Although the new structure made use of local administrators, these merely served to facilitate British colonial exploitation of Kenya's human and natural resources.

Kenyan communities, previously independent but now colonised, witnessed organised destruction of their socio-political and economic systems and the imposition of new value systems. They were made to pay for the cost of administration through forced labour, taxation and alienation of land. Kenyans became a subject people, and even their religions had to submit to the superior god of the colonisers.

During the colonial period, the notion of separation of the secular and the spiritual seemed to exist more in word than in deed. The church (especially British missionary organisations) and the state assisted each other in many areas; to many Africans, the church was an appendage of the state (Chepkwony, 1987). Because of the church's cordial relationship with the state, the budding African nationalist movement did not perceive it as an ally in the struggle to oust the colonial rulers.

At the time when Kenya attained independence, the church had not extricated itself from this collaborative role. The exception was the independent churches that broke away from the mainline mission churches, most of which had embraced the nationalist struggle for independence.

Kenya became a self-governing entity in 1963 after a bloody struggle against Britain's seventy years of colonialism. At the time, Kenya was a multiparty state, with KANU as the ruling party and KADU (the Kenya African Democratic Union) as the main opposition party. One year into independence, however, Kenya became a *de facto* one-party state after KADU dissolved itself and its members joined KANU. Even with this change, the constitutional provision for other political parties remained unaltered.

In April 1966, Vice-President Oginga Odinga, disillusioned by the government, formed the Kenya People's Union (KPU) in a radical split from KANU. Three years later, in 1969, KPU was banned and its entire leadership detained without charge or trial. Although banning KPU brought formal political-party competition to an end, Kenya nevertheless remained a *de jure* multiparty state until 9 June 1982, when the republic's Fifth Parliament hurriedly enacted a constitutional provision that formally rendered Kenya a one-party state.

Despite the constitutionalisation of one-party rule, there had never been a consensus in Kenya on its desirability. In fact, when the constitutional amendment was rushed through Parliament, the immediate intention was to pre-empt oppositionists George Anyona and Oginga Odinga's move to form an opposition party. Anyona was arrested and detained before he could announce the formation of the Kenya Socialist Alliance, while the elderly Odinga was put under house arrest in 1982. It is in light of this clampdown on avenues of free expression and freedom of association that the attempted military takeover of August 1982 should be viewed. After the coup attempt, many Kenyans who held dissenting views were forced into exile and/or adopted clandestine methods of political expression. The universities, which the government viewed as hotbeds of anti-government activities, were purposely targeted for a major crackdown, with many scholars detained or forced into exile.

The coup attempt provided the government with an excuse to step up suppression of every form of dissension. The limited democratic space that had existed quickly collapsed. Meanwhile, the citizenry had of course lost faith and hope in the country's political machinery and leadership. In short, between 1963 and 1992 Kenya experienced high-handed political leadership in dealing with any form of dissent, from murder of opponents to detention without trial. Corruption and mismanagement of public institutions became rampant.

The churches' partnership with the state

With independence in 1963, the church had to redefine its relationship with the new state and its leadership, particularly in view of the role it had played during the colonial era and the struggle for independence. During the independence movement, the church was divided between those who applauded and those who condemned and satanised the nationalists. At independence, these nationalists assumed the reins of power. The new political leadership was quite aware that the church had functioned as the backbone of the colonial state. What, then, was to be the new church-state relationship?

Church leaders were indeed grappling with a critical issue, especially in view of the church's paradoxical history and conflicting theology. The theology of mainstream Protestants insisted on separation of church and state. However, except for the Catholic Church, ties between the church and the state during the colonial era had been close. During this era, and more so during the struggle for independence, the church had learned some lessons and wanted to redefine its relationship with the state.

The political leadership, on the other hand, expected the church to be as loyal to the new authority as it had appeared to be to the old. Since history had shown the church to be complementary to the colonial state, it was not easy for it now to articulate a clear theology on secular power (Chepkwony, 1987); it was much easier for the churches to engage in socio-economic activities and all the better if such activities contributed to empowerment of the people. Thus the Catholic Church engaged in social-transformation programmes (e.g., Development Education Leadership Teams in Action, or DELTA) with a view to empowering the people.

Just as the church was divided on whether or not to support the nationalist struggle, so was it divided on its involvement in national politics. Sections of the Protestant churches, especially those with an evangelical orientation, preferred not to concern themselves with non-spiritual matters, while the Catholic Church put pastoral letters to good use as a mode of articulating its position on issues of national importance. The NCCK and some of the mainline churches intervened at moments of crisis—e.g. during the 1969 illegal oathings after the assassination of popular nationalist Tom Mboya and in 1975, when another popular politician, J.M. Kariuki, was murdered. The church in Kenya was otherwise content to fill in the gaps left vacant by the government.

When Daniel arap Moi succeeded Jomo Kenyatta as President of the country in August 1978, efforts to subordinate the church were renewed. These ranged from harassment of vocal individuals who expressed dissenting views to threats of banning institutions such as the NCCK. Another target of harassment was the Catholic-run DELTA programme, which was forced to disband in 1983. At the same time, the president's enthusiastic church attendance all over the country gave the appearance of a cordial church-state relationship. Before too long, the president had hijacked the pulpit and was busy cultivating for himself an image as a Christian leader. Church leaders were caught up short, not knowing what was in the making.

In response to the mixed message, the church seemed to lower its guard. It was now expected to sanctify the state and its leadership, and indeed, the church blessed the state and called President Moi's leadership God-ordained. Even in the aftermath of the failed military coup in 1982, church leaders pledged their loyalty to the president. But beneath the apparent conviviality between church and state, the masses groaned. Little did the churches know that the repression that peaked from 1975 to 1978 during President Jomo Kenyatta's era would be repeated under Moi, only this time with sharper and more complex contradictions.

The Road to Multiparty Democracy

> Justice be our Shield and Defender
> May we dwell in Unity, Peace and Liberty
> Plenty be found within our borders
>
> *From Kenya's National Anthem*

The first stanza of the Kenyan national anthem invokes "justice" as Kenyans' "shield and defender." Ironically, for many years Kenyans have now known a reality that is quite the opposite of the vision and spirit evoked by their national anthem. This reality has been characterised by:

- Official corruption, with public resources being channelled into private coffers;
- Neglect or deliberate destruction of the potential for viable processes of indigenous development;
- Social engineering to rationalise and sustain political repression manifested in the criminalisation of political dissent. This was perfected through the judiciary by invoking unjust sedition and detention laws; and,
- The systematic destruction of institutions that would normally ensure democracy; for example, (1) the Kenyan Constitution, whose sanctity has been steadily eroded through amendments; (2) the Kenyan Parliament, whose supremacy and/or sovereignty has been whittled down; (3) the Judiciary, whose independence the Executive interfered with by removing security of tenure for members of the bench; (4) the institutions of civil society, which have been systematically undermined through co-opting faculty and students at universities into KANU, and encouraging some churches to splinter from the NCCK and form the Evangelical Fellowship of Kenya (EFK); (5) groups and individuals, who have been patronised as a means of ensuring their loyalty and allegiance (groups that showed dissent had privileges and services withdrawn); and (6) the nation, whose solidarity has been undermined by manipulation of ethno-regional loyalties and nationalism as a divide-and-rule tactic.

These characteristics of the one-party state in Kenya have turned out to be a double-edged sword. Although they were designed as tools of self-preservation for the ruling elite, they also provided Kenyans with ammunition to gun for their "second liberation."

The church as the champion of social change

Kenya's campaign for democracy was spearheaded by several components of civil society, the church chief among them. After church leaders declared their loyalty to the president in 1982, they did not decisively distance themselves from the regime until 1986. Even when the 1983 general elections were brazenly rigged, the churches did not take a clear stand. In 1986 President Moi introduced drastic changes in electoral procedures in a lightly veiled attempt to increase control of the process. The changes entailed replacing the secret ballot at the nomination stage for civic and parliamentary elections with *mlolongo* (queue voting). In addition, a new provision stipulated that any candidate who garnered 70 per cent or more of the votes cast at the nomination stage would be deemed elected unopposed.[1] The church vehemently opposed this move, and the NCCK issued a press statement on behalf of 1,200 pastors who vowed not to participate in queue voting. The head of the Anglican church (known in Kenya as the Church of the Province of Kenya [CPK]), Archbishop Manasses Kuria, described the move as "ungodly," while Bishop Henry Okullu of the Maseno South CPK Diocese argued that the idea should first have been debated, accepted and endorsed by the people before adoption by the ruling party (*Weekly Review*, 1986:2).

When the government effected the queue voting system in the 1988 elections despite the objections, fears that had been expressed about the system were confirmed. Instances of open rigging were meticulously monitored in the See of Eldoret—especially in Nandi District—by the late Right Reverend Alexander Muge of the Eldoret CPK Diocese. Consequently, the churches, through the NCCK newsmagazine *Beyond*, painstakingly documented the rigging.[2] The NCCK's outspokenness led the people to turn to it and other churches to speak for them, not only on the rigged elections but on many other shortcomings of the system.

As long-oppressed Kenyans continued to press for change, individual church leaders also began to speak out. In a sermon to mark New Year's Day 1990, an outspoken PCEA clergyman, Reverend Timothy Njoya, boldly criticised single-party rule in Africa, saying it was outdated and destined to crumble, just as similar regimes in eastern Europe were crumbling. In April of the same year, Bishop Okullu appealed for removal of the infamous Section 2A of the Constitution in order to pave the way for competitive multiparty politics.

In speaking out, both Reverend Njoya and Bishop Okullu embarked on a warpath with the government with unprecedented boldness. During the rest of 1990, church leaders engaged in the raging political-reform debate and used their pulpits as a focal point for popular sentiment. They questioned, criticised and condemned government policies that showed no sensitivity to people's rights; a vivid example was the demolition of shanty dwellings in Nairobi's Muoroto Village on 25 May 1990. On 7 July, various segments of Kenyan society rioted in what is known as the *Saba Saba* (July 7) Uprising. The uprising followed the violent dispersal of a meeting called by Kenneth Matiba and Charles Rubia to discuss pluralism. The government had refused to license the meeting, and the organisers had vowed to go on with it anyway. On the eve of the meeting, Rubia and Matiba were arrested and detained. The ensuing riots in Nairobi and other towns lasted for a week, with many people killed after the government issued a shoot-to-kill order.

After the riots, CPK leaders took issue with the government over their cause. Archbishop Kuria and bishops Okullu and Muge demanded that the government face up to the people's economic and political demands. Bishop Okullu went further by calling upon the government to resign to make way for a new beginning. On 15 July 1990, he urged the government to convene a constitutional assembly and form a transitional government of national unity.

Prior to the *Saba Saba* riots, the government had shown some flexibility on the issue of a national conference. After the riots, the government did not have the stamina to allow such a free public debate. Instead of the national conference, it convened a commission under Vice-President George Saitoti, later named the Saitoti Review Committee (SRC), and instead of inquiring into "The Kenya We Want" (which was to have been the focus of the national conference), the committee reconceptualised the debate and confined it to how to reform the ruling party and its hierarchy. Clearly, the regime was not ready to allow political pluralism. The NCCK, Bishop Muge, Archbishop Kuria and ordinary Kenyans had to make do with what was offered, although they exerted pressure that forced the commission to include several independent thinkers in its membership.

In all the provinces that the SRC visited, most petitioners refused to confine themselves to its agenda and delved into issues that perhaps would have been the focus of a national conference. The SRC reluctantly listened to a litany of complaints centred around tribalism, corruption, land grabbing and unaccountable leadership, as well as the need to limit the presidency to two five-year terms. Church leaders, including those who had initially aired their scepticism about the SRC and its terms of reference, submitted written statements or appeared in person before the Commission.

In December 1990, the SRC report was submitted to a special KANU delegates' conference at the Kasarani Sports Complex in Nairobi. (This conference came to be known as Kasarani I.) From the outset, the delegates were opposed to any political reforms that would limit or end KANU's monopoly. However, the president, in his characteristic populist style, upstaged the delegates and moved for abolition of the queue voting system and the 70 per cent rule. Further, the delegates' conference agreed to suspend the practice of expelling non-conformist party members and allow all who had been expelled from KANU to rejoin.

As pressure to effect change mounted at home, pressure also was exerted from outside. In 1990, the United States' ambassador to Kenya, Smith Hempstone, called for the release of all political prisoners. He also stated that American aid in future would be given only to countries that nourish democratic institutions, defend human rights and practice multiparty politics.

In August 1991, a year after the *Saba Saba* civil riots, the Forum for Restoration of Democracy (FORD) was formed as a pressure group. The founder members took advantage of a constitutional clause that allows for the formation of pressure groups without government registration. On 16 November 1991, in what looked to be a repeat of *Saba Saba*, FORD tried to hold a rally in Nairobi, and the provincial administration refused to license it. On this occasion, opposition leaders were arrested and taken to their respective districts of origin for trial before district magistrates. The reasoning was that by taking the opposition leaders to their remote home districts, tension in the city, where most opposition supporters were thought to be, would be defused. But this move only succeeded in bringing the opposition to the people as opposition supporters all over the country turned out to cheer the accused leaders when they appeared in court. On realising this political miscalculation, the government quickly disbanded the trials.

During the same month, Kenya's principal donors, meeting in Paris, suspended aid and gave President Moi and his government six months within which to institute meaningful and substantive political and economic reforms as a prerequisite to resuming aid. Some political activists, including Reverend Timothy Njoya, had presented written submissions to the donors' meeting in Paris, making a case for suspension of aid. Reverend Njoya and other human-rights activists, among them Professor Peter Anyang' Nyong'o, had made similar submissions at the Commonwealth Heads of State meeting held in Harare, Zimbabwe.

Pressure on the government reached its zenith in December 1991, when the American government issued a travel advisory to American nationals intending to visit Kenya, alleging insecurity in the country. (This advisory coincided with the peak tourist season, which meant substantial loss of revenue for a country in which tourism is the largest earner of foreign exchange.)

Once again, President Moi bowed to pressure. The annual KANU delegates' conference (Kasarani II) was convened on 2 December 1991 for the express purpose of organising the repeal of section 2A of the Constitution to pave the way for political pluralism. With political pluralism legalised, FORD organised a meeting on 18 January 1992 at the Kamukunji grounds in Nairobi.[3] This turned out to be a momentous day in the struggle for freedom and democracy. Gugu Njoroge aptly captures the mood of the people at the time when he states,

> On that day, the historic grounds turned into a scene of ecstasy. It was as if the gourd of oppression had finally been shattered as the people of Kenya streamed into Kamukunji to witness the end of an era and the beginning of another. . . . Thousands carried green twigs, white handkerchiefs and the black, white and green flags of the Forum for Restoration of Democracy. (Njoroge, 1992:4)

Although political pluralism was now legal, single-party diehards who felt threatened by pluralism quickly hatched a scheme to undermine the change process. The scheme became operational towards the end of 1991 at the infamous Kapsabet rally addressed by powerful politicians. At the rally, the idea of *majimboism* (regionalism), debated and rejected at Kenya's independence, was revisited. The politicians argued that they advocated *majimboism* to counter political pluralism, but the regionalism they proposed entailed confinement of all ethnic groups to their areas of origin. Thus, the Kalenjins were instructed to clear the vast Rift Valley Province of all "rubbish"—in this case, members of other ethnic communities. This marked the beginning of politically motivated "ethnic clashes" and heralded the subsequent "zoning" of certain ethnographic areas as off-limits to opposition parties.

This sketchy description indicates the role churches and individual members of the clergy played in Kenya's political-change process. The people transferred their trust to religious leaders at a time when political leaders' credibility had waned. Although the church has had prophetic voices denouncing injustice throughout Kenya's independent period, there was no vigorous effort to co-ordinate and collaborate in this endeavour. During the last four years, the churches' political stewardship has changed, and their efforts have become more systematic. This development has made the role of the church more credible and discernible, in the process helping to build bridges between its leaders and the people.

Institutionalisation of Political Stewardship

> I have indeed heard the cry of my people and I have seen how the Egyptians are oppressing them. Now I am sending you to the King of Egypt so that you can lead my people out of this country.
>
> *Exodus 3:7-8*

The church has a biblical mandate to stand up against oppression. Apart from the oppressive one-party structure that Kenyans have had to live with for many years, the period immediately preceding the return to pluralism was fraught with many urgent concerns. These included the politically instigated ethnic clashes, a worsening economic situation, and heightened abuse of individual freedoms. When the government finally assented to multipartyism, there were also urgent issues such as electoral procedures that needed to be wrested from KANU's control. How was the church to free the people from bondage and oppression under these circumstances?

The Kenya Episcopal Conference articulated its position through pastoral letters, letters which commented insightfully on social, political, economic and ethical issues of the day. They were read to congregations on Sundays, reproduced in daily newspapers and placed in bookshops. The letters always provoked interest in and discussion on national issues among the general public. The CPK issued statements only occasionally, but its leadership and individual members of the clergy were very outspoken. In its turn, the umbrella NCCK relied mainly on press statements (as did other individual clergymen, church leaders and the Kenya Episcopal Conference) and its weekly newspaper, *Target*. In addition, several churches institutionalised their political stewardship through other specific activities.

Electioneering

The elections process commenced on a controversial note. To begin with, when registration of voters was announced, only a very limited amount of time was allowed, even though it was clear that many Kenyans intended to abandon the apathy nurtured by past single-party elections and vote in large numbers. Secondly, no arrangements had been made to issue identity cards, one of the documents required at voting time, to young eligible voters. Thirdly, the government set up the Electoral Commission of Kenya without consulting the opposition parties on its leadership and membership. And, finally, the president strategically withheld the election date and the ruling party controlled the public radio and television, thereby denying the opposition parties both time to prepare, as well as access to crucial media. The Episcopal Conference, the NCCK and CPK bishops objected to and publicly condemned the manipulation of the electoral process by the government.

Ethnic violence

Ethnic violence in Rift Valley Province started as an isolated "land dispute" on a farm in Nandi District and soon became an orgy that engulfed almost the entire Province. Hundreds of people were killed, and thousands were displaced. It affected the electoral process because the government used the violence as an excuse to hamper freedom of association and limit the movement of opposition party members. This was further compounded by the zoning of certain ethno-geographic areas of the country as out of bounds for opposition parties.

The NCCK was first to produce a report detailing the costs, both human and material, of the ethnic violence and the report also identified some of the people behind the ethnic clashes. (The report was submitted to the President.) In the same vein, the Inter-party Symposia (see page 109) commissioned a task force under the chairmanship of the Very Reverend George Wanjau, a former moderator of the PCEA and chairman of the NCCK, to inquire into the causes of the ethnic violence and how it could be contained. The task force came up with a report that corroborated the NCCK's. (This report was discussed at the Second Inter-party Symposium.) The Government reluctantly appointed a parliamentary committee under the chairmanship of the Hon. Kennedy Kiliku to once again go on a fact-finding mission. The report the committee tabled concurred with those of the NCCK and the task force. Just when it appeared that there were enough grounds for punitive action against the perpetrators, the President surprised Kenyans by denouncing the Kiliku Report and accusing the parliamentary committee of having been influenced by the opposition and the churches; the report was quickly rejected by the compliant Sixth Parliament.

Even after the ethnic violence had subsided, the church continued to voice its concern, especially over the plight of the displaced victims. The NCCK, in collaboration with individual churches in the affected areas, documented the atrocities on videotape and with photographs and recorded testimonies. The Kenya Television Network (KTN), then considerably independent and bold in its coverage of controversial issues, agreed to air the videotape. The only copy was given to a news editor at the station for this purpose, but the tape was never aired, and all attempts to get it back failed.

In addition, the NCCK, other individual churches, and Catholic and CPK dioceses undertook relief, rehabilitation and resettlement work among the displaced. More important, however, were the initiatives in peacemaking among the communities affected. (The peacemaking and mediation work of the church are discussed elsewhere in this chapter.)

Notwithstanding the usual confrontational pastoral letters, press statements and other public documents and statements, church leaders also adopted more diplomatic approaches. These entailed visits and representations to the Head of State during which the positions of the churches on particular issues were made known. Some visits to State House involved joint Protestant and Catholic delegations, but at other times, representations were made separately.

Education and training

The churches devised joint civic-education programmes that were implemented during the period leading up to the December 1992 elections. This civic education broadly encompassed voter education, elections monitoring and political education.

NECEP

The National Ecumenical Civic Education Programme (NECEP) was a collaborative venture between the Kenya Episcopal Conference, the CPK and the NCCK. It was initiated at a meeting at the Ukweli Pastoral and Development Centre in Kisumu in January 1992, when several clergymen and scholars, including this author, inquired into the possibility of promoting the democratisation process through a civic-education programme. It was resolved that consultations be held with the NCCK, the Kenya Episcopal Conference and the CPK, whose justice and peace departments had hitherto operated separately. The purpose of the consultations was to discuss modalities for the formation of an ecumenical and nonpartisan civic-education body. After the consultations, long-term objectives for NECEP were formulated. These long-term objectives were:

- Promotion of public awareness and the facilitation of enlightened participation in the multiparty elections as a formal political contribution to the democratic process.

- Encouragement of members of the Kenyan public to involve themselves directly in pluralist democracy as a means of protecting their fundamental human and civil rights.

- Sensitisation of the Kenyan people to the political reality of the public-policy environment and education on the values and virtues intrinsic to peaceful development of a democratic culture consistent with their historical heritage and in affirmation of their aspirations. (NECEP, 1992:3)

To operationalise the long-term objectives, short-term goals that could be pursued and attained within a particular timeframe were also formulated. These were to:

- Seek to empower the marginalised electorate (the rural and urban poor, women, youth, etc.), the majority of whom are afflicted by all sorts of discriminatory political practices.

- Sensitise the public to appreciate the linkages between their basic needs for water, health, education, etc., on the one hand, and government policies and representation through electoral processes on the other.

- Educate the public on the whys and hows of multiparty elections and to equip them with the necessary skills and vigilance to detect and deal with all manner of electoral fraud.

- Restore popular confidence in the ballot box as an instrument of political empowerment, given its erosion in the past.

- Educate the electorate on the significance of parliamentary democracy, given the very fragile configuration of Kenya's nationhood.

- Provide viable fora for dialogue between political parties as a means of building a broad-based, extra-party political consensus on issues of national importance.

- Monitor the electoral process in order to ensure free and fair elections.

- Study and appraise the constitutions and election manifestos of various political parties with a view to evaluating them on the basis of their democratic significance and social-policy import

- Draw public attention to and address issues that may obstruct or frustrate the freeness and fairness of elections.

- Publicize, without fear or favour, the results of its monitoring exercise (NECEP, 1992:3-4)

NECEP was a response to the shift to pluralism and expansion of competitive political space beyond organised and recognised political-party parameters. NECEP's basic mandate was to promote civic education among the marginalised and the impoverished in Kenya. The prominence that civic movements had begun to gain as media for the articulation of public policy prompted the church to work more resolutely in its commitment to social transformation. The momentous changes on the political scene prodded the churches to revitalise their own skills, methodologies and knowledge. These skills had long been developed in the process of implementing community-development programmes such as DELTA and TOT (Training of Trainers). The challenge for NECEP was to adopt and replicate creatively the development-education heritage in the promotion of the democratisation process. To this end, the Freirean method of psychosocial analysis proved very useful to NECEP (Freire, 1972).

In accordance with its short-term operational aims, NECEP produced training and educational materials. These were used to train district co-ordinators, who in turn identified and trained constituency co-ordinators and community animators. In addition, district co-ordinators organised workshops that provided much-needed forums for training and dissemination of skills and information. Initial assessments show that NECEP's efforts went a long way towards ensuring the public's effective participation in the elections. NECEP was able to defy the institutional and personal rivalries that tended to overshadow its vision to register remarkable accomplishments within a brief period of six months. Soon after the December 1992 elections, NECEP was the first local monitoring organisation to produce a report on the electoral process.

NECEP Inter-party Symposia

Besides elections monitoring and civic education, NECEP organised two symposiums aimed at providing opportunities for dialogue between the various political parties. The symposiums were attended by a broad spectrum of constituencies drawn from religious groups, pressure and advocacy groups, and political parties. They sought to provide a forum within which the different political parties could meet with discerning Kenyans and articulate their proposed policies on specific national issues. They also provided a forum through which the burgeoning civil organisations could share a platform with the political parties and therefore lend a hand in development of a national agenda. The forums were perceived, initially, as a possible mediation facility between the ruling party and the opposition parties, especially given the hostility against the opposition prevailing at the time. Unfortunately, the ruling party did not attend any of them but sought instead to portray the churches as sympathetic to the opposition. As the dialogical process was now limited to the opposition parties, the churches decided not to convene the long-awaited national convention as KANU had shown no intention of participating. Instead, Symposium II resolved to establish a working group to co-ordinate the activities of participating organisations and find appropriate mechanisms for implementing resolutions passed by the two symposiums. The working group remained functional after the elections and continued to consult with the churches on compensation and resettlement of victims of the ethnic violence.

Education for Participatory Democracy (EPD)

The NECEP steering committee was composed of representatives from the CPK, the NCCK and the Catholic Justice and Peace Commission (JPR). In one meeting with Kenya-based donor agencies, the steering committee agreed that the member organisations would discontinue individual programmes that duplicated what NECEP was doing. The NCCK and the JPR, however, continued their individual programmes.

The NCCK's Education for Participatory Democracy (EPD) was established in 1991 and functioned under its Justice, Peace and Reconciliation Department. One of EPD's basic aims was to educate Kenyans on how to participate in and manage change. Like NECEP, EPD employed the learning-for-social-transformation model in its seminars and workshops. EPD placed great emphasis on voter education and produced many educational materials in several Kenyan languages.

In summary, through education and training, the church sought to bridge the wide experience gap in people's awareness about the operations of the multiparty system. In this way, it became a reassuring and comforting agent. Among the major problems the church faced in this endeavour was how to reach the many illiterate people. Educational materials were published and reproduced in daily newspapers, but these only reached those who could read. In addition, given the short timeframe within which so much had to be done, the number of facilitators was not commensurate with the task at hand. The zoning of some areas to keep out the opposition did not help, either. The church as an institution has not been a role model in participatory and representative democracy within its structures, a fact that tended to put it in an awkward position as an advocate of democracy in political life. In the end, the efforts of the church would have yielded greater results had all the initiatives been co-ordinated by one body.

Peacemaking and reconciliation

The churches have been weakest in this area due mostly to lack of skills and the absence of a corporate will. Nevertheless, alongside ecumenical civic-education and elections-monitoring efforts, the churches also attempted peacemaking and reconciliation on two fronts.

The first was within the opposition, particularly when FORD (by then a political party) began to disintegrate. Church leaders worked behind the scenes to encourage FORD's leaders to subordinate their personal interests to those of the nation. Other church leaders, including Reverend Njoya, were fairly outspoken in their quest to keep the original FORD intact. Despite these efforts, FORD split into two.

At another level, the churches engaged in mediation and intervention in the spiralling ethnic violence through sermons, prayers, personal visits to the victims and delivery of relief assistance. Opposition leaders were called upon to restrain themselves, even when it appeared that government officials were deliberately provoking them. Many churches throughout the country held prayers for peace, although on occasion such prayer meetings were cancelled by the government.

Many prayers grew out of a hunger strike by mothers of political prisoners seeking to have their sons released. The mothers chose to stage their strike in the corner of Nairobi's Uhuru Park (which had only recently been restored to the public after KANU yielded to pressure and shelved plans to build its headquarters there). The government, obviously embarrassed, reacted by violently evicting the striking mothers from the park. The mothers then sought refuge in the CPK All Saints' Cathedral nearby. Nevertheless, the police, in a blatant violation of the law, invaded the cathedral, forcing the mothers to seek refuge in a bunker in the cathedral. The church maintained solidarity with the mothers for many months in the protracted standoff with the government.

The Church's Balance Sheet

For many Kenyans, the struggle that led to the December 1992 multiparty elections in Kenya ended in disappointment. Nevertheless, the church's role in the change process included both successes and shortcomings.

Pointers towards success

As a concomitant to their involvement, the churches during recent years have sharpened and collectively developed their political ethics, morals and values. As far back as 1984, Bishop Okullu wrote about the need for the church to contribute to national values. Furthermore, the effort to develop political ethics was strengthened by ecumenical efforts to institutionalise the church's advocacy role (Okullu, 1984). There appears to have been a move from individualised prophetic ministry to an institutional/collective approach.

Civic-education endeavours helped restore the citizens' confidence in the ballot box after many years of one-party elections. The educational endeavour also sensitized the people to corruption in politicians seeking their votes. Although the government did not approve of the Inter-Party Symposia and their theme (Come Let Us Reason Together), only the churches were able to bring the opposition political parties together for national dialogue. Through such efforts, the churches facilitated and encouraged coalition-building within the civil society with a view to holding the government accountable.

The "federal" structure of the NCCK and the CPK makes it easy for individual leaders to exercise autonomy without heavy institutional restraint. This, of course, also has disadvantages. The CPK, for instance, has had painful experiences with a clergy at liberty to speak out on its own. The government and politicians have conveniently interpreted individuals' statements as those of the CPK.

In a turbulent and volatile situation, the churches ensured a relatively peaceful transition as catalysts for mediation and reconciliation. Finally, having monitored the electoral process, the churches were able to convince opposition members to take up their parliamentary seats, even though they were fully aware of the rigging that took place in some places during voting and of the administration's bias against opposition parties during the electioneering period.

Shortcomings and constraining factors

In spite of its achievements, the church encountered many obstacles. First, there is the dire need for the church to fully and continuously define the theological basis of its involvement if it is not to become a victim of triumphalism.

Second, because the churches advocated political ethics, they evoked the wrath of the state. The President at one point asked the NCCK to show cause why it should not be deregistered or outlawed. Moreover, the state used ethnic propaganda to divide the churches. Many churches have been harassed and denied "privileges" such as duty-free allowance that have been accorded more compliant ones. The government has also accused churches of being partisan, the main reason being its displeasure that during the church-sponsored Inter-party Symposia, many pressure groups were able to speak openly for the first time. In other words, the involvement of the church is not without cost.

Third, even an alert church is equipped to do only limited political work. It has to listen and minister to the interests of those from different social strata who, but for their membership in the church, have nothing else in common. The task of arbitration is made difficult because of the church's mandate to be in solidarity with the poor, the oppressed and the marginalised. The delicate balance that must be struck renders the church ambivalent in the eyes of the public and steeps it in opposition to political authorities of the present day.

Fourth, the church clearly learned that it can hardly be a credible advocate of democratic rule if it remains an undemocratic institution. The church is more than ever challenged to provide a model of democratic leadership and guidance.

Fifth, the church as an institution has had to cope with a situation in which some members (and even entire churches) do not understand political stewardship, while others refuse to relate religion to life or doctrine to conduct.

Sixth, the near absence of independent churches from the national political scene robbed many rural Christians of the opportunity to participate fully in the recent dialogue about change.

Seventh, the churches are constrained by institutional rivalries that became more apparent in the ecumenical process of civic education. As E. Oyugi observes in his evaluation of NECEP, while the concept was noble and viable, "the entrenched denominational interests on the ecumenical landscape did not undergo corresponding shifts in order to accommodate its institutionalization" (1993:11-12). Oyugi further states that within the church, "pro-government forces embarked on a rearguard action against NECEP, thereby preferring to see it as an ecumenical front for the opposition" (1993:11).

As discussed earlier, the resolution to bring all civic-education endeavours under NECEP failed to take effect, creating "confusion arising from the duplication of civic educational concerns and operational overlaps" (1993:11). An external factor that further eroded NECEP was donor assistance. On this issue, Oyugi's evaluation report states,

> NECEP's fundraising capacity, apart from suffering from the programme's disarticulation, was low and further rendered ineffective by local donor agencies and misinformed speculation. It was further frustrated following the programme's embroilment into party-ethnic political rivalries, jealousies, intrigues and manipulative donor interests (1993:14).

As things now stand, hardly any work is being undertaken to complement the few successes. Even civic education came to a standstill after the 1992 elections.

Finally, the persistent menace of ethnic clashes and the reconciliation work it necessitated depleted the churches' already inadequate resources.

All in all, the churches in Kenya brought concern for democracy to the political agenda and kept the movement for social change alive at a time when it was anathema to discuss the subject. This process has yielded important breakthroughs and lessons. It has also exposed serious endogenous and exogenous weaknesses and obstacles in the church.

Conclusion: Challenges

Many of the churches on the forefront of the Kenyan church's involvement in the democratisation and change process were the same ones that had for a long time been engaged in socio-economic projects. From these experiences, they had already developed a rapport with the people as well as transferrable methodologies. Even though these churches do not always represent the will of the people, they nevertheless are closer to the people than the government machinery. Because of the varied political positions among congregations, some of the faithful are rather critical of the clergy's use of the pulpit to delve into political discourse. By virtue of being active in socio-economic activities, however, the churches were in a better position to appreciate and be concerned about the impoverishment of the people. In addition, the same vocal churches are endowed with national urban and rural infrastructure that renders them powerful, unlike the small, fragmented NGOs and independent churches.

The clustering of the churches into evangelical, ecumenical (NCCK) and Catholic groupings helps in discerning and understanding their attitudes and stances on political issues, as well as their theological orientations. The wide spectrum of theological persuasions provides rich and varied interpretations of what involvement in politics should entail for churches. Even though church leaders have attempted to bring their faithful on board by institutionalising advocacy, the distance between the two remains large.

While Adubia may be correct when he states that the church must be contextual because it is still held in high esteem and still sufficiently independent to redefine the rules that govern African societies, for the churches to be effective in this role, a number of challenges will have to be faced head-on. The first challenge is the possible emergence of new sources of conflict as a result of democratisation. The church will have to undertake mediation and reconciliation so that losers and winners in competitive elections work together for the good of the nation. Second, the Kenyan experience of 1992 brings to the fore the need for the churches to be totally non-partisan and work on consensus building if they are to have any impact. Third, it is imperative that churches, along with other civil organisations, engage in a search to identify aspects of African tradition that can nurture democracy in an African setting. Fourth, more deliberate ecumenical effort must be focused on furthering democracy and developing a democratic culture. Fifth, the churches must begin to take economic justice seriously and build it into the democratic process. It is vital that the churches be fully informed about the consequences of the type of market economy being sold to Africa, which advocates democracy amidst poverty and misery. Sixth, gender issues in democratisation have not received their due attention. Here the church should improve its record before attempting anything at the national level. And finally, the church needs to work at a clearer understanding of what participatory and representative democracy is all about. The church's experience during the democratisation process may have been difficult, demanding and gruesome. But the next phase, unlike the previous one, requires consistency, clarity of vision, continuous analysis and, above all, collaborative efforts that will carry both the weak and the strong.

Notes

1. Criticism of the new system centred around the fact that voting by queueing behind candidates would make people vulnerable to reprisals from politicians who were either rejected or rigged into office. In the heyday of single-party hegemony, powerful politicians and the administrative arm made it clear who the "favoured" candidate was. Thus, in queue voting, the people would have to vote for these favoured candidates. The alternative was to abstain from voting. Mass abstention, however, would easily allow the favoured candidates to garner the 70 per-cent vote needed to go to Parliament "unopposed"—albeit on a minority vote.
2. *Beyond* was subsequently banned.
3. Kamukunji gained symbolic importance during Kenya's struggle for independence as a place where nationalists addressed public gatherings.

References

Bratton, M. 1992. "Civil Society and Political Transition in Africa." Paper presented at the International Conference on Civil Society in Africa, Jerusalem, 5-10 January 1992.

Chepkwony, A. 1993. "Democracy as the Last Rescue for Africa." Paper presented at the German Kircheutag, Munich, 9-13 June 1993.

———. 1993. "Gender Issues in Democratization." Paper presented at a seminar on The Role of the Church in Democracy in East, Central and Southern Africa," Nairobi, 15-17 March 1993.

———.1993. "The Duties and Responsibilities of National Christian Councils in Discharging their Political and Social Stewardship." Paper presented at a seminar on The Role of the Church in Democratisation in East, Central and South Africa, Nairobi, 15-17 March 1993.

———.1993. *The Quest for Democracy in Africa*. Nairobi: National Council of Churches of Kenya.

———.1987. "The National Council of Churches of Kenya (NCCK): The Challenges of Our Times." Paper presented to the NCCK, Limuru, Kenya, 24 September 1987.

———. 1987. "The Role of Non-Governmental Organizations in Development: A Study of the NCCK 1963-1978." *Studia Missionalia* XLIII.

Freire, P. 1972. *The Pedagogy of the Oppressed*. New York: Herder and Herder.

National Council of Churches of Kenya (NCCK). 1990. "NCCK Memorandum to the KANU Review Committee." Photocopy. Nairobi.

Njoroge, G. 1992. Untitled article. *Finance* (February 15):4.

Okullu, H. 1993. "The Role of the Church in the Democratization Process." Opening speech at a seminar on The Role of the Church in Democratization in East, Central and Southern Africa," Nairobi, 7-15 March 1993.

———.1984. *The Church and State in Nation Building and Human Development*. Nairobi: Uzima Press.

———.1976. "Church-State Relations in Kenya," in *Opening Ecumenical Dialogue*. Geneva: World Council of Churches.

Oyugi, E. 1993. "National Civic Education Programme: An Evaluation." Mimeograph. Nairobi.

Tengatenga, J. 1993. "The Church As an Instrument of Justice, Peace and Reconciliation in Times of Rapid Change." Paper presented at a seminar on The Role of Churches in Democratization in Eastern, Central and Southern Africa. Nairobi, 7-15 March 1993.

Weekly Review. (September 26):26.

7

From Independence to Multiparty Democracy in Zambia
A Personal View from Inside the Church

Foston Dziko Sakala

The Zambian people chose a new president on 31 October 1991, after almost twenty years under one-party rule. This brought the rule of Kenneth Kaunda and his United National Independence Party (UNIP) to an end. The defeat was humiliating in that UNIP got only about 25 per cent of the popular vote and managed to win only 25 of the 150 parliamentary seats.

The post-elections transition from one-party to multiparty democracy was peaceful, and this isolates Zambia as one of the few countries that have had a smooth transition to a multiparty system. The church (including Catholics and Protestants) has worked together on political and social issues in Zambia and can perhaps claim to have contributed substantially to the peaceful transition.

There are many lessons to be learned from the process of political development and social change in Zambia and the initiatives taken by religious leaders. Has the church confined itself to a peacemaking role, or has it gone beyond its limit? Did it do only a little, when in fact it was supposed to do more? What should be the future role of the church in Africa?

Major Political Events and Church Involvement

Zambia attained its independence on 24 October 1964. There were high expectations among the people of Zambia when colonialism, which had politically and economically oppressed and exploited them, came to an end. The people who occupied political positions, however, were not only political amateurs, but were also economically poor. This meant that to them political power became a means to economic power.

Zambia gained independence with a multiparty constitution, a constitution which stipulated that general elections for parliament and the office of president be held every five years. However, as political power meant access to economic power, those who ascended to power made sure that they retained their positions at any cost.

The night without a president

In 1967, UNIP held its general conference at Mulungushi Rock near Kabwe to elect a new central committee:

> Of the seven contested seats, three were particularly important: those of the national Vice-President, the national Secretary and the national Treasurer. The contestants divided into two main camps: a primarily Bemba/Tonga-speaking alliance under the leadership of Kapwepwe, Foreign Minister and the incumbent UNIP Treasurer; and a Lozi/Nyanja-speaking alliance which ranged behind Reuben Kamanga, the party and national Vice-President. In a bitter campaign the party was almost torn apart by the intense sectionalism of its leaders (excluding, of course, Kaunda himself) and their followers. The Kapwepwe group dubbed their opponents intellectuals and alleged that they were CIA agents; the Kamanga group responded by accusing the Bemba/Tonga Alliance of having sold out to the communists. (Tordoff, 1974:112-13)

The division within the party was to remain for quite some time.

> After August, 1967, however, the split within UNIP went too deep to be healed by what had become a familiar balancing device, by which President Kaunda had successfully balanced the various factors within his party in making appointments to both the Central Committee and the Cabinet.... Personal recriminations within UNIP, with their tribal and provincial overtones, had not abated by February, 1968, when the National Council held a stormy meeting in Lusaka. On 5 February a disgusted Kaunda announced his resignation as national president. (Tordoff, 1974:114)

The real cause of the problem during the National Council meeting at Chilenje was the fact that the new central committee elected the previous year at Mulungushi was not recognised by people from Eastern, Western and North-Western Provinces (Wina, 1982:35). When it was time for the National Council to discuss resolutions, all were read and adopted. According to Sikota Wina,

> One floor delegate stood up and said there was a serious omission in the entire structure of the draft resolutions. I refer, of course, to the complete omission of any mention of the recognition of the Central Committee.... At this stage it became very apparent that everybody also had been waiting for this opportunity to declare to which group he belonged and the debate was going to re-open and drag on, leaving behind a trail of bitterness which was completely new with the rank and file of UNIP. (1982:33-34)

The party vice-president, Simon Kapwepwe, the man who was at the centre of the whole problem, openly backed the group that wanted recognition of the new central committee included in the Chilenje resolutions. Most of the people who spoke opposed the committee's inclusion because they were convinced that its members were not genuinely elected (Wina, 1982:36).

There was only one man who could save the situation, and that man was Kaunda. This evening he was badly hurt, a disappointed and disillusioned leader who was witnessing before him the apparent disintegration of what had taken him more than seventeen years to build. And he was hurt because he himself did not believe in tribalism.

The amended resolutions, which included the recognition of the central committee, were read. "As I sat down," recalls Sikota Wina, "pandemonium broke loose on the convention floor. There were cries of 'Resolution accepted,' countered by 'We do not recognize the Central Committee—resolution rejected'" (1982:39).

> While this confusion was still raging, Dr. Kaunda moved to the microphones and the Council fell dead silent. "Fellow countrymen, I have for the past several hours listened to the views expressed in this hall. I must say how deeply divided the party is—and even more shocked to learn that this division is purely along tribal lines.
>
> "During my tenure of office as your President, I have done all I could to try and point out that if we fall prey to tribalism, we might as well write off the Republic of Zambia. I had hoped, with God's help, that I would succeed, but it is now clear that all my efforts have been in vain. . . . This afternoon I sent a note to the Attorney-General, James Skinner, asking him what legal steps are necessary before a Head of State can resign. . . ." There were unanimous shouts of "No, No, No, No—we need you." Now, having cleared the legal technicalities, Dr. Kaunda said: "I wish most sincerely to thank all of you for the cooperation you have given me in the past. I have known some of you for well over a decade and it is with a very heavy and sad heart that I, hereby and forthwith, tender my resignation as President of both UNIP and the State." (Wina, 1982:42,43)

Kaunda walked out of Chilenje Hall and headed for the old Government House, where he stayed for the night. Meanwhile, Simon Kapwepwe and Grey Zulu, Chairman of the National Council, followed Kaunda and tried to persuade him to come back. The president returned for a brief moment to say he was not a man who took decisions lightly: "I am very much touched by your devotion to me, but it is too late (Wina, 1982:45).

News of Kaunda's resignation travelled fast to the homes of some clergymen for whom Kaunda had very high regard. A procession of church ministers invaded State House to appeal to Kaunda to reverse his decision.

In an interview, former President Kaunda recalled:

> At the National Council which met in Chilenje, Lusaka, in 1968, people were shouting at each other. I saw tribalism at its worst. When I started to speak, I told them that I could not lead a party which was divided along tribal lines, then I announced my resignation. As I was walking out of the room, Patterson Ngoma, one of the members of the council, blocked my way and shouted, "Ken, Son of David, please come back!" I did not come back. I went to the old Guest House which is near State House. As I was going out, mothers were crying.
>
> Later, I saw a group of church leaders who were led by the Anglican Bishop of Lusaka, Philimon Mataka. They told me that they appreciated the problems which made me to resign. However, there was need for me to see how much the country would suffer if I did not decide to go back. After about two hours with church leaders, I decided to go back. What made things easier ... was the fact that I had not yet taken the constitutional step of submitting my resignation in writing to the chief justice.
>
> When I emerged into the room where the council meeting was taking place, there was ululating and wild cheering. I told them I did not want history to hold it against me, and because church leaders pleaded with me to go back, I reversed my decision (Kaunda, 1993).

The deaths of the family of five

In 1971, a family of five was petrol-bombed in Matero township, Lusaka, and all its members perished. Investigations revealed that the bombing was politically motivated. The man who died, together with his family, belonged to the opposition party. He was a potential challenger of the person who was the member of parliament in the area.

After this incident—one of several all over the country, I wrote to President Kaunda suggesting to him how the political killings could be minimised. The letter read, in part:

> The present political situation in Zambia has compelled me to write to your Excellency in my capacity as both an ordinary citizen and a minister of the Reformed Church. Experience during the last seven years of independence in Zambia has shown that the system of Democracy which we have (adopted) in Zambia is contrary to the actual way of life of the Zambian people. It is too western than African. I, therefore, feel that there is a very urgent need for the introduction of a One Party State in Zambia, failing which Zambia is bound to face more political disturbances in the not too distant future.
>
> The African democracy works better where there is no legal opposition political party. Opposition parties in Africa are there not for constructive opposition. They will not appreciate anything the party in power does. People could still enjoy democracy in the One Party State. (Sakala, 1971)

In writing to President Kaunda, I was motivated by the political situation that then prevailed in Zambia. I felt that introduction of a one-party system was the only way to avert further deterioration.

Zambia did become a one-party state by consensus through the Choma Declaration. Unfortunately, this political system was soon abused, and the suffering of the people took a different form as they were denied democratic participation; those in office arrogated to themselves the power to decide who should and should not participate in the political life of the country.

Scientific socialism

On 27 April 1967, the National Council of UNIP, meeting at Matero, adopted "Zambian humanism" as a philosophy for national development. According to this philosophy,

> man is the centre of all human activity. All of us are God's creatures and this is a firm enough foundation to see us through what we are about to do—that is to lay down a solid foundation on which to build One Zambia, One Nation.

President Kaunda pronounced an affinity between Zambian humanism and Christianity, calling the philosophy "Christian humanism," by which term he meant that

> we discover all that is worth knowing about God through our fellowmen and unconditioned service of our fellowmen is the purest form of service to God. I believe that man must be the servant of a vision which is bigger than himself, that his path is illuminated by God's revelation and that when he shows love towards his fellowmen, he is sharing the very life of God, who is love. (Meebelo, 1973:18-19)

Christians in Zambia did not find any problem with the philosophy of humanism. A letter from the leaders of the church in Zambia to their members about the president's seminar on humanism and development, dated 11 May 1982, states,

> We accept Zambian Humanism and a Socialism based on it which agrees very well with our Christian beliefs about God and man. We wish to emphasize traditional African Social values and Gospel values in accordance with them. We will collaborate in teaching Humanism.

The introduction of scientific socialism, however, was unacceptable to Christians, and church leaders were prepared to fight its emergence at all costs. In October 1979, church leaders wrote a letter to all their members on scientific socialism titled "Marxism, Humanism and Christianity." In part, the letter said:

There is much talk today about advancing to Humanism through Scientific Socialism. Christians have been advised not to worry about this because there is no intention of introducing atheism or attacking religion. Indeed we have been assured that one can be a Scientific Socialist and a Christian as well.

The letter then points out,

> On the other hand we know that Scientific Socialism normally treats religion as an enemy to be destroyed. Governments who follow it usually try to wipe out belief in God and place many difficulties in the way of the church.

After receiving this letter, the government appeared to abandon the idea of introducing scientific socialism. In 1982, the President invited the churches to discuss with him matters of national concern on which agreement was difficult. When he referred to scientific socialism again, church leaders wondered whether Zambian humanism had failed, so that there was a need to import a new ideology from outside. They argued,

> We have failed Humanism due to lip-service to its ideals, greed among leaders, laziness, inefficiency, lack of discipline, unfair distribution of wealth between rich and poor, dishonesty and theft in government offices, corruption, and intimidation of non-Party members. (ZEC, CCZ and EF, 1982)

The objectives of church leaders were to prevent the introduction of scientific socialism in schools and ensure that Zambian Christians were not robbed of their belief in God. Since 1982, the government has made no further attempts to introduce scientific socialism. The secret of the churches' success in this particular case was that they acted together and spoke with one voice.

The 30 June 1990 coup attempt

Early on the morning of 29 June 1990, a radio broadcast announced that the military had taken over the government. This "takeover" lasted about four hours. At 7.30 a.m., the announcement came that the coup had failed. All of this happened when President Kaunda was in the Copperbelt to open an agricultural show.

On Monday, 2 July 1990, I made an appointment to see President Kaunda two days later. When I entered his office, an unusual thing happened. I had been to see the President on previous occasions but on this visit, the President seemed to be in a state of shock. We hugged, emotions rose and tears began to drop. After about a minute, we sat down. I asked the President how he had been informed of the army takeover. He explained that the police officer who looked after him knocked at the door of his room and told him. The bodyguard suggested that the President fly to Lusaka that same night. Kaunda declined and said he would remain in Ndola. He advised the officer that if the soldiers came to look for him, he should not attempt to protect him. Asked what he did next, Kaunda said, "I dropped on my knees to pray." The president then said, "I think I have been too lenient with those who have attempted to stage coups d'état in the past. I should send Luchembe [the army officer who led the 30 June coup attempt] to the gallows."

"Please do not dare do that," I said. "Do you know what has made you survive the previous two coup attempts?" He corrected me and said that, in fact, there had been three previous attempts including one in 1967 unknown to many people. "You survived these coup attempts because you never shed the blood of those who rose against you," I continued. "Remember that 'Those who kill with the sword will die by the sword'. If I were you, I would do the unexpected, something that would surprise the whole world. I would release all the political prisoners, including Luchembe himself. Do not think that an act like that would be an act of weakness, although some people might perceive it that way. If anything, it would be a sign of strength."

Two weeks later, Kaunda released all those who were alleged to have staged the 1981 and 1990 coups, including a prominent lawyer, Edward Shamwana, and Luchembe. The release was televised, and the President shook hands with his enemies in person.

The national convention of 15 and 16 March 1990

UNIP called a national convention at the height of agitation for political reforms to discuss national issues. Many people, including Zambia's ambassadors abroad, were called back to participate in the convention. Church leaders were also invited to attend. During this conference, people openly differed, although they were all UNIP members and in the end, the convention called for the re-introduction of multiparty democracy in Zambia. The state responded by proposing that the decision to change the political system be put to the people of Zambia by referendum, an exercise that would cost the nation about US$ 2 million.

The Zambia Episcopal Conference (ZEC) and the Christian Council of Zambia (CCZ) instructed their social justice and peace committees to discuss the issue of the referendum and advise their parent bodies on an appropriate response. The CCZ social justice and peace committee found that there was no need to conduct the countrywide referendum since it was quite clear that the people of Zambia wanted political change.

The referendum did not take place. Instead, a commission was appointed to revise the constitution to allow for the change to multiparty system. Members of the commission, appointed by the President, included one Catholic bishop and the chairman of the Christian Council of Zambia. (The commission, headed by Professor Mvunga, is referred to as the Mvunga Commission).

In December, 1990, Article IV of the Zambian Constitution was repealed, allowing the creation of other political parties. Within six months, more than ten new political parties had been created.

Soon after the Mvunga Commission presented its report in the form of a draft constitution, it became clear that the opposition parties, particularly the Movement for Multi-Party Democracy (MMD), were not happy with some of the proposed amendments. They threatened to boycott the first multiparty elections, the date of which was yet to be announced. The reactions to the draft constitution and the aggressive election campaign practices caused a feeling of uneasiness and tension in the country.

The "Mvunga Commission Report" pointed out a drift towards serious political trouble in the country. "People and politicians are turning towards the churches for guidance," the report said, adding that there was need to examine what church leaders could do "to preserve unity and peace."

A consultative meeting on the political situation

On Saturday, 13 July 1991, church leaders from the Christian Council of Zambia and the Zambia Episcopal Conference met at the Catholic Secretariat. Participants in this meeting felt that the situation in the country was explosive. "We needed to examine what we could do as churches and what might happen if we took no action," said one Catholic bishop.

Philip Simuchoba, one of the Protestant church leaders, also was a member of the Mvunga Commission. He admitted that the commission had had very little time for good consultation. The meeting resolved that a delegation be sent to seek an audience with the President. Archbishop Adrian Mung'andu, Bishop Dennis de Jong, Father Ives Bantungwa (representing ZEC), Bishop Stephen Mumba, Bennet Nkonga (acting General Secretary of the CCZ), and two other CCZ delegates met the President on the afternoon of 19 July at State House.

According to the press statement released the following day, the delegation met the President "to discuss the current political situation in the nation and ways in which the churches could promote reconciliation and peace." The press release ended by stating that, at the earliest convenient time, we will host a meeting to discuss the proposed constitution and ways to facilitate an orderly election. This meeting, to which representatives of all the parties will be invited, will be held in a neutral venue (e.g. one of our Cathedrals), and will be chaired by neutral persons (e.g. a church leader). (Catholic Secretariat, 1991)

The committee of experts on the constitutional bill

On 24 July 1991, the meeting to hear arguments on both sides of the constitutional issue, chaired by Anglican Bishop Stephen Mumba, was held at the Cathedral of the Holy Cross. It was attended by representatives of the government and the Movement for Multi-Party Democracy (MMD). Participants were to come up with specific recommendations concerning the new constitution and how the parties could promote a spirit of unity and reconciliation. The joint meeting came up with a number of resolutions, among them

1. That ministers be appointed from Members of Parliament.
2. a. That the President considers lifting the State of Emergency immediately.
   b. That the subject of the lifting of the State of Emergency be discussed between the President and the MMD President, Mr. F. J. T. Chiluba.
   c. That the period of a State of Emergency declared by the President by proclamation be reduced from 28 days to seven (7) days and a declaration approved by resolution of Parliament be reduced from six months to three months.
   d. That the President could, in consultation with the cabinet, declare war and the State of Emergency could then continue until the cessation of hostilities.
3. That a constitutional court would not be formed.
4. That the nominated Members of Parliament should not be more than eight (8).
5. Immunity of a President From Prosecution—that civil proceedings could be instituted against a president after leaving office and criminal proceedings could be instituted only with approval of Parliament by a simple majority.
6. General Powers of the President—that the role of the Cabinet should include policy-making and being advisory to the President. (GRZ/MMD, 1991)

The coming together of the two parties under church leadership provided a solution to the problem of who should approve the proposed constitutional amendments, since Parliament at that time comprised people from one political party, UNIP.

Formation of the Christian Churches' Monitoring Group

The breakthrough Committee of Experts on the Constitutional Bill, facilitated by church leadership, did not end political tension between the GRZ and the MMD. The fear was that if nothing was done about it, the country would plunge into a civil war. There were rumours that some people were preparing to wage a bush war if the presidential and parliamentary elections were rigged.

So widespread was this fear that many people started to buy and hoard food in readiness for the period of trouble. On 19 September 1991, church leaders met again at the Catholic Secretariat to discuss the role they would play to ensure that elections were conducted in a peaceful atmosphere. They agreed to form the Christian Churches' Monitoring Group (CCMG), and I was elected its chairman.

Four days later, the CCMG merged with other local monitoring groups: the law association, the press association, the women's lobby, non-governmental organisations and the University Union. This new body adopted the name Zambia Elections Monitoring Co-ordinating Committee (ZEMCC). The new organisation resolved that the chairmanship should remain in the hands of church leadership, and I continued as chairman of the larger ZEMCC.

During the six-week period between creation of the ZEMCC and election day (31 October 1991), I met with President Kaunda, either alone or together with the executive, to discuss a number of issues:

Lifting of the state of emergency

Members of the opposition parties complained that the many policemen and army officers, especially those from the Para-Military Wing, stationed in almost all townships in Lusaka and in the Copperbelt, rendered free campaigning almost impossible. The ZEMCC team appealed to the President on a number of occasions to lift the State of Emergency, which he did not do until the day of the elections.

Allegations about a weapons cache

The rumour that President Kaunda had a store of weapons hidden on the border with Malawi was so strong that the ZEMCC had to send a delegation to State House to discuss it. The story was that the weapons were for UNIP to use against the new government that would take power. The President denied any knowledge of this.

The proposed meeting between Kaunda and Chiluba

Local monitors felt that President Kaunda and Frederick Chiluba, President of the MMD, needed to meet under the supervision of ZEMCC before the day of the elections to discuss the handover of power to the winning candidate, since this had never happened before in Zambia. Kaunda refused to meet Chiluba. Our last attempt at persuasion was two days before the elections. This time, President Kaunda agreed to meet Chiluba, but not until after the elections.

The detention of Bishop John Mambo

Bishop Mambo, an executive member of ZEMCC, was very vocal in the affairs of the nation. The state alleged that Bishop Mambo was not a citizen of Zambia since he was born in South Africa of parents who were not Zambian. Immigration officers were sent to his village to interview his parents, the headman and the local chief. Shortly afterwards, Bishop Mambo was detained, and the government made plans to deport him to South Africa or Swaziland, the country of his mother's birth.

ZEMCC members' first reaction was to organise a big demonstration to demand Bishop Mambo's release. Since I had been invited to a luncheon at State House, I asked the board members to give me a chance to speak to the President about the bishop. Following a meeting arranged for that evening, President Kaunda released him.

Results of the Involvement of Religious Leaders

Zambia is said to be 80 per cent Christian, and the tremendous influence the church has had on Zambian politics is not in doubt. President Kaunda was of the view that, in the absence of opposition parties, the church had a crucial role to play. He referred to the church as "our mirror into which we can look and see where we did not do well," a phrase that later became a slogan, which he referred to in many speeches.

The Zambian situation is unique in that the church has spoken with one voice on important national issues since Zambia's independence. In addition, President Kaunda never developed an ideology or practical policy that antagonised or alienated the church (Hastings, 1979:187). When the regime planned to introduce scientific socialism in Zambian institutions of learning, the Christian Council of Zambia, the Evangelical Fellowship of Zambia and the Zambia Episcopal

Conference acted together as signatories to the letter, "Marxism, Humanism and Christianity," which was sent to all three churches' members in 1979, and to another letter that followed. The same spirit of co-operation prevailed during the transition to multiparty democracy.

After the 1991 presidential and parliamentary elections, President Chiluba invited a few church leaders to meet him at Government House, where he first stayed. I was among the five he invited to thank for the role the church had played during Zambia's transition to multiparty democracy. He pointed out that the story would have been different if the church had not played that role.

The people of Zambia are now used to turning to the church whenever there is a crisis in the country. During this time of many political parties, some political leaders have come to church leaders to ask them to do something about a given situation. The church and its leadership have won the confidence and trust of the people of Zambia.

In some cases, however, the church appeared to compromise with the state on certain issues. The impression may have been that "the churches have been, in fact, gently harnessed to the ruling system and the Catholic Bishop Mutale even agreed to serve as a member of the commission for instituting a One-Party State" (Hastings, 1979:188). I want to strongly state that the church in Zambia has never compromised with the state. In fact, Bishop Mutale became strongly critical of the prolonged imprisonment of those held responsible for the 1981 coup attempt. When Bishop Mutale died tragically in a car accident in 1989, there was strong suspicion that the state may have wanted to get rid of its critic.

The church refused to keep silent on examples of injustice. If the church had kept silent on established evils, it would have identified itself, and the Christian religion, with injustice. When it was deemed necessary to co-operate with the state, yes, the church co-operated—but in all cases it acted independently.

Conclusion

The church in Zambia has a proud record in the area of guiding the nation during times of crisis. This is also true of the church in some other African countries. There will be more for the church to do during this time of the "second liberation" of Africa. Will the church continue its present strategy of coming in when the nation is in crisis? Or is the church coming up with a new approach to its involvement in national issues?

The time has come when churches in Africa need to discuss how they can guide African nations so as to minimise crises. Now is the right time since the people still have great confidence and trust in the leadership of the church in Africa.

The All Africa Conference of Churches should come up with new strategies to meet the new challenges. The second liberation of Africa by means of the democratisation process needs to be supported. The church in Africa is well placed to play this role.

A new AACC department to deal with social and political change, which could involve Christian social and political scientists in Africa, could be an answer to this challenge. An AACC initiative would be enhanced by the establishment of similar departments in all of Africa's national councils of churches. These departments would be responsible for drawing up programmes of action.

Throughout its known history, Africa has never enjoyed social and political stability. Now economic instability is haunting Africa in the form of the debt crisis. The attainment of independence—for many African states, three decades ago gave Africans a lot of expectations. But it was not long before it became clear that "the beautiful ones were not yet born." How long is Africa going to wait for the beautiful ones?

We cannot wait another three decades before we see the Africa that will know peace and live in peace. This is the challenge of the church in Africa: Blessed are the peacemakers for they will be called children of God (Matthew 5:9).

References

Catholic Secretariat, Department of Communication, 1991. Press Release, Lusaka, 20 July.

Fortman, Bastiaan de Gaay 1969 *After Mulungushi* Nairobi: East African Publishing House.

GRZ/MMD 1991. Resolution of the Meeting of the Joint GRZ/MMD Committee of Experts on the Constitutional Bill, 1991, Cathedral of the Holy Cross, Lusaka, 24 July.

Hastings, A. 1979. *A History of African Christianity* Cambridge: Cambridge Unversity Press.

Humanism in Zambia and A Guide to its Implementation. Part I. Lusaka: Zambia Information Services.

Kaunda, K.D. 1993. Interview with the author, Lusaka, 17 February.

Meebelo, H. 1973. *Main Currents of Zambian Humanist Thought*. London: Oxford University Press.

Okullu, H. 1984. *Church and State in Nation Building and Human Development*. Nairobi: Uzima Press.

Sakala, F.D. 1971. Letter to Kenneth Kaunda, 21 October.

Tordoff, W.D. 1974. *Politics in Zambia*. Manchester: Manchester University Press.

Wina, S. 1982. *The Night Without President*. London: Oxford University Press.

Zambia Episcopal Conference (ZEC), Christian Council of Zambia (CCZ) and Evangelical Fellowship (EF) 1982. Letter to Kenneth Kaunda, Lusaka. 11 May.

8

Churches and the Struggle for Democracy in Zaire

Philippe B. Kabongo-Mbaya

Since 1990, Zaire has been facing a considerable socio-political crisis triggered by tremendous pressure for political change, pressure that challenged the legitimacy of the Mobutu government. A transition mechanism has been deadlocked, further deepening the crisis.

Churches and other groups working within the context of the church have played an important role in the present crisis. As each Christian denomination acts, it seems to seek recognition as an important social force in the face of the on-going changes. But what is the real involvement of these churches? Who are the real actors and what are their modes of action? Are there specific strategies and styles of operation peculiar to each denomination? What is the nature of alliances between the various churches, and how do they function?[1]

Profile of Churches

The three main churches in Zaire are the Roman Catholic Church, the Church of Christ of Zaire, and the Church of Jesus Christ on Earth founded by Simon Kimbangu.[2] Each has a social physiognomy that is relevant to its involvement in the country's current socio-political developments.

The Roman Catholic Church (RCC)

About 17 million Zaireans out of a national population of 37 million are Catholic. The church has forty-seven dioceses and fifty-one bishops (*Voix d'Afrique*). Preferential treatment from the Belgian colonial power enabled the Catholic Church to establish many institutions and schools. During the last two decades, it has been involved in development projects in various socio-economic sectors such as rural personnel and arts and crafts training and in a flourishing university project centred around the church's Faculty of Theology at Kinshasa University. Two generations of elites were marked by a strongly Catholic upbringing: hence most Zaireans in positions of power between 1960 and 1980, including Marshal Mobutu Sese Seko and many of his generals, ministers and diplomats, were from a Catholic background.

The Church of Christ of Zaire (CCZ)

The CCZ groups together more than fifty Protestant denominations with about 12 million followers. Among these denominations are the Baptists, Congregationalists, Presbyterians, Methodists, Mennonites, Pentecostals and Lutherans. Some Protestant denominations are not members of the CCZ, most notably the Anglican Church.

Three main features distinguish the Protestant groups from their Catholic counterparts: the discrimination that affected them during the colonial era, the otherworldly legacy and very often the fundamentalist nature of their testimony, and the fragmentation of their institutions. However, the formation of the CCZ has helped to correct the fragmented image of Protestant churches. Fragmented or not, the projects and activities Protestants undertook before the onset of the Zairean economic crisis in the mid-1970s were numerically and qualitatively noteworthy, and these were sustained in the 1980s. However, Protestant representation among the power elites of the country remains low. This apparent under-representation of Protestants is aggravated by the quiet discretion that characterises Protestant executives when it comes to their religious identity. In 1960, however, two of the three principal political figures of Congo-Kinshasa, including Patrice Lumumba, were Methodists (Kabongo-Mbaya, 1992:100-101; Williame, 1989).

The Church of Jesus Christ on Earth (CJCSK or Kimbanguism)

The CJCSK claims to have 5 million members and is also established in Congo, Angola and Zambia. The CJCSK grew out of a prophetic movement led by Simon Kimbangu that was severely suppressed during colonial rule and only recognised as a church in December 1959. It is a member of the All Africa Conference of Churches (AACC) and is affiliated with the World Council of Churches (WCC).

The charisma and reputation of Simon Kimbangu, as well as the CJCSK's feudalistic centralised organisation, dynamism and popularity, and the discipline of its members, gives the church a strong presence. It made considerable progress in establishing social, school and agricultural projects between 1960 and 1980.

The Kimbanguists are represented in government to an even lesser degree than the mainstream Protestants. However, CJCSK sympathisers among the senior executives, and the CJCSK itself, have acknowledged support from Marshal Mobutu.

Strengths and Limitations of the Churches

A close look at the Catholic Church reveals a higher and a lower church. The former is represented principally by the Zairean episcopate and its official leaders; the latter could be defined as the entire community of laymen and women who recognise themselves as Catholics and who act and involve themselves in society, through their church as well as other organisations. The lower church takes initiatives, and very often the ordinary clergy operate at this level. Other times, bishops too try to channel, direct or harness the commitments of the lower church. (The same breakdown applies to Protestants and Kimbanguists as well.)

As a result of a religious renewal in Zaire, there is an extraordinary consensus on the importance of Christian religious practice. It is as though civil society and the religious communities are wholly overlapped and are now evolving through a form of synergy. In the face of this phenomenon, distinguishing what Christians do on account of their spiritual convictions from the general actions of society becomes difficult.

Towards a Multiparty System

The most recent Zairean socio-political transformation is considered to have begun on 24 April 1990. On this date, Marshal Mobutu made a speech authorising the introduction of multiparty politics in the country. However, the battle for democracy did not start with the speech of the dictator. A powerful opposition led by the Union pour la Démocracie et le Progrès Social (UDPS) had already broken the legitimacy of the one-party system.

By 14 January 1990, when Mobutu announced a major national convention to discuss the situation of the country and the functioning of its institutions, civilians had already lost confidence in the government. (Only a few days earlier, Mobutu had vehemently asserted the undesirability of a multiparty political system in

Zaire.) Since in Zaire there is no separation between the ruling party—the Mouvement Populaire de la Révolution (MPR)—and the government or even the nation itself, this convention naturally was to be an MPR affair. Zaireans could convey their memorandums to the president of the republic through his faithful collaborator, Mokolo. Almost 800 memorandums were deposited in Mokolo's office (*Elima*, 1990).

Mobutu, knowing quite well what was at stake politically, made extensive tours of the country to publicise the convention and received petitions directly from prominent individuals as well as from ordinary citizens. Memorandums from churches were among the documents addressed to Mobutu, including one letter from the Permanent Committee of Catholic Bishops (*Jeune Afrique*, 1990:20-25). The accompanying cover letter, dated 15 March 1990, was signed by Monseigneur Monsengwo Pasinya, Archbishop of Kisangani and President of the Committee. This memorandum, consisting of an introduction and two main chapters addressing the roots of the crisis in institutions and suggesting some solutions, deserves a closer look.

In the first chapter, the bishops denounce the present political system, which they describe as a hybrid:

> We dare assert that the principal cause or if not the principal the root of the paralysis of the national institutions and the structural crisis of the republic is the result of a hybrid political system. This system combines the advantages of liberalism, such as private property, even though to a minority, with the methods of conquest and maintenance of power borrowed from totalitarianism. (*Jeune Afrique*, 1990:21)

In the same chapter, the bishops also criticise the MPR and its institutionalisation as a state-party:

> Apart from the desire to create one people and one nation, which is praiseworthy in itself, the MPR advocates revolution. History has confirmed that revolution implies refusal of any permanent standard of reference. It sets in motion a process of a series of reversals of acquired status and a range of social, ethical and moral values. (*Jeune Afrique*, 1990:21)

Although the Catholic bishops criticise "revolutionary" dynamics as an ideology and socio-cultural situation that brings about general instability and moral and spiritual destabilisation, they do not question the "praiseworthy desire to create one people and one nation." This contradiction is in no way foreign to the corporatist mindset of totalitarianism. It is in the name of national unanimity that dictatorship rejects pluralism. Could the fact that the Catholic bishops did not touch on this point be due to the church's own monolithic institutional culture? (On the other hand, pluralism based on the recognition of the right to be different is inseparable from the democratic ideal and Protestantism.) This distinctive element is characteristic of the Catholic approach.

In their criticism of the party's misuse of state institutions, the bishops stress that

> the [institutionalisation] of the Mouvement Populaire de la Révolution (1970) and its transformation into a state-party (1974) is the first among the ambiguities and inconsistencies resulting from our hybrid political system. Wherever it was introduced and organised, whether in schools, economic or financial institutions, public administration, government or the army... it tended to [reverse the values] with regard to criteria for recruitment, evaluation and promotion. Solidarity among leaders, nepotism and militancy have generally prevailed over virtue and competence. (*Jeune Afrique*, 1990:22)

Besides the absurdity of recognising the MPR as a political party when it rejected pluralism outright, the Catholic prelates were justifiably concerned about the fate of ethical values in the Mobutu regime. Three sub-chapters analyse the excessive concentration of power in the hands of the head of state which, according to the Catholic leaders, creates irresponsibility in subordinate officers and corrupts the entire state system. For this reason, the bishops emphasise the importance of distinguishing between the roles of the legislature, the executive and the judiciary with regard to financial management. The bishops openly criticise the plundering of national resources:

> The National Bank, the parastatal institutions and the whole portfolio of the state satisfy political demands and function as the cash desk of the state-party, left at the disposal of individuals, especially the authorities of the country... each one fetching as much money as he pleases. (*Jeune Afrique*, 1990:22)

The bishops extend their concern to the problem of the national debt and international responsibility:

> The functioning of our institutions, as described above, is known and encouraged by Zaire's foreign partners. In effect, they know very well with whom they signed the contracts and where the money given as credit to Zaire goes. It is therefore unfair for the same people who established a financial system that diverts capital to their advantage to demand repayment and create budgetary restrictions that result in the impoverishment of the population. (*Jeune Afrique*, 1990:22)

Protests against the policy of structural adjustment for most of the Third World during this period were virulent, and these comments from the episcopal memorandum should be viewed in this light.

The second part of the bishops' document addresses the need for urgent remedial measures. It stresses, first of all, the necessity for profound reform of the system. While acknowledging the neutrality of the church with regard to political systems and their inability to define a concrete line of action, the bishops justify their approach by stating that the light of the gospel enabled the church to illuminate and facilitate any worthwhile project of human society. Furthermore, as mother and educator of people, the church has a mission to train and question individual and collective consciences (*Jeune Afrique*, 1990:23).

While priests, lay leaders and militant followers conceive the struggle for change as solidarity with the people, members of the church hierarchy base their approach on the magisterium of the church. They perceive themselves as mother and tutor of the people. Historically, the tutelary vocation the Roman Catholic Church claims for itself has often been a problem because it negates the intrinsic autonomy of human societies. (Such a tutelary conviction does not normally exist in Protestant doctrine, and herein lies a difference in motivations and approaches in the various churches' socio-political commitments.)

The last two sub-chapters of the memorandum deal with general political options and priority reforms. The bishops first single out the maintenance of the dearly acquired peace (the Mobutu propaganda machinery has always hammered this point, attributing peace to the regime and rejecting political pluralism as a threat to peace) and then address unity and national integrity, fundamental rights and the need for justice in the exploitation and enjoyment of national wealth. Among priority reforms that they suggest are:

- drafting of a new constitution to be submitted to the entire nation for approval.
- separation of the ruling MPR from the state.
- limiting state involvement in certain sectors that could be handled by other institutions (e.g., schools, hospitals, etc.).
- freedom of expression.
- change of attitude in tune with changes in social structures.

However, nowhere in the bishops' memorandum was there a proposal for a multiparty system, yet a second political party already had been demanded as early as 1982.

Interestingly, a copy of the bishops' memorandum seems to have found its way to other countries before the original was submitted to Mokolo's office, and the government was reluctant to consider the Catholic letter among the other memorandums that it received between March and April of 1990.

Although the memorandum was not the Catholic Church's first denunciation of injustice in the Mobutu regime, its text really contains nothing offensive and is neither subversive nor revolutionary. Nevertheless, Mobutu and his advisers seemed to have been terrified by the avalanche of criticism from the other working institutions in the country; certainly the regime has never been pleased with the manner in which the Catholic episcopate puts Mobutu to task.

The Protestants also spoke up. Among the documents that they made public are one by the CCZ Eastern Kasai Regional Synod and another by the CCZ National Council (CCZ Regional Synod, 1990; CCZ National Secretariat, 1990; Kabongo-Mbaya, 1991). The document by the Regional Executive Committee, dated 25 February 1990, criticises the accumulation of power in Mobutu's hands, the existence of partisan structures that serve the interests of supporters of the regime, and the economic collapse and other social evils, but it does not question the regime itself in any radical manner. Rather, it makes proposals that could help the regime out of the crisis; for example, it does not demand a multiparty system, but proposes tolerance and diversity within the single party of Mobutu.

On 30 March of the same year, the National President of the CCZ, Monseigneur Bokeleale, addressed a memorandum to President Mobutu on behalf of the entire CCZ. The memorandum begins with generous salutations to Mobutu:

> [CCZ] seizes this opportunity to praise and appreciate . . . your high degree of patriotism and your political courage to have initiated the popular consultation. . . . This is an act of high political significance which shows, on the one hand, the height of the responsibility of he whom God has placed at the leadership of the country for the past twenty-five years. (CCZ National Secretariat, 1990:1)

The memorandum then notes that the consultation had shown "on the other hand the legitimate worry of Zaireans in participating, for the first time, in the conception and elaboration of fundamental principles which will govern their destiny" (CCZ National Secretariat, 1990:1). In this way, the CCZ made clear where its sentiments lay.

In the preamble, the memorandum notes some of the achievements of the regime such as unity, peace and Zairean nationalism. In its social and economic analysis, the memorandum also notes with much circumlocution,

> Faced with the difficulty of installing a fair social politic, the appeal to the presidential magnanimity becomes too much especially that the presidential inventions . . . remain very often without follow-ups by the beneficiaries." (CCZ National Secretariat, 1990:4)

The memorandum states, more directly, that "too many top civil servants behave very often in a selfish manner by enjoying privileges, funds, government lands, furniture and buildings." It proposes that the President of the republic make the government "responsible for its acts before the people (the Parliament).

In this way, the President would be spared all criticisms related to the daily running of the country" (CCZ National Secretariat, 1990:4).

Unlike its Catholic counterparts, the CCZ took an explicit stand on the multiparty system, stating that "the President of the Republic should authorise the existence of two or three political parties whose scope of action should be defined by the constitution" and that "the church considers the institution of a pluralist corporate trade unionism to be auspicious" (CCZ National Secretariat, 1990:5). While the document acknowledges, in its conclusion, the difficulties of multiparty systems in developing countries, it asserts "that no country in the world can remain isolated from evolutionary processes in world history" (CCZ National Secretariat, 1990:6). The conclusion further develops the theme that only Mobutu can lead the country towards a multiparty system:

> Ride on. We will support you in prayers and you will succeed! May God help us overcome this important stage for the honour and dignity of our President, of our country and of our people created in God's image." (CCZ National Secretariat, 1990:6)

The memorandum from Kasai lacks the idolatory tone of the CCZ National Council's document. Although the national CCZ document addresses political and trade-union multipartyism, it does not deal with revision of the constitution as explicitly as the Eastern Kasai document. The National Council proposals suggest institutional reform with the retention of President Mobutu's personal authority; it reflects the attitude, strongly established with the national leaders of the CCZ, that Mobutu and his regime are not to blame for the national malaise, but rather the politicians and administrative officials as well as the general attitude of the people. This also reflects the tendency in many religious circles to accord priority to changing people's hearts, so that they accept the prevailing order, rather than disrupting political and social structures.

In 1958-59, the CJCSK and Mobutu forged a link that took the form of a prayer of benediction by Diangienda, predicting that Mobutu would become a great person. Throughout the 1970s and 1980s the Kimbanguist leaders' loyalty to Mobutu was based on the theological doctrine of respect for all authority. All the same, Diangienda asserted the liberty of every Kimbanguist to join the party of his or her preference. Upon Diangienda's death in June 1992, a section of the population of Kinshasa wailed as the funeral procession went through the city, "*Hibou aye* —Here comes the agent (owl) of Mobutu." Despite this close association, some personalities and Kimbanguist pastors have joined the opposition. The best known among them is Dr Bazinga, a lay Kimbanguist preacher who is now a member of the national committee of the UDPS.

The National Conference

With the Catholic Church the only force other than the army capable of posing a threat to Mobutu's regime, it was natural for his advisers to turn their attention to the episcopacy. By refusing to accept their memorandum, they hoped to undercut the prelates' impact by portraying them as motivated by ill-will at a time when Mobutu finally was on the verge of listening to the people and taking care of their well-being.

Between 1989 and 1990, however, the Zairean Catholic Church was not a very stable institution. The death of Cardinal Malula, the Archbishop of Kinshasa and the key figure in the anti-Mobutu campaign, brought out internal conflicts revolving around succession. Old rivalries and hostilities among top-ranking clergy were revived. This was particularly pronounced around the Malula Foundation, as well as in the private Catholic universities that were to be set up in Mbuji-Mayi, Kinshasa and Mbandaka.

As had happened in previous decades, the regime tried to exploit differences and weaknesses among the clergy with the aim of finding alliances among the bishops and the clerical elite. Against all expectations, Monsengwo, the Archbishop of Kisangani, failed in his candicacy for the Cardinalship. (Mobutu recommended Archbishop Etsou, who had just succeeded Malula as Archbishop of Kinshasa.) Two bishops, Moke and Tshibangu, who were considered friends of the regime, were excluded from the episcopal nominations for Kinshasa.

Few bishops were really opposed to Mobutu; many were said to depend on financial aid from him as the decolonisation of missionary work had left some local bishops materially insecure. Foreign donations and grants went to heads of religious congregations, who, legally speaking, could in no way be required to render accounts to Zairean bishops. (Material poverty was even more pronounced among the Protestants.) This precarious dependence weakened the episcopacy, involving the lower clergy and other ecclesiastics of the country in a predatory economy in which profit-making is the norm:

> The Mercedes-Benz car has become the episcopal vehicle par excellence, attributed to church leaders and elders and making them elites in the prominent places within the . . . post colonial state. In 1970, the Catholic bishop of Lisala shared this privilege with only two other dignitaries: the commissioner for territorial administration and a rich merchant." (Bayart, 1993a:139)

With the upper church characterised by a moderate reformist line and this de facto clientelism, impatience in the lower church grew, and its demands became increasingly radical. Moreover, certain bishops had misgivings about the regime, which they equated with Mobutu himself.

Besides numerous warnings from Rome against socio-political involvement that could compromise the church's role in Zaire, other factors forced the issue with the Zairean episcopacy. At the beginning of 1980, political opposition was getting organised and gaining popularity. Opposition leaders from Kasai certainly played an instigating role; Cardinal Malula and a significant number of the clerical elite and ordinary priests also were known for their sympathy for the political opposition. According to some sources (Dungia, 1992:202-211), diplomatic initiatives in favour of the opposition were conferred on Father Tshiamalenga, a Professor at the Faculty of Theology.

Mobutist propaganda portrayed the opposition as tribalist from the very beginning. (Malula and a good number of priests who were sympathetic to the UDPS were of Kasai origin.) The Archbishop's uncompromising attitude towards the regime was supported by a handful of bishops who were convinced that, above all, Malula's stance had to do with ethnic solidarity. This perception, coupled with many prelates' material dependence on the regime, prevented the development of a strong and consistent anti-Mobutu inclination within the hierarchy of the Catholic Church. The leadership of the CCZ and the CJCSK had clearly declared their support for Mobutu for many years. From 1987 to 1988, an unenthusiastic desire to disassociate themselves with the regime developed among the clergy, with indirect criticisms levelled against the regime's human-rights policy. This development caused the CCZ, as some Catholic bishops, to adopt an inconsistent stance two years later.

Just as the political elite, the working class and the churches were trying to come to grips with Mobutu's 24 April speech (in which he announced the separation of the MPR from the state, resigned as president of the MPR and announced a limited multiparty system), trade unions and other forces carried out their deliberations at the Congo's Sovereign National Conference on the other bank of the river Zaire. Congo's example (of setting up transitional institutions to enable democracy to regain its rightful place through peaceful means) became a source of inspiration for Zaireans (Mpundu, 1990:26). In addition, the citizens of Togo, Cameroon and Madagascar were pressing their respective regimes for similar conferences.

As the whole of francophone Africa became engulfed in the fever for democracy and the search for peaceful political transitions, Zairean public opinion overwhelmingly favoured this same route. The debates and public revelations in the Congolese Sovereign National Conference were a source of intense excitement in Kinshasa. The public pressed more and more for a Zairean sovereign national conference modelled on the Congo's. Since a Catholic archbishop skillfully presided over the Congolese Sovereign National Conference, many people felt that a church personality should do the same in Zaire, particularly given the numerical strength of Christians in the country.

For several months, the regime resisted the idea of a sovereign national conference and instead pushed for a constitutional conference. But, taking note of prevailing public opinion between 1989 and 1991, the regime began to seek possible sympathetic contacts within the Catholic hierarchy as well as among other religious dignitaries. The opposition and trade unions did the same. The net effect was renewed competition and rivalry within the episcopacy. A climate of distrust and mutual suspicion arose among the bishops, aggravating the difficulty of arriving at a common position as a church, with some members and some clerical elites having a strong aversion to the possibility of the presidency of a sovereign national conference going to a non-Catholic.

Meanwhile, the regime, terrified by the turn of events, tried to reassert its authority through violent intimidation. In May 1990, dissident students at the University of Lubumbashi were violently attacked, with many lives lost. The leadership of the Catholic Church in Lubumbashi, particularly the Catholic members of the university staff, were unanimous in their condemnation of the massacre.

This incident swayed international opinion and contributed to the consolidation of resolve against the regime. Religious authorities, Catholic as well as Protestant, seemed decisive in their resolve to abandon Mobutu. For the first time, many leaders of the CCZ adopted an openly nonconformist attitude. But still all was not clear. On 29 July and 1 August 1990, the national executive committee of the CCZ met in Goma. (According to some sources, President Mobutu, who had established his residence at Goma several months back, initially instigated this meeting.) With national and international opinion still shocked by the student massacre at Lubumbashi, the meeting came at a sensitive time. Positions were quite divergent within the National Executive Committee, with Archbishop Bokeleale advocating moderation, even neutrality, on the question of the Lubumbashi affair. At the same time, he urged the National Executive Committee to pay a visit to Mobutu. On the other side, Pastor Mbiya-Mulumba, Regional President of the CCZ in Eastern Kasai, emerged as the spokesman for those who found such a visit ill-timed and wanted the Executive Committee to take a stand on the country's overall political situation. He went on to condemn the Lubumbashi Massacre and other killings committed on university campuses.

Fortunately, the late arrival in Goma of a delegation representing the CCZ in Shaba (whose capital is Lubumbashi) with first-hand accounts of the massacre from student survivors helped delegates appreciate the facts better. The Shaba delegation was severely critical of the regime, and its stance helped rekindle antiregime sentiments, which had been on the wane.

Marshal Mobutu, discredited locally and internationally, appeared to be overwhelmed by events. He agreed to accept unlimited multiparty politics, which he had rejected not long before. The opposition and the trade unions realised then that they could force acceptance of the sovereign national conference by increasing pressure on the regime.

A few days after Mobutu's 24 April speech, new political parties had begun to emerge with surprising rapidity, many of which were formed with the financial support and blessing of the regime. This was also true of a number of newspapers and several associations set up by the regime in the hope of infiltrating civil society. Now the growing and irresistible strength of the anti-Mobutu forces obliged many parties, media associations and other organisations to disassociate themselves from the regime in order to establish their credibility and gain public support. The Catholic Church founded *La Conscience*, a newspaper committed to ecumenism.

After Goma, developments on the political scene were rapid. Up to 24 April 1990, the UDPS had been the only opposition force that could boast of a public following comparable to that of the MPR in 1980. Many new organisations now feared that the UDPS, whose popularity continued to grow, would completely overshadow them. Among the new parties, a force worth mentioning was the Social Christian Democratic Party (PSCD), comprised of a handful of former politicians—notably Joseph Ileo—and influential Protestants, which included Kalonji Mutumbayi, Bosunga Loombe Infinde, Professor Jean Masamba Ma Mpolo and Kimbanguist Pastor Luntadila. Informed of this political grouping, Mobutu threatened top Kimbanguist and Protestant leaders, forcing Luntadila and Kalonji to withdraw from the organisation. Masamba left and created the National Democratic Front, which was regarded as a specifically Protestant party, while Bosunga held on and became influential in the PSCD leadership.

For many people, the awakening of religion to politics filled the vacuum created by the disappearance of the totalitarian ideology with its promises of secular salvation. As in South Africa, Haiti and Poland, spiritual energies brought about a Christian revival in Zaire that proved to be a precious means of mobilising society in the fight against dictatorship.

Many "Christian" parties such as the Federalist Christian Democrats (FCD) under the leadership of Professor Ngoma, and the National Federation of Christian Democrats (FENADEC) began to flourish. These Christian parties were conceived as a way of containing the political resuscitation of the lower church, with the blessing of some Catholic bishops. There is no evidence that

Christians were especially attracted to these parties. In reality, people joined or became activists in parties on the basis of criteria such as friendship, socio-ethnic affinities and other interests of all sorts. Political ideologies drew the most support, which explains the success of the UDPS (Mpundu, 1990:25).

It is difficult to assess the Christian parties and how different denominational inclinations contributed in winning party affiliates since religious fervor in the form of prayers, exhortations, singing church songs and Bible reading punctuates the meetings and rallies of all parties (including those previously under Marxist influence!) (Biebe, 1991).

In June 1990, under pressure from their constituents, trade unions and political parties organised a day of protest in reaction to the student massacre in Lubumbashi. Cardinal Etsou, the Archbishop of Kinshasa, advised Christians not to take part in the protest. Public opinion at this time was for change, and the majority of Catholics in Kinshasa vehemently criticised the prelate's attitude; from this point, Etsou would be regarded as an ally of the regime. His loss of credibility seems to have allowed for new initiatives by priests under his jurisdiction. It also ensured that he did not feature among the candidates for the presidency of the sovereign national conference.

After several months of avoidance, Marshal Mobutu finally authorised a sovereign national conference to be held towards the end of June 1991. The prime minister, Professor L. Mulumba, assisted by a preparatory commission, had the responsibility of organising the conference. The conference eventually opened on 7 August 1991, accompanied by a frenzy of political and religious activity launched a few days beforehand. The CCZ and a network of prayer groups close to Kalonji Mutambayi held prayer campaigns around the People's Palace (where the conference was to be held) to exorcise it from supposed demons.

Having failed to prevent the Sovereign National Conference (SNC) and in fear of being only a small minority at the national forum where radical decisions were likely to be made, the regime tried to find ways of controlling it and swelling the ranks of its supporters. It also attempted to introduce into the provisional board of the SNC some individuals whom it could manipulate easily. A group of associations and parties opposed to the regime, the Sacred Union, immediately saw through the ploy and decided not to participate. Representatives of the Catholic episcopacy, including Etsou and Monsengwo, took part in the first two sessions before also withdrawing.

After long negotiations at a crisis meeting at the Nganda Catholic Conference Centre in Kinshasa, the Sacred Union and the Catholic bishops resumed their participation. Soon after, however, disagreements arose on the question of the registration of participants. Supporters of the regime were adamant in their position and opposed the call for transparency by resorting to obstructive tactics and motions. Prime Minister Mulumba succeeded in getting Kalonji Mutambaya appointed president of the provisional board of the SNC. Kalonji, a former President of the Senate and the Protestant University of Zaire and the rich son of a Presbyterian pastor, was well-known for his political ambitions. Even though Kalonji himself was not a pastor, the prime minister referred to him on the occasion as a "great spiritual head... and a pastor." The aim was to split the Luba community, which overwhelmingly supported Etienne Tshisekedi, the charismatic leader of the UDPS. Overtly manipulated by Mulumba and overstretched by the confused dynamics of a visibly ill-prepared assembly with insufficient physical and intellectual resources, Kalonji was completely overwhelmed. Protestants were both humiliated and frustrated; their buildings and premises in Gombe and Limete were even attacked.

Seizing the opportunity yet again in this confused chaos, the Sacred Union asked Kalonji to step down. Monsengwo Pasinya, Archbishop of Kisangani, was then proposed as president of the conference. He indicated that he would accept the role, provided it was conferred on him legally. Reassured about this, the assembly retired peacefully from the conference room.

Monsengwo, Archbishop of Kisangani since 1981, has had fluctuating relations with Mobutu's regime. During his episcopal enthronement in Kisangani, he actively solicited Mobutu's presence, but the latter's preference for Archbishop Etsou as Cardinal led to a downturn in their relationship. Two days after Monsengwo announced his acceptance of the presidency of the provisional board of the SNC, serious trouble broke out in Kinshasa and was followed by similar events up-country. The French Government worked to get the opposition and the regime to reach an agreement. Etienne Tshisekedi, a foremost opponent of the regime, was appointed prime minister. This first Tshisekedi government was to last for only two days before it fell victim to acts of destabilisation orchestrated by the regime.

In the meantime, the SNC was able to resume its deliberations with Monsengwo's candidacy assured. All the same, Mobutu's allies went on a campaign intended to divide the Christian churches on his candidacy, with considerable pressure brought to bear on Pastor Marini Bodo, Vice-president of the CCZ, to challenge Monsengwo. Marini appeared inclined to move the CCZ towards a more reformist and prophetic line and away from a pro-Mobutu stance. In October 1991, he issued a statement on the Zairean crisis ("Message...", 1991:9). Many people saw this document as a sign of real change in the official position of the CCZ, which previously had refrained from attacking the regime publicly. (Since 1990, any institution that failed to prove its non-alignment with the regime was perceived badly by the public.) How did Archbishop Monsengwo come to be endorsed, despite the intrigues of Mobutu's allies? A crashing victory was needed to underscore the will for change. Many senior Protestants in the anti-Mobutu political parties and associations exerted pressure on Marini to withdraw his candidature. Other Protestant leaders did the same. However, Vice-president of the CCZ was not willing to follow this line; he was in favour of an opposition personality of proven integrity assuming this role. For the Protestants, having one of their own at the head of the SNC would help correct the image of incompetence that had surrounded the Kalonji presidency, and put them in an advantageous position at a decisive moment in the history of the nation. (Indeed, Zairean Protestants, especially Kimbanguists, still suffer a feeling of social and cultural exclusion.)

Monsengwo eventually won the day, with J. Ileo Amba as his Vice-president, thereby defeating the machinations of the regime. To avoid further conflicts, Monsengwo insisted on co-opting members of the Mobutu camp. A few weeks afterwards, Prime Minister Karl-I-Bond Nguza, Tshisekedi's successor and a supporter of Mobutu, interrupted the SNC, saying that the conference was too costly and that national elections should be called instead. A showdown ensued between the workers and the churches on the one side and the regime and a handful of small parties on the other. What struck most people during this period, however, was the determination with which the leadership of the Catholic Church reacted to the crisis.

Efforts to Save the Democratic Transition

In a declaration made on 27 January 1992, the Catholic hierarchy pleaded to continue the SNC:

> Several times and in various ways, our people have expressed and continue to express their desire for a peaceful transition to democracy. For the majority of Zaireans and many other people of the continent, the best way to transit to democracy seems to be the Sovereign National Conference.

When the government questioned the legality of the SNC, the episcopate asserted that the search for a new national consensus made it necessary to go beyond the framework of the usual institutions, which are too limited and ineffective in a crisis of rare and extraordinary magnitude: "It is advisable to find a solution by means of an equally rare and extraordinary assembly [the SNC]".

Mobutu's supporters and their allies, however, focused on political justification of the SNC. For them, organising elections in order to attain democracy would suffice. On the other hand, the bishops insisted that holding elections before the people had had an opportunity to discuss and restructure their society was tantamount to reversing the process of democratisation.

As matters came to a head, Catholic ecclesiastical leaders were convinced that Mobutu's refusal of the sovereign national conference could only lead to violence; the lower clergy and mainstream Catholics felt that their bishops were not doing enough, or that there were too many moderates among them who were indulgent towards the regime. In the meantime, in both Kinshasa and the provinces, the lower church became dynamically mobilised involving the whole Catholic population in the struggle for democracy, with the immediate objective of restarting the SNC. A Catholic group in Kinshasa known as Amos especially distinguished itself in this regard. In Kisangani, (the seat of Archbishop Monsengwo), prayer-support groups such as Justice et Liberation, Les Amis de Nelson Mandela and Lotus proved very dynamic.

Many other peaceful-resistance initiatives were going on elsewhere. Monsengwo's appointment as temporary head of the SNC aroused renewed commitment among Catholics. In a long declaration published by *La Conscience*, the priests of Kinshasa went a bit further than their bishops by calling on the Catholic faithful and people of goodwill to abandon their fear and become more concretely involved in the struggle for change.

The most remarkable event confirming this renewed commitment was the demonstration held on 16 February 1992. After their church services, Christians—men, women and children, the young and the old, priests and pastors—a multitude of people all holding Bibles, candles, rosaries or crosses and singing songs of praise, walked along the roads of the capital. Their common purpose was to express their desire to see the People's Palace re-open its doors for an immediate and unconditional resumption of the SNC and an end to dictatorship. None of the participants threw stones at the soldiers or beat them but strictly maintained the discipline of non-violence throughout the walk. Still, the authorities decided to quell the demonstration with violence (Mpundu, 1990:27-28).

The protest march did not have the blessing of the area archbishop, Cardinal Etsou, but neither had he formally denounced it as he had with the demonstrations of June 1990. The CCZ had advised Protestants not to take part in the demonstration; after the repression, Bokeleale expressed regret that he had not been listened to. The Kimbanguist leaders simply forbade their members to participate. This apparent difference between church leaders and followers provided the government with the excuse it needed to justify the violence it perpetrated on the demonstrators, attributing all responsibility to "political and subversive evil" (Mpundu, 1990:28).

Despite this repression, internal pressure increased, and the government continuously resorted to violence and acts of intimidation. Throughout the country, the majority of people went on strike, staged demonstrations and put up barricades, paralysing activities in the towns. Apart from these activities, Christian groups also carried out quite remarkable activities such as alternating chains of intercession, prayer, fasting and hunger strikes, as an expression of solidarity with the oppressed. In Kisangani, there were appeals to boycott the information broadcast over the national radio and television and calls for peaceful demonstrations.

On the international scene, Mobutu became more and more isolated. The European Economic Community and the Belgian, American and French governments made moves to pressurise the regime into re-opening the SNC.

The Christian groups committed to the struggle for democratic transition were strongly inspired by the philosophy of non-violence, with priests trying to inculcate the people with the ideology and techniques of evangelical non-violence. Moreover, the churches made a particular effort to ensure reflection and analysis of the political situation. This was carried out through conferences and training workshops in which Catholic priests played a very important role (Badidike, 1992). Very often, this conscientisation through education on democracy, human rights and passive-resistance techniques was the creation of the priests and missionary workers.

In towns such as Kisangani, the mobilisation of Christians was so effective that the militants of the former regime carried out a strong campaign of disinformation with the aim of dividing the population. Some of the literature in this campaign reads:

> Moslem friends, Kimbanguists, Protestants and others, the hour has come for us to come together with the neutral forces whose objectives remain: Change in peace and in unity. The Catholics favoured by the Mobutu regime are today in the opposition and preaching violence, division and civil war between sons and daughters of this country with the goal of seizing the leadership of Zaire. Warning, warning and warning! Neutral forces are preparing to face these political activist priests at Kisangani. Let us unite ourselves and sow pillage, lifting desolation in the camp of these false missionaries.
>
> *Neutral forces*

The authors' strategy was to isolate the Catholic groups from other Christians and Muslims. Some of the leaflets attacked the Catholics directly and sought to intimidate them. One states,

> You, priests and religious people, we have done all you asked us to do but there is no change. This time around, we will turn on you. We will take all the money of

the procurator and rape all the sisters and the legionary mother. Since you seem to like politics, we will follow you very closely.

Mr Mâchoir de la Chèvre

The virulence and tone of the threats these leaflets contain show the impact of Christian action. In most cases, the initiative came from the lower church, but at Kisangani—the episcopal seat of Archbishop Monsengwo, grassroots mobilisation was seen as a sign of Catholic solidarity with the bishop and the President of the SNC.

The pressure on the regime eventually paid off, and on 6 April 1992, the SNC re-opened (*La Référence Plus*, 1992:1, 11) with twenty-one working commissions. After twenty-four months, Etienne Tshisekedi was elected transition prime minister. In the interim, a permanent executive committee managed the SNC, with Monsengwo as its president. The SNC eventually elected a High Council of the Republic (HCR) from among its delegates and finally adopted a transition programme that specified a judicial framework for the country and detailed its functioning.

Archbishop Monsengwo, who was elected President of the HCR, seemingly had "accepted" the position of leader of the opposition, but those close to the Vatican did not hide their reservations. Neither did Mobutu and his allies hide their displeasure with the SNC. Consequently, the regime renewed its efforts to derail the SNC, which indeed ended abruptly for three main reasons:

1. The release of compromising reports from the SNC's Commission on Assassinations and Commission on Ill-Acquired Property.
2. The boycott of the SNC by Mobutu and his allies.
3. The withdrawal of the 5,000,000 zaire banknote and Tshisekedi's move to control the Central Bank.

The lower church, the working people and the political parties did all they could to convince the prelate to carry on. Nevertheless, on 6 December 1992, the SNC ceased functioning, mainly due to threats from the regime.

At the re-opening of the SNC earlier, in April, a sort of national consensus, strongly encouraged by religious leaders, had been moving the country towards reconciliation and a lessening of socio-political tensions. The collapse of the SNC led to a grim crisis in Zaire. Gradually, the role and the speeches of Archbishop Monsengwo began to change considerably, aggravating the crisis and creating doubts about his abilities. Mobutu, in a show of force in Kinshasa at the end of January 1993, brought his rebellious army under control with the help of his special division. The aftermath was a terrible period during which opponents were hunted down, printing presses of independent newspapers were destroyed, and a climate of terror was installed.

In the political arena, Mobutu dismissed Tshisekedi, his government and the Supreme Council of the Republic. The previous Parliament made up of supporters of the dictatorship was reactivated, and Mobutu organised a conclave of his party's politicians and adherents to form a new government headed by Faustin Birindwa. Nevertheless, the Supreme Council of the Republic, the people and foreign governments refused to recognise this new government, leaving Zaire on the verge of civil war.

In spite of innumerable attempts to get Western governments with interests in Zaire to support the democratic process, Archbishop Monsengwo now appeared to be playing several chords at the same time. He asserted his loyalty to the institutions set up by the Sovereign National Conference, but went to great pains to explain why it was necessary for Tshisekedi to head the government, even though he had been appointed by the SNC. Later, he rejected both the Tshisekedi and Birindwa governments.

Monsengwo's inconsistency exasperated the public. Seeing the danger of being grouped together with Monsengwo and, above all, weighing the eminent crisis, the Zairean Episcopal Conference issued a statement on 23 April 1993. It stated, in part,

> In the deadlock created by the present situation, we are calling for dialogue between the political figures. Even in the midst of war, men feel the need to negotiate. This must, however, have as its ultimate goal the well-being of the people." (*Le Phare*, 1993)

Although Monsengwo was a signatory to the statement, the public and the media expressed doubts about his sincerity.

The bishops' concern about the need for dialogue and negotiation showed the priority they put on the values of peace and tolerance. But this call for dialogue was also interpreted in two other ways: (1) Mobutu's supporters, their allies and some important members of the opposition had severely criticised Tshisekedi's intransigence and call for dialogue, which, in this context, appeared to be a criticism of Tshisekedi's attitude; (2) Mobutu, having recently brought the army under his control, may have interpreted this call as *de facto* recognition of his authority at the expense of the legal institutions set up by the SNC.

The involvement of the Zairean Churches in the socio-political unheavals remain a large area for research. We, however, have to move away from this reality and draw a few lessons.

Major Directions and Questions for the Church

The church in Zaire can be described only with superlatives such as Africa's largest Catholic community, the world's most influential francophone Protestant movement and, in terms of numbers, the continent's biggest "independent" church. Together and separately, the churches delineate the social space. The dynamics of the religious revival described above show the possibilities for the church to influence socio-cultural realities in Zaire. Just as the weight of the church is obvious at the summit of political life—in the SNC, in the Supreme Council of the Republic and in the political parties—the pervasive spiritual awakening also impacts upon the social mentality from below. But can the representatives of the Zairean churches speak and act with the same authority? Is this desirable?

In the deepening crisis and stalemate of the moment, a real initiative embracing all the churches can serve as a testimony of hope for the people as a whole. The church's major handicap is the acute self-awareness within each denominational entity. The internal contradictions of each community and the influences of their own histories and socio-cultural heritage render the churches of Zaire prone to manipulation for political gain.

Even though church leaders remain suspicious of ecumenical co-operation, ordinary Christians cross the barriers of denomination to form a community with one common destiny. The prayer groups, various associations, and political parties seem closer to this lower church than church leaders—although the Catholic hierarchy exercises more control over its followers than the Protestant and Kimbanguist churches.

The churches and socio-political pluralism

To the extent that the practice of democracy challenges unanimity and encourages political competition within society, the church finds itself in a new situation in Zaire. Preferences and tendencies appear within communities and tensions and conflicts emerge as a result of different political persuasions, and the groups may rapidly become antagonistic to each other. How can the church work for social liberty and pluralism while managing the divisive situations that the latter tends to engender within their communities?

Very often, church leaders advocate neutrality and prefer preserving internal unity by avoiding the political challenges that society poses. This was the official line of conduct that the Kimbanguists adopted. But in extreme situations such as Zaire's, doesn't the church risk being marginalised and discredited by adopting a neutral stance?

In the West, Protestantism is identified with dynamism and initiation of political modernity and democratic values. At present, African Protestantism, like her ecclesiastical institutions, is gerontocratic and static. How can a church that shows little sign of life and democracy in its internal functioning authentically contribute to the development of democracy in the socio-political field? This is as much a burning question for the Church of Christ of Zaire, as it is for the Catholic Church.

The Catholic Church in Zaire is at the forefront of the movement for democratic change, but the Catholic Church has never identified itself with democratic practice. Its ecclesiology and structures of authority are monarchical; indeed, Catholicism often tends to equate legitimate pluralism with dismemberment of the church. In what form, then, can the Catholic hierarchy go along with the fight for democracy within society without giving rise to demands for democracy within the church?

Christian responsibility and political exigency

The Catholic bishops' involvement in setting up the new state and political institutions in Zaire is considered "political priesthood." In Benin and Congo, the political involvement of bishops was transitory. Because of the complexity of the political situation and the determination of the regimes in Zaire and Togo to retain power, it became necessary for Catholic prelates to become more involved.

In the case of Zaire, the partisan and antagonistic logic has been taken to the extreme. What room remains for church leaders to place themselves as much as possible above the conflict and foster dialogue? Can a church leader preach evangelic values within an institutional reality that makes him or her both the guarantor and the defender of the gains in the struggle for democratic change? Can the same church leader strike up, renew and maintain relations with the representatives of the old regime, who, very often, hardly believe in the nonpartisanship and good intentions of the church? Is there room to act in accordance with personal convictions and analyses of the situation? Questions like these illuminate the political deadlock in Zaire and suggest why it was necessary for someone like Archbishop Monsengwo to assume the political priesthood.

Notes

1. In addition to published sources cited in this text, other information was obtained in confidence from reliable oral sources.

2 Information on other churches is negligible, and this includes Muslims, who comprise 1.4% of the population.

References

Asch. 1983. *L'Eglise du Prophète Simon Kimbangu de ses Origines à son Rôle Actuel au Zaïre.* Paris: Karthala.

Badidike, J.P. 1992. Rapport no. GA/JL/02/92.

Bayart, J.F., ed. 1993. *Réligion et Modernité Politique en Afrique Noire.* Paris: Karthala.

Biebe, J.C. 1991. Conversation with the author.

Diangienda, K. 1984. *L'Histoire de Kimbanguisme.* Kinshasa: Editions Kimbanguistes.

[Church of Christ of Zaire] Eglise du Christ au Zaire. 1991a. *Chrétiens Lumière du Monde, Procès-Verbal du Synode National de 1987.* Kinshasa: Cedi.

———. 1991b. *20 Ans d'Unité, Tenez y Fermement, Procès-Verbal du Synode National de 1989.* Kinshasa: Cedi.

———. 1985. *La Mission de l'Eglise Aujourd'hui, Procès-Verbal du Synode National de 1985.* Kinshasa: Cedi.

Church of Christ of Zaire (CCZ) National Secretariat. 1990. *"Mémorandum de l'Eglise du Christ au Zaïre du Président Fondateur du Mouvement Populaire de la Révolution, Président de la République du Zaïre".* Kinshasa-Gombe. Photocopy.

Church of Christ of Zaire (CCZ) Regional Synod of the Kasai-Oriental. 1990. *"Réflexion du Comité Exécutif Régional de l'Eglise du Christ au Zaïre sur le Bon Fontionnement du MPR et ses Organes."* Mbuyi-Mayi. Photocopy.

La Conscience 72 (February 1992).

Dungia, E. 1992. *Mobutu et l'Argent du Zaïre.* Paris: L'Harmattan.

Eboussi, B. 1993. *Les Conférences Nationales en Afrique Noire.* Paris: Karthala.

Elima 136 (25 April 1990).

Jeune Afrique 1527 (9 April 1990).

Jewsiewicki, B. 1991. "De la Prestidigitation, de la Démocratie et des Morts sans Qualité Particulière." *Politique Africaine* (Paris) 41 (Mars).

"Justice et liberation, appel a la liberation, lettre aux chrétiens et aux hommes de bonne volonté." n.d. Document received from Kisangani.

Kabongo-Mbaya, P. 1992. *L'Eglise du Christ au Zaïre: Formation et Adaptation d'un Protestantisme en Situation de Dictature.* Paris: Karthala.

———. 1991. "Protestantisme Zaïrois et Déclin du Mobutisme." *Politique Africaine* (Paris) 41 (Mars).

"Message de l'Eglise du Christ au Zaire au peuple Zaïrois en Détresse." *Mission* (Paris)18 (15 Décembre 1991):9.

Mpundu, I. 1990. "Le Zaire en Marche vers la Démocracy." *Cahiers de la Reconciliation* 3:25.

Mulumba, M., and M. Makombo. 1986. *Cadres et Dirigeants au Zaïrois qui Sont-ils? Dictionnaire Biographique.* Kinshasa: Editions du C.P.R.

La Phare 228 (23 April 1993).

La Référence Plus 50 (6 April 1992).

Schotte, J.P. 1993. "L 'Eglise en Afrique et sa Mission Evangelistrice vers An 2000. Vous Serez Mes Témoins." Document de travail, Synode Spécial des Evèques pour l'Afrique. Paris: Centurion-Cerf.

Toulabor, C. n.d. "Le culte Eyadéma au Togo." In *Religion et Modernité Politique en Afrique Noire*, edited by J.F. Bayart. Paris: Karthala.

Voix d'Afrique (Bulletin of African Missionaries [Pères Blancs]) 11 (December 1991):14-15.

Williame, J.C. 1989. *Patrice Lumumba, Premier Ministre: La Crise Congolaise Revisitée*. Paris: Karthala.

"Zaïre un Pays à Construire." 1991. *Politique Africaine* (Paris) 41 (Mars).

9

The Christian Council of Churches in Madagascar (FFKM) and Its Commitment to Social Change

Josoa Rakotonirainy

Background History

In 1975, sixteen years after independence, Madagascans elected Didier Ratsiraka their president and, by referendum, adopted a socialist constitution. The Madagascan Socialist Revolutionary Charter of this Second Republic called for nationalisation of key sectors, among them banks, financial services, internal distribution networks of consumer goods and external trade.

From 1979, the government pledged to facilitate the creation of some public enterprises. This policy was largely responsible for the ensuing catastrophic economic situation, which was characterised by acute indebtedness and aggravated by corruption, inefficiency and world-wide recession.

In 1980, the government held negotiations with the International Monetary Fund (IMF). After the first standby loan the IMF granted, no further credit was forthcoming due particularly to the alarming debt rate. In 1982, the World Bank intervened, and the country adopted a structural adjustment programme (SAP).

Radical reforms adopted in 1986 to facilitate a new investment code, a new privatisation policy and liberalisation of imports failed to improve the social and economic situation. By 1989, the unfortunate effects of delayed economic reforms had plunged a sizeable proportion of the population into greater poverty and created social insecurity. Politically, however, the liberalisation measures the government adopted in 1986 lifted the 1975 ban preventing organisations that did not belong to the Front Nationale pour la Defense de la Revolution from participating in political activities.

In March 1989, after opposition parties failed to field a single candidate to face the President, Ratsiraka was re-elected for a third seven-year term. Nevertheless, the FFKM's appeal prior to the elections for Christians to pledge their support to the search for justice was received enthusiastically. New organisations that had been formed to join in the struggle to establish democratic practices contributed as elections observers. The opposition also voiced the need for a new constitution and a new electoral code.

In 1990, on the advice of its Commission des Affaires Nationales (FIEFIP), the FFKM announced its intention to organise a national convention to be attended by the various groups in the country. This national convention was the first of three that FFKM was to help organise.

Subsequent to the second national convention, the opposition parties organised themselves as the Forces Vives. In May 1991, the Forces Vives started organising popular movements and multiple strikes, using the principle of non-violence to seek the resignation of President Ratsiraka. The President, however, was determined to remain in power despite the pressure. Eventually, the entire administrative structure crumbled, and the national economy collapsed.

In the strikes, about 10 members of the Forces Vives died, 188 were injured and 57 disappeared. On 10 August 1991, the presidential guard cracked down hard on hundreds of thousands of demonstrators marching towards the presidential palace. Now, a solution had to be found.

The political crisis partially abated, thanks to a third national convention held on 31 October 1991, in which the government agreed to a transitional period during which the FFKM was to have the responsibility of organising a National Forum to facilitate formulation of a new electoral code and constitution. The new constitution was submitted to the people and approved by referendum on 16 August 1992.

In February 1993, Professor Albert Zafy, a Forces Vives candidate, was elected President of Madagascar's Third Republic.

The Church and Its Evolution in Madagascar

The first Christian mission to arrive in Madagascar was the London Missionary Society in 1812. Others followed suit:

- The Roman Catholic Church (1855).
- The Society for the Propagation of the Gospel, or SPG (1864). (The SPG gave rise to the Eglise Anglicane Malgache in 1918.)
- The Lutheran Mission of Norway (1866), followed by the Evangelical Lutheran Church, or ELC (1888), the Lutheran Board Mission (1890) and

three other Lutheran missions. These missions formed the Eglise Lutherienne Malgache (LMS) in 1961.
- The Friends Foreign Missionary Association, or FFMA (1867).
- The Mission Protestante Francaise, or MPF (1897).

The LMS, FFMA and MPF created three Madagascan churches, which in turn formed the Eglise de Jesus-Christ a Madagascar (FJKM) in 1968.

In spite of open conflicts between the various denominations and their members, the history of churches in Madagascar is characterised by a constant search for reconciliation. In fact, in 1913—three years after the historic meeting of missionary societies in Edinburgh—Protestants and Anglicans formed the Conference Intermissionnaire de Madagascar which, in 1958, made way for the Federation des Eglises Protestantes de Madagascar. In 1961, the various churches that were the offspring of Lutheran missions achieved unity and formed the Eglise Lutherienne Malgache. The same is true of the three churches that grew out of the three reformed missions and formed the Eglise de Jesus-Christ a Madagascar. The desire for conciliation is perhaps attributable to the country's *fihavanana* ("solidarity between various elements of society") tradition, which is deeply embedded in the mentality of the people.

Churches are often obliged to collaborate, as observers, on national political and social issues. From 1966 to 1968, a joint social commission, the Ecumenical Commission for Social Affairs (FEMES), brought together representatives of various denominations and established a forum within which churches could seek solutions to national problems. Although initially informal, FEMES is currently extending its activities to other areas that require intervention; for instance, adapting church training to Madagascar's economic and cultural realities.

In 1970, the Commission Oecumenique Nationale de Theologie (FET) was created. The new organisation, in some ways, was an outgrowth of the Protestant churches' Commission de Theologie, which it emulated. The FET reunited the representatives of the four main churches with an initial objective of co-ordinating a week of prayer for the unity of Christians and jointly translating the Our Father, the Apostles' Creed and the Nicene Creed.

In May 1973, the FET supported church leaders in their talks with government leaders during popular uprisings. Church leaders intervened in the tussle between security forces and demonstrators marching to the presidential palace, preventing a pointless blood bath. The success of these interventions encouraged church leaders to assign the responsibility of formulating constitutional documents to the FET to facilitate the creation of the Christian Council of Churches of Madagascar (FFKM). The first of these documents was submitted to the national synods of the four FFKM founder churches (Roman Catholic, Anglican, Church of Christ and Lutheran) for approval in 1974, and the FFKM was established in December 1979 and made official in January 1980.

The FFKM and the Origins of Activism

The Christian Council of Churches of Madagascar (FFKM) represents some 6 million Christians out of Madagascar's total population of 12 million. The rest of the population comprises a Muslim minority (about 3%) and practitioners of traditional religions. The elite of Madagascan society, however, are generally found within the Christian population owing to the fact that the churches are committed to educating the people through various programmes undertaken separately or jointly by the various denominations.

In 1982, the FFKM organised a national congress in Antsirabe with the theme Christians' Role in National Rehabilitation; a similar congress organised in 1987 in Fianarantsoa dealt with The Prophetic Role of the Church Within the Nation. These congresses served to mobilise the people but hardly caught the attention of political leaders who were preoccupied with other problems. The FFKM nevertheless continued to grow, while the activities the churches undertook increased in moral authority. In 1982, for instance, educational leaders within the FFKM were actively involved in meetings organised by the Conseil Supreme de la Revolution in an effort to find solutions to problems emanating from the application of Ordinance 78 040, which provided for the insertion of socialist ideology into Madagascar's entire educational and cultural system. Thanks to the appropriate involvement of FFKM leaders in these meetings, the political leaders of this period made concessions that limited the damage caused by the politicisation of educational and training structures.

Generally speaking, the FFKM makes its stand on issues known; for example, in August 1989, church leaders addressed an open letter to President Ratsiraka and President Frederick de Klerk when the South African leader visited Madagascar. The letter expressed church leaders' hope that relations between the two countries would be strengthened to a greater degree than political leaders anticipated at that time. They expressed the hope that progress in the struggle against apartheid would be boosted.

The FFKM, however, does not confine its involvement to political issues. It conducts research and exchange activities that touch on various aspects of church life, with national commissions and regional and sub-regional structures that handle these activities. FFKM's doors are open to non-member churches. As of

1993, the number of full-fledged member churches remains four, a number that remains low more due to the reluctance of other church organisations to join the council rather than to prevailing FFKM policy. Often, however, matters of doctrine prevent churches from seeking membership in the FFKM, as is the case with the Adventist Church. Nonetheless, whenever the opportunity arises, non-member churches collaborate with the FFKM on specific projects. An example is the independent churches' and Muslim community's attendance of the national conventions in 1990.

Religious leaders in Madagascar have long enjoyed a moral authority that has earned them the title *raiamandreny*, or "wise parent." The fact that religious leaders have managed to establish a common ground where political leaders have generally failed reinforces their authority. The FFKM's member churches thus constitute a pressure group that has proved effective over the last few years.

The First National Convention

The First National Convention organised by the FFKM between 16 and 19 August, 1990, is the most significant of church leaders' involvements in events leading up to the formation of the Third Republic. The theme of this first convention was based on Exodus 33:12 ("Bring up this people. . . ."). Discussions revolved around five major issues: education, training, health, the economy and politics.

Origins of the convention

In 1989, FIEFIP undertook the task of continuous review of the national situation, particularly the impact of Madagascar's structural adjustment programme within the context of assistance from the World Bank. From its reviews, FIEFIP concluded that for meaningful national reconstruction to be achieved, all influential parties needed to work together to convene a national conference. This idea received the blessing of FFKM leaders, who gave FIEFIP the responsibility of drawing up plans for the convention.

The aims and objectives of the national convention are expounded upon in a series of papers presented by leaders of the FFKM during the convention's preparatory stages and during the opening ceremony. In the main, the FFKM's motivation was related to specific theological ideals. Owing to its role as the nation's prophet, the FFKM believes, the church is responsible for spreading the living word of God to the nation: "The earth is the Lord's and the fullness thereof, the world and those who dwell therein" (Psalm 24); "For there is no authority except from God, and those which exist have been instituted by God" (Romans 13). The church therefore has a responsibility to oversee the well-being of the nation.

The principle of separation of church and state, which is often invoked and exploited by selfishly motivated individuals, has been a source of discontent and debate. Christians hold that God's transcendental authority over every earthly thing commands them to be "the salt of the earth and the light of the world" (Matthew 5:3-16). The church is also the living testimony of Christ, who "came that they may have life, and have it abundantly" (John 10:10). The same church, therefore, cannot remain indifferent to people's suffering and misery. It must be involved in the search for solutions to human problems at national and global levels.

Political groups' dismal performance in alleviating the suffering of the people also gives credence to the need for church participation, particularly at the national level. The ruling political party's attempts to reform the system came too late to mitigate the suffering into which the socialist regime had plunged the country. Opposition parties have had little or no success in reaching a common understanding, and political leaders who are old hands in the game continue to jeopardise the little success others achieve by sowing distrust. This state of affairs helped prompt the FFKM churches into taking the initiative by organising a meeting for all influential groups—*forces vives*—in the country.

A preparatory committee of twenty-eight persons representing various social and political groups and presided over by FFKM leaders formulated preliminary documents that served as the basis for the proceedings of commissions and plenary sessions. Participants formed four commissions, which in turn formed subcommissions, each dealing with a topic pertaining to the major issues.

A document formulated beforehand by the FFKM provided ground rules for procedures and decision-making. The objective was to facilitate fruitful exchanges and enable participants to rise above differences of opinion, thus safeguarding the *fihavanana*, the link that keeps the nation's unity intact. The document also accorded great significance to the contributions of church leaders and their representatives and to motions of order (e.g. limiting verbal contributions to three minutes to avoid unnecessarily lengthy speeches). In the event of irreconcilable differences with no hope of reaching consensus, the document stipulated that the various opinions would be noted.

The most essential co-ordinating role involved management of the proceedings. Four FFKM members from the executive board of the FIEFIP Commission, who were selected for their roles within the FFKM and their ability to lead discussions, presided over the plenary discussions. They were authorised to allow the leaders of the four main churches to speak whenever they wanted to. Other commission and sub-commission proceedings were conducted by boards selected by the participants themselves. The deliberations of the commissions and sub-commissions were attended by leaders from either the FFKM Executive Board or the FIEFIP Commission. In general, church leaders intervened whenever it became necessary to steer debates along the objectives defined by the convention and in the spirit of solidarity. There was always the concern that debates might focus on the parochial interests of a particular group.

Each plenary session started with an ecumenical prayer service. In addition, joint prayer services were held in the independent Protestant Temple of Antanimena, a few hundred metres from the convention venue. These services were open to all participants and to the public. On Sunday, 12 August 1990, four days prior to the official opening of the convention, six parishes of the four FFKM churches within the city and in the outskirts conducted ecumenical intercessional prayers. The convention proceedings started on 16 August with an ecumenical service of thanksgiving. The proceedings concluded with another solemn public service in the Catholic parish of Antanimena on 19 August, a Sunday afternoon.

The FFKM was able to fund the convention in full, partly with funds raised locally and partly with grants provided by Action Chretienne pour Madagascar (ACM-France) and the Federation Protestante de France. These funds were adequate for the expenses of co-ordination since food and accommodation were the responsibility of all participants except those from outlying provinces.

The 474 participants were distributed as follows: 150 delegates from the four FFKM member churches (including church leaders and members of the executive board, as well as those of the various national commissions and regional and sub-regional structures), 39 from the FFKM General Secretariat, 19 from certain administrative and judicial bodies (magistrates, bailiffs), 33 from 16 political parties, 24 from various unions, 31 from civic organisations, 103 from professional associations (lawyers, pharmacists, journalists, academics), 40 from the media (print, radio, TV and press agencies), and 14 from other religious communities (Muslims, Jews, independent churches, etc.). The rest comprised various personalities attending in their private capacities, as well as some invited dignitaries.

Some political parties and presidential lobby groups boycotted the convention despite written and personal invitations to the President. (On 16 August 1990, the President finally conceded to church leaders' request for an audience after vacillating for a long time.) The same was true of the majority of ministries and public services. The President, however, did send delegates to attend the opening ceremony.

Expectations for the convention

In organising the First National Convention for all *forces vives*, the FFKM hoped to provide a forum within which all elements could unite to foster national development. Such unity was considered a prerequisite for surmounting the problems of national reconstruction.

Opposition parties were invited to the convention, not by virtue of being the opposition, but because of the role they had played in initiating the debate on political reform. Social and economic organisations' enthusiastic response to the FFKM's invitation reflected their desire to be viewed as significant actors representing civil society in national development efforts. Their response also confirmed the FFKM's view that national rehabilitation cannot be the preserve of political parties alone, and the meeting proved not to be simply political, aimed at discrediting or overthrowing the government as the president's supporters alleged at the time.

Problems and constraints

The First National Convention met with several problems that emanated mainly from the presidential lobby groups' boycott and subsequent attempts to derail it. The President and his sympathisers were not satisfied to simply stay away from the convention; they also tried to divert attention from it in order to downplay its impact. Thus, the Indian Ocean Island Games held in Antananarivo almost coincided with the convention dates. In addition, South Africa's President was unexpectedly invited to Antananarivo for a few hours during the convention.

The President's retinue, however, was not the only source of problems. Among FFKM member churches, certain people created problems by voicing their reluctance to see the initiative succeed. One particular Catholic bishop's partiality to the President was evident and most disturbing. Even within the FFKM, certain leaders were reluctant to see the convention succeed because of their allegiance to the President. This internal division proved to be a major obstacle.

Other obstacles emanated from the fact that many church leaders, particularly those from the interior, simply did not have enough information to appreciate and accept the difficult responsibilities the FFKM had assumed. In the face of a systematic campaign to discredit the organisation, this lack of basic information enabled the convention's detractors to create an unfavourable atmosphere for its implementation. Likewise, the FFKM had insufficient experience to convince certain church leaders of the merits of collective action. In addition, the absence of adequate means of communication isolated FFKM churches from others in

Africa and from similar organisations in other parts of the world. (Since the rest of the world had hardly any information about the situation in Madagascar, the FFKM was deprived of indispensable support from churches elsewhere).

Time was another constraint. The preparatory committee and FFKM leaders had only a few weeks during which to formulate and prepare the documents that served as the basis for the proceedings. Besides this, the time allocated for the proceedings amounted to only a few days. The problem of time was aggravated by detractors, including some church leaders who engaged in negative pamphleteering.

Outcome and consequences

On the whole, the First National Convention met its objectives. Participants in the proceedings defined the basic principles upon which a new constitution would be based. These principles included:

- belief in God, but with the principle that the government would remain secular.
- national sovereignty.
- separation of judicial, legislative and executive powers.
- neutrality of government with regard to all ideologies.
- pluralism and freedom of speech.
- protection of the environment.
- limiting the presidential term to five years.
- a bicameral parliament with a national assembly and a senate.

These principles were formulated with the realities of the first and second republics in mind.

In some areas, issues seemed to require more deliberation and clarification before they could serve as a basis for national policy. Table 9.1 briefly outlines some of the issues discussed and the proposals that emerged.

The resolutions of the First National Convention presupposed that a second would be convened. FFKM church leaders were given the responsibility of communicating the convention's resolutions to the Head of State. They were likewise assigned the responsibility of convincing the President and his sympathisers to attend the second convention.

First National Convention—Issues and Proposed Solutions

ISSUE	PREVAILING REALITY	CONVENTION PROPOSALS
TRAINING/ EDUCATION	• Lack of skills among Madagascans • Training structures not adapted to the realities of socio-economic development in Madagascar	• New approaches to adapting the training sector to Madagascan realities • Phasing out ordinance 78 040—the basis for establishing the training system along ideological lines • Re-evaluation of the teaching profession • Giving priority to technical training for middle-level officers • Phasing out the employment of graduates of the National Military Service as trainers • One ministry of education for primary, secondary and university levels • Creation of a national committee for education
HEALTH	• The cost of medicines and medical care too high in proportion to people's low standard of living • Alcohol and drug use on the increase	• Lowering of health insurance cost • Campaign to raise citizens' awareness of the fact that they are the primary custodians of their own health and equally responsible for others • Stern measures in the application of laws regulating the use of alcohol
ECONOMY	• Failure in the economic management of the country • Total nationalisation and investment policy responsible for the system's failure • Reduction of the masses to destitution • Escalation of debt • Increase in unemployment rates	• Campaign to increase production in order to raise GNP • Strategies to generate employment • Proper use of the government inspectorate • Creation of a commission of inquiry on investment

The Second National Convention

The Second National Convention was held from 5 to 9 December 1990 at the same venue as the First National Convention. The number of participants increased from 474 to 534, with 522 of the delegates representing 138 organisations. Political parties were still in the minority. Presidential lobby groups again boycotted the proceedings. Thus, the convention faced similar problems to those encountered during the first convention.

The objectives of the convention were:

- To clarify and further develop the general principles defined by the first convention.
- To formulate political strategies to facilitate application of the principles enumerated.
- To minimise differences of opinion among all those willing to attend the convention.
- To enable those who kept away from the first convention the opportunity to attend and participate.

One outcome was a set of resolutions aimed at inspiring further motivation. Another was the creation of a new forum by the name of Forces Vives that was intended to bring together all entities represented. The Forces Vives was expected to replace the old opposition platform, which had proved ineffective. One disadvantage of the second convention, however, was that management of this forum, comprising a larger proportion of political actors than any other, created a feeling of frustration among the non-political elements. The Forces Vives was supposed to be capable of defining and applying political strategies to effect national rehabilitation. The FFKM, in a statement issued by church leaders, made it clear that it intended to detach itself from the Forces Vives. Below are excerpts from the salient points of the statement:

1. The FFKM regrets the failure of certain entities to respond to its appeal. The FFKM cannot claim that the resolutions emanating from the conventions have been endorsed by everybody. However, the FFKM affirms confidently that the ideas that have been expressed reflect the aspirations of the majority of Madagascans. Additionally, the FFKM believes that a minority of people or a few groups representing a limited number of people cannot by themselves explain the reasons and causes of the dire poverty affecting the entire country. It is imperative that the voices and aspirations of all the people be listened to in order to arrive at proposals that could lead to the rehabilitation sought by all.

2. The FFKM feels compelled to make it clear to all that it does not wish to acquire political power. The FFKM has no intention of forming a political party as that is inconsistent with its mission and would amount to supporting political personalities during elections. The role of the FFKM is relegated to facilitating the exchange of ideas and the holding of conventions, as is the case now. However, it is also incumbent upon the FFKM to disseminate, as extensively as possible, the outcome of such conventions.

3. The FFKM wishes to underscore its commitment to the amendment of the constitution with a view to facilitating actual and effective national reconstruction. These amendments should be based on the following principles: respect for the culture of Madagascans; affirmation of belief in God; respect for human rights in conformity with the UN and OAU charters; economic and social development, taking into consideration the rights of the individual; and, respect for discipline. The resolutions made at the Forces Vives meetings, which pertain to the economy, education and training, and health, will be communicated by the FFKM to all those empowered to improve on and apply them.

4. The FFKM urges churches, political organisations, leaders at all levels and all other groups to consolidate the unity achieved by adopting the proposals of the Forces Vives and applying them within the fraternity in order to uplift the people. We are hopeful that all organisations will permanently promote unity, in order for *fihavanana*, justice and peace to be established in the country and for actual rehabilitation to be effected in a democratic manner.

5. For its part, FFKM will, after the Second Convention, make a point of studying the proposals of the Forces Vives to see what responsibilities it could assume. The study of the proposals will be effected in the course of co-ordination of activities that the Executive Board of the FFKM is supposed to carry out. In all national rehabilitation activities, the FFKM will steadfastly play the role of *raiamandreny*, a factor of unity and national reconciliation. The FFKM will also strive to establish contacts between church leaders past and present as well as future decision-makers.

The FFKM's decision to remain on the sidelines caused some disappointment within the Forces Vives. The disappointment is not however, quite captured in the statement the Forces Vives made at the end of the meetings, but it deserves mention and is excerpted below:

1. The Forces Vives, having been summoned by the FFKM to attend the two national conventions of August and December 1990 at the FALDA Antanimena under the theme "Bring Up This People," and having heard the fine statement read on behalf of the FFKM by its Chairman, express their profound gratitude to the FFKM for all the efforts it has put forth and for what it continues to undertake and wish it the best of luck in its future undertakings.

2. The Forces Vives are convinced that the FFKM represents, in the eyes of the nation, moral authority and deserves credit for the role it has played. This

explains the FFKM's success in organising a peaceful convention in a very brief period of time and bringing together all these organisations with varying shades of ideas. Churches and Forces Vives must jealously guard the spirit of unity in order to ward off disappointments that would be difficult to heal. For the Forces Vives, conciliation among the churches themselves, on the one hand, and the church and the government, on the other, are part and parcel of history.

3. The Forces Vives affirms its readiness to always join hands with the FFKM to play their role in national rehabilitation.

The FFKM and Management of the Political Crisis

The political crisis remained unmitigated after the national conventions. The positions of the political group around the President (le Mouvement Militant pour le Socialisme Malgache, or MMSM) and the Forces Vives hardened. From 1 May 1991, when the Forces Vives demonstrated its ability to mobilise the masses, work boycotts became increasingly intensive, both in Antananarivo and in the provinces. These paralysed the administrative machinery and increased pressure on the President to resign. Since the President refused, the Forces Vives announced a transitional government, with Professor Albert Zafy as Prime Minister. Confronted with this state of affairs, the government of Colonel Ramahatra (installed by President Ratsiraka just before the political crisis of 1990) imposed a State of Emergency.

Due to the seriousness of the situation and the heightened threat of civil war, FFKM church leaders, in an open letter dated 19 June 1991, urged the two parties to reconcile in order to seek solutions to the crisis. The FFKM offered itself as mediator. On 20 June 1991, the President received the church leaders, who communicated to him the proposal for reconciliation.

The dinika santatra *and the Tripartite Committee*

From 2 to 9 July 1991, the FFKM organised a meeting at the FALDA Antanimena (a Catholic lay training centre near Antananarivo) for MMSM and Forces Vives representatives. The meetings, referred to in the Madagascan language as *dinika santatra* ("mutual initial exchanges"), were attended by 30 MMSM representatives, 30 participants from the Forces Vives and 22 from the FFKM (including the four principal church leaders). Co-ordinated by the FFKM leaders, the initial agenda of the meeting was Analysis of the Current Situation and Solution to the Question: How to Manage the Current Situation Within the Context of a New Society. Three commissions were formed, each with a composition of 10 MMSM, 10

Forces Vives and 7 FFKM representatives. Representatives of the FFKM presided over the commissions, with members of the MMSM and the Forces Vives serving as co-chairmen and co-secretaries. The plenary session was held during the second half of each day.

The most notable outcome of the *dinika santatra* was the creation of the Tripartite Committee composed of representatives of the MMSM, Forces Vives and FFKM. This committee was charged with finding solutions to the impasse between the Forces Vives and the MMSM.

The government announced by the Forces Vives meanwhile had attempted to seize ministries by storming ministerial offices. On 25 July 1991, the Ramahatra government reacted by detaining some of the insurrectionary government "ministers," notably Albert Zafy and Mrs Andriamanjato Rahantavololona of the Ministry of Transportation and Public Transport. On 26 July, FFKM church leaders proposed a truce to the Tripartite Committee and suggested a halt to detentions, cessation of hostilities, an end to the State of Emergency, and an end to seizure of ministerial offices by the Forces Vives. The FFKM further proposed the dissolution of the parallel governments of Ramahatra and Zafy in order to pave the way for a transitional government for a period of three to four months. During this time, preparations would be made for a third national convention and formulation of a new constitution and electoral code. This would be followed by a referendum and fresh elections soon after. According to the FFKM proposal, a transitional government emanating from the Tripartite Committee would be vested with special powers and headed by a director who would double as chairman of sessions. The transitional directorate would appoint ministers on the commendation of the MMSM and the Forces Vives. The FFKM would abstain from proposing individuals for appointment, but would have a say in the appointment of ministers, who were to have no links to the two dissolved governments.

After receiving these proposals, the parties requested time to reflect on the issues. On resumption of discussions, the Forces Vives demanded an indefinite suspension of the meeting and threatened to withdraw unless their fellow campaigners for justice were released from detention.

On 1 August 1991, the Tripartite Committee resumed talks, focusing on a search for solutions to the prevailing situation. On 6 August, participants received a draft constitution prepared by the Tripartite Committee, but differences between the two camps (heightened by events) led to the early demise of the committee. The MMSM felt that the Forces Vives should make concessions since the government had already accepted redrafting of the constitution, freeing detainees and dissolving Ramahatra's cabinet. The Forces Vives, for its part, felt the only solution was for the President to give power back to the people. This standoff led to the blood bath at Iavoloha on 10 August, during which presidential security forces used hand grenades on a crowd of more than 500,000 people who were marching peacefully towards the presidential palace. This incident sounded the death knell for the Tripartite Committee, and some people felt that its untimely demise signified failure of the FFKM and its efforts.

The Convention of 31 October 1991

By 10 August 1991, the parties had reached a stalemate despite the appointment of Guy Willy Razanamasy as Prime Minister on 8 August 1991. All political leaders felt the need to reach a consensus. The result of the desire for conciliation was myriad proposals for a convention. More than twenty proposals focusing on specific points were made. No political party or organisation expressed willingness to act as mediator for the various camps.

As attempts to find a solution failed, the impact of the general strikes that had gone on for months became painfully apparent. At the same time, advocacy for federalism, spearheaded by some of the President's supporters, enjoyed a resurgence. A rift developed within the Forces Vives, which splintered into the Forces Vives Rasalama and the Forces Vives de Madagascar. Tensions also ran high within the armed forces as a faction loyal to the President threatened to start an uprising if his legitimacy continued to be challenged. Some of the senior officers were particularly eager to bring the factions to an understanding in order to avert this threatened catastrophe.

On official invitation from Prime Minister Razanamasy, the MMSM, the two Forces Vives and the FFKM met for a third convention at the Hotel Panorama from 29 to 31 October. Two senior officers in the armed forces, General Ramakavelo (Minister of Defense in Razanamasy's government) and General Soja, insisted on attending the debates and contributing to resolutions. Although church leaders did not initiate this meeting, they were called on to co-ordinate the discussions.

This third convention defined the objectives and conditions of the transitional period, during which new elections would be held, institutions restructured, and a new constitution and electoral code written. The convention recognised the government of the Forces Vives and planned to allow the president of the republic to remain in power, although there would be a significant reduction in his powers. According to the convention, the institutions with authority during the transitional period were to be:

- The High Authority of the State (HAE).
- The Council for Economic and Social Recovery (CRES).
- The transitional government.
- The Constitutional High Court (HCC).

After protracted negotiations between representatives of the political parties on the issue of who should chair these institutions, Albert Zafy, a representative of the Forces Vives Rasalama, was chosen to head the HAE, while Pastor Richard Andriamanjato of the Forces Vives Rasalama and Manandafy Rakotonirina of the Forces Vives de Madagascar became co-chairmen of CRES. The MMSM had fewer members than the two Forces Vives, but Guy Willy Razanamasy, who had been appointed by President Ratsiraka, headed the government. Razanamasy's confirmation as Prime Minister helped strike a balance since he was seen as representing the interests of the Head of State, who trusted him and expected his support.

One of the most important points from the third convention was the responsibility given to the FFKM. Article 6 of the convention states in part,

> The Prime Minister should assist the FFKM in the organisation of the 'Fihaonambem-pirenena' [national forum] and the preliminary meetings to prepare the new Constitution and the new Electoral Code for the approaching Third Republic.

In addition, Article 11 states,

> As soon as the Convention is signed under the responsibility and guidance of the FFKM, the HAE and the CRES will be created and they will proceed with the appointment of their committee members.

The post of Secretary-General of the HAE was given to the FFKM. This responsibility did not initially please church leaders, who felt that the FFKM should not be involved in the transitional institutions. However, after pleas from all parties, church leaders accepted this post as a duty of the FFKM.

The prolonged effort to find solutions to the serious political crisis Madagascar had experienced since 1989 culminated in the convention of 31 October 1991. It brought the consensus that all the people who wanted to see justice and peace had sought for a long time and guaranteed that a new era of democracy and pluralism was on the way. In practical terms, adoption of the convention meant a return to normal life and resumption of the administrative machinery of the state, which had been brought to a standstill by the six-month-long countrywide general strike. It also ended a long period of widespread psychosis caused by threats of a military coup. By involving the FFKM, the political authorities invoked the moral authority of the church to prove that they were serious about their desire for peace.

Soon after the signing of the convention, a problem arose. Albert Zafy, who was appointed chairman of the HAE, had been out of the country when the convention was signed. Upon his return, Zafy declared that he did not agree with the convention and disowned the meetings that led to the signing. According to some people, he rejected the convention because it allowed the president to remain in power. Tensions quickly dissipated when he and the Forces Vives Rasalama accepted some modifications of the initial text that did not alter its general orientation.

Soon it became clear that the outcomes of the Convention of 31 October could not satisfy all expectations. The clauses of the convention were vague on the issue of whether the HAE or the government had the prerogative when it came to some issues, especially if partisan political interests were at stake; the majority of members and the chairmen of the HAE and CRES were from the two Forces Vives, while the government was made up mainly of people who sympathised with the president. (The most significant disagreements between the two camps came to the fore in 1992, when international tenders were solicited for the supply of petroleum products.) The convention was also unclear on the duration of the transition period.

Nevertheless, the convention managed to accomplish the mission of setting up a transitional government. It adopted a spirit of give and take, thus preventing disagreements between those with divergent political tendencies from degenerating into armed conflict. Threats of civil war were quelled, and the Third Republic, with its spirit of democracy and *fihavanana*, eventually was ushered in smoothly.

The FFKM and the National Forum

As provided for in the Convention of 31 October 1991, the National Forum was to provide the framework for preparation of the new constitution and electoral code. Before its dissolution by the Convention of 31 October, the National Assembly of the Second Republic made some modifications to the constitution. These were considered cosmetic and aimed only at securing the interests of the leaders of the time. Eventually, even those in power accepted the need for a new constitution and electoral code.

The issues to be considered in preparing the constitution were not to be the monopoly of political parties or a few leaders. Rather, all classes of society were to participate in designing the basic constitutional instruments. Indeed, the objective of the National Forum (initially recommended by the FFKM) was to ensure maximum participation by people with different opinions in order to arrive at a national consensus.

Another objective the FFKM envisaged for the National Forum was to follow up on the proceedings of its national consultations of 1990 to prepare guidelines for a national policy on the economy and the social and cultural development of the country.

As set out in the Convention of 31 October, the prime minister was to help the FFKM organise the forum. Six people from the FFKM, 4 from the Forces Vives Rasalama, 2 from the Forces Vives de Madagascar, 4 from the MMSM, 2 from the Office of the Prime Minister, 6 from civil society, 3 from the armed forces and the national police, 6 from social and cultural organisations, 2 from universities, 2 from women's associations, 2 from youth organisations, 4 from rural people's organisations, and 6 from regional organisations made up the Organising Committee of 47. This committee elected an executive committee of 7 whose chairman, vice-chairman and secretary were from the FFKM. The Committee of 47 was aided by the Permanent Administrative Committee (CAP) made up of FFKM technicians and divided into five technical departments: organising, communication and information, leading, finance, protocol and security forces, and logistics. The Secretary-General of the FFKM was to be the overall head of these CAP departments.

The National Forum was to take place in two stages. At the regional level, the forum was to take place in 110 centres countrywide, corresponding to *fivondronana* (the equivalent of the former districts [*sous-prefectures*]). Before the regional forum took place, the Committee of 47 sent a team to check each centre. These prospecting teams had to identify church leaders who could lead the proceedings of the forum and set up the necessary structures. This prospecting phase mobilised about 50 people who worked in twos or threes in the organising centres situated in the most problematic areas. In this preparation stage, some church leaders were sent to the regional centres to prepare the people psychologically and familiarise those appointed to conduct the proceedings with management techniques. (These 150 leaders included 40 people each from the Catholic and Lutheran churches and the FJKM, and 30 from the Anglican church.) The regional preparatory phase took about a month, from mid-December 1991 to mid-January 1992.

The regional forums took place from 9 to 15 February 1992 under the leadership of local representatives of the FFKM. Participants at each regional centre included 20 people from the FFKM, 20 from other church organisations or religious communities other than the FFKM (e.g., the Adventist Church, MET, Independent churches, Muslims, etc.), 8 from industries or local enterprises, 20 from peasant organisations, 20 from youth organisations, 10 from teachers' organisations, 10 to 30 from legalised associations, 2 from each regional section of each political party (or 20 in all), 4 from the civil society, 18 from civil servants and employees in the private sector, 10 from the regional university, and 20 from associations or organisations that had taken part in the mass movement. In total, each regional forum had about 150 participants.

The proceedings of each regional forum were conducted using documents prepared beforehand by the Committee of 47 and CAP. Ideas proposed in the basic documents were analysed and new propositions collected, debated and finalised. Any points peculiar to each region were discussed. When all proposals for the constitution from the regional forums were combined, the result closely approximated the general principles that had emerged from the FFKM's national consultations of August and December 1990.

At the national level, the forum took place in Antananarivo from 22 to 31 March 1992. The meeting opened with an ecumenical service at Mahamasina Stadium on 22 March, which was attended by at least 30,000 people. The official participants in the forum numbered 1,400 (12 representatives from state institutions, 60 from public ministries, 8 from private services, 16 from the courts of justice, 79 from political parties, 60 from trade unions, 28 from economic organisations, 28 from parastatal organisations, 12 from civil organisations, 5 from women's organisations, 6 from peasant organisations, 15 from cultural organisations, 23 from the special schools of higher education, 6 from the national directorate of schools, 29 from youth associations, 7 from health organisations, 47 from social organisations, 4 from associations of the handicapped, 10 from the press, 12 from all kinds of professionals, 10 from the armed forces and gendarmes, 5 from the national police force, 90 from private and semi-private associations, 22 from other religious communities, 50 from the FFKM (executive committee, commissions and regions), 47 from the organising committee, 672 representatives from regional centres of the forum [at least 6 per region], and 11 from associations or groups that had taken an active part in the people's movement).

The participants were divided into five big commissions, which in turn were divided into several sub-commissions dealing with important subjects related to the constitution, the electoral code, the economy, health or education.

Each commission combined the findings of the sub-commissions before submitting them to the plenary session. Before resolutions could be adopted, the sub-commissions and commissions had to reach a consensus. Any issues that could not be reconciled were submitted to the plenary session as alternatives.

The budget for the National Forum was 1.3 billion Madagascar francs. The government provided this amount through the Ministry of Finance. The Embassy of the United States of America donated photocopying machines, computers, typewriters and duplicating machines, and the Swiss Confederation and Norway gave subsidies amounting to 125 million Madagascar francs.

Problems

As with the preceding conventions, the biggest problem encountered in the organisation of the National Forum came from parties who supported the President. These parties had been practically silent since the tragic events of 10 August 1991, but they had now begun to gain strength as they found support in the coastal regions where certain people were demanding that the six regions of Madagascar become federal states. They claimed that the state had neglected the coastal population and that it had favoured the people from the highlands and the capital, where power was concentrated.

The abusive concentration of power around the centre did indeed create an imbalance between the regions, making it imperative that Madagascar decentralise as soon as possible to enable the various regions to develop in an equitable manner. During preceding regimes, decentralisation had remained anathema, ignored even by those who preached socialism. The regime's sudden push for federalism came as a surprise, since during sixteen years in power, it had never advocated decentralisation. Thus, the campaign for federalism was at its hottest during the national and regional forum meetings. Its advocates demanded that they be allowed to present a proposal for a federal constitution alongside the Committee of 47's amalgamated proposal.

In the regional centres where the MMSM and the federalists agreed to participate, the two groups were allowed to present and defend their proposal. But those who favoured the federal option appeared to have difficulty in explaining how their constitution differed from the unitarian one recommended in the basic documents of the forum, which contained clauses on full-fledged decentralisation. For those who defended the unitarian constitution, the unity of the state, which guaranteed the unity of the nation, was to be safeguarded. They claimed that the country's present demarcation into six regions—a colonial legacy that the federalists now proposed to make permanent by creating six federal states—did not correspond with sociological and economic realities. Making these six regions autonomous states would have doomed them to isolation and possible tribal clashes since almost all contained a mixture of tribes. Some of these groups such as the Zafisoro and Antaifasy, neighbouring tribes from the south-eastern region who engaged in fighting in 1988, have a history of hostility towards each other.

At the regional forums, the MMSM and the federalists united to try and prevent the meetings from taking place. They threatened physical harm to participants, and when this failed, they tried to foment disturbances. These attempts at sabotage continued and reached their peak during the National Forum when some members of the MMSM and the federalists tried to force themselves into the venue. The plenary sessions, initially planned for the Ampefiloha School complex, were transferred to the covered Mahamasina Stadium and then to the Military Officers' Mess (CEMES) at Fiadanana. In spite of barricades, the troublemakers tried to force their way into the CEMES, and the security forces protecting these grounds (considered a national security zone) opened fire. Several supporters of President Ratsiraka were killed, and dozens were wounded. This unfortunate incident put a hurried end to the meetings of the forum. The closing ceremony was cancelled, but the participants had already adopted the final text of the new electoral code and constitution, with a few last details entrusted to a special *ad hoc* committee that was to finalise the documents.

In this way, the proceedings of the National Forum almost came to naught just as they ended. The hard-core supporters of the President rejected the proceedings as a bloc, even though church leaders and the FFKM had done everything they could to make the forum a success. FFKM leaders in the Committee of 47 had held working sessions with delegates of the MMSM who had been sent by President Ratsiraka to find out how the principles on territorial communities that had emerged from the regional forums could be aligned with those advocated by the supporters of federalism. These meetings, which were held almost in secret at the beginning of the National Forum, helped to prepare Chapter VII of the constitutional proposal, a compromise between the federalist and unitarian positions. Neither these initiatives nor the participation of the MMSM and federalists in all of the proceedings were able to dispel the misgivings that the supporters of the President had about the FFKM. The former custodians of power could not accept the fact that the majority of participants in the National Forum were not from the political and administrative structures already in place. The FFKM's involvement of people who had never before been consulted about major decisions related to the state made it an easy scapegoat.

The President's supporters led campaigns aimed at disparaging the FFKM. In several regions, they went as far as attempting to kill some FFKM leaders or burning down buildings that belonged to FFKM churches. The Protestant Temple of Antarandolo in Fianarantsoa, the FJKM Temple of Tsiroanomandidy, the Androva Vaovao Temple in the centre of Majunga and the Benjamin Escande School at Ambositra were all burned. All the big towns in the country had graffiti accusing the FFKM in indelible ink of partiality and of causing the disturbances.

Results

In spite of the numerous problems and attempts at sabotage, the anticipated results of the National Forum were achieved. At the regional level, participants were totally free to choose between the federalist and unitarian constitutions. Of the 110 regional centres, only one in the province of Toamasina opted for the federalist constitution.

The general spirit of the new constitution can be summarised in three points that reflect the aspirations the people expressed during the FFKM's national consultations of 1990:

1. The separation of the judiciary, executive and legislative powers.
2. The importance of the will of the people (i.e., it is the members of Parliament, who have been elected by the people, who are to choose the prime minister—not the head of state, as in the past).
3. The autonomy of territorial communities or decentralisation of power, with provisions to guarantee the unity of the state in order to foster national unity.

After the Ad Hoc Committee of the National Forum finalised the constitution, it was subjected to a referendum on 19 August 1992. The federalists' idea of presenting two constitutions at the referendum was rejected by the transitional government. The results of the voting were monitored by national and international observers. The referendum passed with 72.29 per cent of the vote (2,330,641 votes out of a total of 3,206,126), marking the end of the Second Republic.

Conclusion

The eighteen months of transition seemed exceedingly long, and the economic and social situation in Madagascar has not improved. Deteriorated conditions have been aggravated by instability during this period. The minister for internal affairs, in an interview in January 1993, said there were 19,024 complaints to the police during 1992, 1,400 crimes recorded and 728 arrests. There has been a marked increase in the activities of the *dahalo* (organised bandits who plague the villages and urban centres). Under the poor conditions of the rural areas, the young people, who have no jobs, see *dahalo* as a way of earning a living.

Yet Madagascar has immense resources including gold, emeralds, mercury and uranium that could be exploited. The country's potential is already attracting foreign investors encouraged by the recent economic liberalisation. Dozens of free enterprises set up in favourable economic zones have yet to blossom to their full potential. The election of Albert Zafy as President—with 66.74 per cent of the vote, on 10 February 1993—may just guarantee the stability that the country needs and justify the people's excitement at the advent of a new era.

In spite of everything, the leaders of the transitional government succeeded in dissolving the tension between the federalists and the government and between the federalists and the Forces Vives. Although some people feared that the communities affected by gradual decentralisation following the National Forum might be incited by leaders of the former regime who had lost their privileges into causing disturbances, these did not go beyond verbal exchanges. Before the first presidential elections, the Prime Minister negotiated the Fanambana Contract with advocates of federalism in four provinces to stop hostilities so that elections could take place.

As their influence waned, the federalists of Antsiranana started to settle scores with local members of the Forces Vives. These conflicts were brought under control by a special brigade sent to Antsiranana by the transitional government. Was the fact that the often explosive situation did not degenerate into armed conflict between supporters of Ratsiraka and those of the Forces Vives due to *fihavanana*, the solidarity that binds the members of society despite their differences, which is highly respected by Madagascans? Or was it because people respect the moral authority of the churches?

The organisation of the National Forum in 1992 was the final duty entrusted to the FFKM. The member churches are now evaluating their common enterprise on behalf of the nation. Only the churches' joint activities have stopped as they now take stock of their common situation. The Fifteenth National Committee meeting of the FFKM, held in Antsirabe from 2 to 8 November 1992, had on its agenda papers on the theological position of each church and its Christian commitment on national issues. The discussions that followed the presentations indicated that the four churches have different theological interpretations of their recent involvement in national politics.

Certainly the churches' intervention helped people become more aware of the responsibilities they needed to assume for national recovery to take place. The churches of the FFKM will continue to study the areas that can enhance their common witness as they seek to unite Christians in Madagascar. For this reason, the Antsirabe committee meeting made plans to set up mobile training institutes on ecumenical matters in the near future. The FFKM's recent election of a Secretary-General suggests that the organisation will give priority to strengthening national and regional structures for better mutual understanding and service to the nation.

Churches will participate in the work of national recovery, although they will not be directly involved in politics as they were during the conventions and the National Forum, they will continue in their role of educating and training citizens. The FFKM has undertaken a vast programme of civic education through the Teachers Commission. Projects in other areas will help to correct any misperceptions about the church that may have arisen from the FFKM's involvement in the change process and reassure those who questioned its intentions.

Postscript: November 1995

Madagascar on the eve of the second millennium

After some thirty years of independence, Madagascar is suffering ever more deeply from a disease with deep and invisible roots. As one of the thirteen poorest countries in the world, with per capita GNP of US$ 230 in 1992, Madagascar faces huge economic and financial difficulties. The purchasing power of the people in general continues to crumble, while overnight a minority class of millionaires has appeared.

Since the events involving the FFKM described above, social and cultural problems have increased dramatically. Madagascans live in a climate of insecurity, with chronic shortages of basic necessities, increasing violence and wanton destruction of the environment. Every year, several hundred million hectares of our forests burn, and acts of robbery and plunder grow increasingly profane (as in the theft of human bones from tombs to feed a mysterious and macabre trade or in the loss, allegedly by arson, of the Queen's Palace at Manjakamiadana).

At times it has been said that our island nation suffers—quite naturally and unavoidably, some would say—from insularity. We must get out from under our isolation, we are told, make our way into the outside world and fit our mentality to the modernism that real development requires. Currently, the people of Madagascar are waiting for the announcement of a new round of agreements with the World Bank and the International Monetary Fund. The agreements, made in good faith, are supposed to provide the miraculous remedy that the country urgently needs. But Madagascar established relations with these institutions in 1983, and the country's submission to the prevailing world economic and social system has not improved its economic situation so far. On the contrary, according to the IMF, Madagascar's financial situation has worsened, with the country's debt now topping US$ 4 billion.

A common practice is to attribute problems such as ours to those who govern and their corruption, incapacity or lack of political willingness to bring about change. Yet the establishment of the democratic Third Republic in 1992 under Professor Albert Zafy has not remedied the country's problems. The solutions of free trade and democracy offered to the Malagasy people do not seem adequate to fulfil their expectations for a better life. The people's disappointment in the political class is evident in their abstention rate, on the order of 40 to 60 per cent, during the recent constitutional referendum and municipal elections.

Julio de Santa Ana, a well-known churchman from Uruguay, has written eloquently in *Concilium: Revue Internationale de Theologie* not only about the plight of Madagascar's 12 million citizens but that of millions of men and women burning for justice and equity throughout the world:

> Some surprising contrasts characterize the world situation at the end of this century. A minority of the planet's population owns the capacity to accumulate wealth, which allows them to enjoy overwhelming material privilege when a high proportion of the inhabitants of the globe are struggling for survival. . . . Now, the system is seen as a lump entity. But those who are governing and harvesting the profits, the production process, the circulation of goods, the commercialization and the financing are not only from the West. The ruling class is made up of people and economic groups from plenty of nations.

Having tried to give a bit more definition to the "system" and provide an understanding of its origins, Santa Ana goes on to denounce the misdeeds of the market economy in these pertinent terms:

> The weight of the *exclusion principle* [emphasis added], fit for systemic logic, is borne as a terrible violence. It is a source of agony. It has a baleful effect on the lives of the poorest, who, in order to survive are often compelled to do things contrary to their own dignity. You meet this violence not only in international relations and interethnic or intercultural relations, but through its irregular demonstrations in big cities, Northern as well as Southern.

Whatever credit is given to this understanding of our problems—and the facts are there, perturbing in their verity—it does not explain all things. The question, then, is what to do in such a situation. What are our alternatives?

Sandra Granjow, an American who recently visited the offices of the FFKM—the Christian Council of Madagascar—declared, "I know of no country like Madagascar, where the church can influence the life of the nation." Already, in August 1982, the FFKM had given its First National Congress the evocative theme, Christians in the Forefront of the National Recovery—an allusion to the prophetic role the organisation has played in Madagascar, mainly in mediation tasks.

The churches in the FFKM, facing the serious realities of our nation, feel the need to establish a culture of peace in Madagascar in order to overcome violence and achieve harmony among the various groups as the government sets about implementing the decentralisation measures defined in the new constitution. For this reason, the churches chose as the theme for the FFKM's Third National Congress, held in Mahajanga from 4 to 8 October 1995, The FFKM in Its Education of the Citizenry Toward a Society of Peace for Lasting Human Development.

It is the FFKM's task to prove that the church cannot remain indifferent in the face of human alienation. As the theme of the last convention indicates, the FFKM is planning to take part in the change in mentality Madagascar needs with efficient development plans, including the search for solutions to poverty and ecological problems.

References

Santa Ana, J. de. 1995. "Today's Socioeconomic System: The Reason for Ecological Imbalance and Poverty." In special issue "Ecology and Poverty: Cry of the Earth and of the Poor." *Concilium: Revue Internationale de Theologie* 261.

10

Peacemaking and Social Change in South Africa
The Challenge of the Church

John Lamola

The period after February 1990 was a very special epoch in the political and social history of South Africa. It was a period of transition, with negotiations aimed at creating a free, democratic and non-racial South Africa out of the morass of apartheid's oppression, dehumanisation and exploitation. This positive process of political transformation in South Africa was, however, proving to be uniquely complicated and protracted.

Many complications dotted and punctuated the course of this transition, but political violence proved to be a major obstacle to timely realisation of a non-racial democracy. Of critical interest was the manner in which the church in South Africa managed to transform its public ministry from outright resistance to support and nurture the process of change. In positioning itself as an interlocutor acceptable to both the liberation movement and forces that still seek to maintain the *status quo*, the church also faced the challenge of maintaining its commitment to a prophetic ministry.[1]

The Church in South Africa

As elsewhere, the church in South Africa has a divided profile when it comes to its response to issues of a socio-political nature. The section of the church that identified itself with the struggle against apartheid was generally represented by the South African Council of Churches (SACC). Other religious faiths that took part in the struggle were collectively represented by the South African chapter of the World Conference on Religion and Peace (WCRP).

Note: The views expressed in this paper are the author's personal analysis and do not in any manner represent the official views of the South African Council of Churches, except where specifically so stated.

Very strangely, in South Africa, even within the "progressive" section of the church, there is an institutionally identifiable line of division. This division was more visible in the period around 1986, when the Kairos Document and its theological analysis, which emphasises justice and liberation of the oppressed, were first placed before the South African public. A movement of theological activists who were willing to subject their faith to a more revolutionary view of South Africa's problems began to emerge over and against the formal institutional church represented by the SACC. As a matter of fact, the "*Kairos* theologians" went so far as to conclude that the institutional church's resistance of the brutalities and injustices of apartheid was theologically defective since it was based on a flawed social analysis of the conflict in South Africa.

Only during late 1988 and early 1989 did the two streams of church resistance begin to move together as they joined in a common campaign that required both institutional church leadership and masses of lay Christians to come together. Finally, in November 1991, Christian leaders from across the spectrum gathered at the Rustenburg Conference, which was held under the theme Towards a United Christian Witness in a Changing South Africa. Rustenburg signalled a historic détente (*toenadering*) between the traditionally left and right factions of the Christian family in South Africa. In the words of Dr Louw Alberts, a conference co-chairman,

> The most important direct result . . . [was that] the failures of the churches, to a greater or lesser degree, in allowing or even condoning the development of the serious social ills that have befallen the country over the past years were acknowledged and confessed (Alberts and Chikane, 1991:9)

This narrowed the gap between the two streams, and the relationships that developed out of this process proved very useful in some of the assignments the church carried out at critical points in the negotiations and transition period.

The Church and the Struggle for Freedom and Peace

The South African church's involvement in the struggle against apartheid and its emergence after 1976 as the chief challenger of apartheid is well known. Since 1960—in the aftermath of the Sharpeville Massacre and the outlawing of the African National Congress (ANC) and the Pan Africanist Congress (PAC)—the church has evolved a series of theological paradigms and methods of resistance aimed at three goals: (1) to refute all attempts at justifying apartheid on biblical and theological terms; (2) to expose the immorality and inhumanity of apartheid as a social system; and (3) to empower and support people who resist the system.

This process contributed significantly to bringing the minority National Party government to the realisation that it could not continue to govern unjustly with impunity. Throughout its ministry in this regard, the church succeeded in robbing the apartheid regime of the support base it had intended to create out of the Christian community (about 75% of the population). Also, the South African church established the moral and legal illegitimacy of the South African government and thereby controverted the regime's right to demand allegiance from the populace (SACC, 1988). Through its pledge of solidarity and support for the liberation organisations in exile, the church, together with the World Council of Churches, served as the major source of succour for the liberation movement, enabling it to withstand the difficult conditions of exile and grow into an intact force for struggle. It consistently called for the ban on the PAC and the ANC to be dropped and for Nelson Mandela, as well as all the incarcerated leaders of the national democratic movement, to be released. It led the call for economic sanctions against apartheid South Africa when it was treasonable to do so. This act of civil disobedience proved, in the end, to be the single most decisive blow against the strident self-confidence of the apartheid rulers.

From 1988 to 1989, the church mounted its most illustrious challenge to the apartheid government of P. W. Botha. In June, 1986, the government had proclaimed a nationwide State of Emergency, and by the beginning of 1988, more than 20,000 people were held in prisons without trial, the press was severely censored and no form of public extra-parliamentary political activity was allowed. In February 1988, Botha sought to complete his clampdown by sealing any remaining loopholes that opposition groups could still exploit. He issued house-arrest restrictions on key leaders of the United Democratic Front, effectively banning any remaining organised black political self-expression.

This jolted the church into new forms and levels of protest. On 17 February 1988, church leaders and leaders from other faiths defied the State of Emergency and marched to Parliament to give notice that they would defy Botha and take over where the banned organisations had left off their peaceful protest (Chikane, 1988). Despite the fact that these leaders were briefly arrested and later bitterly attacked by the state-owned media, in May the churches launched a defiance campaign, Standing for the Truth. For the first time since 1977, when all public demonstrations were legislatively prohibited and the police given powers to disperse such demonstrations with violence, public marches led by church leaders became the order of the day in South Africa. This unleashed from the mass democratic movement a wave of various forms of defiance that the government found very difficult to contain (SACC, 1988).

All of these actions culminated in the political crisis that forced the regime to seek a negotiated surrender of absolute power to the whole people of South Africa. This period started in earnest in August 1989, when Walter Sisulu and others were released from Robben Island Prison. Then came F. W. de Klerk's famous speech of February, 1990, which announced the unbanning of the liberation organisations and the release of Nelson Mandela. In April 1990, the ANC and the South African government held their first official meeting at Groote Schuur in Cape Town.

Framework for a negotiated change

Throughout its opposition to the racist regime, the church actively proclaimed its preference for a peaceful and negotiated end to apartheid rule. It called for a non-racial society in which all the people of South Africa would be afforded equal opportunities to participate in all areas of South African life, a society in which the worth of all human beings is recognized and protected by a bill of human rights in accord with the spirit and values of the gospel. It had further maintained that a process of racial and political reconciliation between the races in South Africa should be accompanied by a process of restitution in the form of a just economic order. The church articulated these positions as early as 1973 in the form of the conclusions of the Study Programme of Christians in Apartheid Society (SPROCAS), conducted by the SACC and the Beyers Naude's Christian Institute.

The framework for the African National Congress (ANC), the main negotiating counterpart to the South African government, was initially and seminally articulated in a document called the Harare Declaration. This was drafted by the ANC in July 1989 and soon adopted by the OAU Ad-Hoc Committee on Southern Africa and, in December 1989, by the General Assembly of the United Nations.

The Harare Declaration specifically proposed a negotiated end to the conflict in South Africa. Through it, the ANC explained that the drive for negotiation was motivated by the need to end bloodshed and protracted conflict and by the pressing requirements of peace and justice. Echoing the South African liberation movement, the international community declared in the Harare document,

> We believe that a conjuncture of circumstances exists which, if there is a demonstrable readiness on the part of the Pretoria regime to engage in negotiations genuinely and seriously, could create the possibility to end apartheid through negotiations. Such an eventuality would be an expression of the long-standing preference of the majority of the people of South Africa to arrive at a political settlement.

The declaration proposed that negotiations aim to formulate a new constitution and proceeded to lay down principles that should be incorporated in it:

- South Africa should become a united, democratic, non-racial state.
- All its people should enjoy common and equal citizenship and nationality, regardless of race, colour, sex or creed.
- All its people should have the right to participate in the government and administration of the country on the basis of universal suffrage, exercised through one-person-one-vote, under a common voters' roll.
- All shall enjoy universally recognised human rights, freedoms and civil liberties, protected under an entrenched bill of rights.
- There shall be created an economic order which shall promote and advance the well-being of all South Africans.

The Harare Declaration also suggested guidelines for the negotiating process: first, discussions should be held between the liberation movement and the regime for the purpose of achieving suspension of hostilities on both sides. After this, during negotiations on a constitution, the parties would agree on an interim government to supervise negotiations as well as effect the transition to a democratic order, including holding elections.

"After the adoption of the Constitution," states the declaration, "all armed hostilities will be deemed to have formally terminated." Following this, the international community "would lift the sanctions that have been imposed against apartheid South Africa" and see to the integration of a democratic South Africa into the world community.

By and large, the international community's vision and programme, proposed by the liberation movement, concurred with the perspective of the church.

Dealing with Obstacles to Negotiations

Crisis on the preconditions to talks

Besides the constitutional principles and guidelines for the negotiating process, the Harare Declaration laid down preconditions for the liberation movement's participation in the negotiations. The preconditions summarised the need to create a political climate conducive to free political activity. As preparatory steps to negotiations, the Pretoria regime was required to:

- Release all political prisoners and detainees unconditionally.

- Lift all bans and restrictions on all proscribed and restricted organisations and people.
- Remove all troops from black townships.
- End the state of emergency and repeal all legislation designed to circumscribe political activity.
- Cease all political trials and political executions.

In short, the regime was to cease its police violence and harassment and allow the liberation organisations to establish and organise themselves as normal political institutions in civil society.

The fulfilment of these conditions created a major political crisis that lasted from February 1990 to September 1992. Matters came to a head in April 1991, when the ANC National Executive Committee issued a statement declaring that "should the Government not meet our demand for the release of political prisoners and the return of exiles, we would have to decide whether to continue talking about further negotiations" (ANC). Apart from the ANC's concern about violence and concerted efforts to counter it, a serious disagreement on the release of political prisoners had developed between the ANC and the regime. For this reason, the April statement included a demand that the government meet all demands for the creation of a climate conducive to talks and end the violence by 9 May 1991; otherwise the ANC would withdraw from participating in the negotiations.

The church, through the SACC, worked hectically, shuttling between the ANC leadership and President de Klerk's office seeking to work out a compromise that would be acceptable to both to help keep the negotiations on course. The reality that there was no alternative for the country other than peaceful negotiation and some form of mutual accommodation between the regime and the liberation movement ensured that the process proceeded. These "talks about talks"—i.e. talks on problems relating to conditions that would allow the liberation organisations to be at least politically equal negotiators with the government—continued even after the startling revelation of June 1991 that the government had been secretly funding the Inkatha Freedom Party (IFP), thereby lending partisan support to what was portrayed as a struggle between the IFP and the ANC. (Later revelations indicated that the government had even taken about 200 IFP members for specialised military training in a secret military base; the trainees later were alleged to have spearheaded the killings in some parts of South Africa.)

Making sense of violence

When violence of a nature never before seen in South Africa erupted in earnest around April 1990, the struggle to get the regime to co-operate in the creation of a climate for negotiations assumed a very complicated form. This situation presented a new task for the church and sparked extensive activity centred around the following programmes:

- The search for an understanding of the actual nature, causes and objective of the violence.
- A systematic proclamation for peace and an offer of the services of the church for mediation and other peace efforts.
- The provision of material assistance to victims of violence.

Due to the spread of violence throughout the country, the presence of church leadership in parts of the country most affected by violence and the added advantage of the SACC's workers' special devotion to this type of work, the church found itself well placed to understand the dynamics and import of this violence.

The dominant mass media as well as the government claimed the incidents were internecine black-on-black violence resulting from rivalry between the ANC and the IFP. Contrary to this, the SACC's monitoring indicated that:

1. The violence was of a character that indicated its primary source was outside the black community. The overt clashes between supporters of rival black organisations were only a secondary phenomenon following on acts of violence initiated from elsewhere.

2. The violence was politically motivated, with an ebb and flow parallel to major political developments around the negotiations process. With each indication of a major breakthrough marking a step away from apartheid rule, a major incident of violence made the news.

3. Those opposed to change were sowing fear and discord through violence, seeking to prove that South Africa was not ready for free democratic politics and making people afraid of political choices of any kind.

By the middle of June 1991, church leaders came to the adamant conclusion that the violence was aimed at slowing down the pace of negotiations or derailing them altogether.

The National Peace Accord and beyond

In the period around June 1991, church leaders, together with leaders of big businesses, initiated an independent national peace effort intended to provide the ultimate basis for the control of violence and help pave the way for constitutional negotiations to begin in earnest. This led to the formulation of the National Peace Accord negotiated with all of the country's political parties and with the government. The accord was signed and launched on 14 September 1991. It established a National Peace Committee represented by the major parties and chaired by Bishop Stanley Mogoba, Presiding Bishop of the Methodist Church in Southern Africa, and John Hall, a business leader from Barlow Rand. The Committee embarked on the establishment of regional and local peace committees, which included all the political parties who were signatories to the accord as well as the police.

To the disappointment of all concerned, the period following the signing of the National Peace Accord continued to be marked by incidents of serious violence. Unlike the earlier vigilante incidents, the violence now assumed a form that indicated professional killers were involved. People were indiscriminately shot with automatic rifles in trains and other public places by people who mysteriously eluded the police. At the same time, allegations and revelations about the involvement of the state security establishment continued to mount.

The SACC concluded that the regime was publicly committing itself to negotiations while at the same time actively working to weaken the organisational capacity of its main negotiating rival, the ANC. This was done by sowing fear and social discord in communities where the ANC had a chance of being greatly supported. SACC General-Secretary Frank Chikane noted in his address to the SACC Round Table Conference in November 1991 that, while the government had accepted the reality that negotiations with the ANC were the only way forward for South Africa, it appeared to be determined to entrench much of the past in the new settlement in order to retain its influence. This dual strategy, in the end, could only have devastating repercussions for the country.

Concern for a number of developments related to this reality led church leaders to seek and hold a series of three meetings with President de Klerk during 1991. At these meetings, church leaders proposed a number of measures that would curb violence, restore the public's faith in negotiations, and secure the negotiations process against any possible derailment:

- Speedy installation of the interim government.

- Joint control of security forces.
- Police apprehension of all perpetrators of violence.
- Invitation of an international monitoring force.
- Disclosure of all past covert operations to selected church leaders.
- Disbanding of all special military formations such as Battalion 32 and Koevoet, which had been used in Angola and Namibia and were now deployed in South African townships.
- Suspension of government officials and security personnel implicated even *prima facie* in acts of violence.

Although the meetings with the President did not produce immediate results, they proved very beneficial because they gave the public a sense that something was happening, that someone was speaking to the government.

Besides speaking to the regime from a prophetic posture, church leaders used every opportunity to voice their concerns to liberation organisations and other partners in the process. A notable event was the summit meeting of leaders from all communities affected by violence that the SACC co-ordinated and hosted in April 1992 under the leadership of Archbishop Desmond Tutu, Bishop Mogoba and Khoza Mgojo, President of the SACC. The purpose of the summit was to consider black organisations' particular responsibility in ensuring the country's peaceful transition. Its declaration calling for the involvement of the United Nations in the peace process in South Africa became the first collective expression of all the country's political parties.

Real constitutional negotiations began in November 1991 with the agreement to set up the Convention for a Democratic South Africa (CODESA) as a negotiating forum. Since the formation of CODESA, the negotiations' chances of success have oscillated dramatically. The ANC's withdrawal from CODESA in May 1992, after disagreeing with the regime on the decision-making process during the adoption of the new constitution, the massacre of 43 residents of Boipatong on 17 June 1992, and the assassination of Chris Hani, was a major setback. Alongside these events, the National Party government took a number of actions (including piloting a self-indemnification decree through Parliament) aimed at securing its members' position in power in the future and manipulating the negotiations process in their favour. The church continued to issue critical public statements in response to these developments and to play an active public pastoral role.

Development of a new theological paradigm

The church's engagement in the political process was taking place hand-in-glove with an active process of theological reflection centred on the exact nature of the church's mission in a situation such as South Africa's. The nature of the challenge made it clear that the church's mission would need to be laid out in very specific and programmatic terms.

In October 1991, Emilio Castro, General-Secretary of the World Council of Churches, paid a pastoral visit to South Africa. An international ecumenical conference organised to coincide with this epoch-making event (no WCC official had visited South Africa since the furore that accompanied the establishment of the Special Fund of the Programme to Combat Racism in 1972) met under the theme Towards an Ecumenical Agenda for a Changing South Africa. The conference was the occasion of a rigorous ecumenical review of the situation unfolding in South Africa, and its participants devised a programme of action to guide the country's churches and the ecumenical movement.

A second occasion for theological reflection took place in January, 1992. The General Secretary of the SACC facilitated a theological colloquium on the implications of current political developments on the mission of the church, held in Johannesburg. The colloquium produced a working document, the "Koinonia Minute," for the SACC's National Executive Committee.

The conceptual framework that emerged from these two conferences included the following elements:

- The situation in South Africa cannot be considered adequately changed until there is an interim government that legally replaces the apartheid regime. The church should continue to put pressure on the government, ensuring that it does not remain an obstacle to change.

- The only morally legitimate and politically acceptable forum for negotiating a new South Africa must be an elected constituent assembly.

- There should be sufficient recognition of the changes taking place.

- While taking credit for these changes, the church should focus on dealing with a wide range of political and socio-economic problems that emerged during this period.

- The church should not lose sight of the eschatological motive of its mission: that it will not equate attainment of a non-racial and democratic South Africa with consummation of the rule of God.

- The church should be prepared to defend the rights of the poor and the marginalised who are in danger of not benefiting from the kind of settlement being hammered out in the constitutional negotiations.

Flowing from these points, SACC proceeded to codify for itself a set of affirmations of its mission in relation to life and service in a period of political transition. These affirmations were accompanied by a programme of action that outlined the future thrust of the Council of Churches' work:

- The unbanning of the liberation movements in February 1990 and the gradual re-establishment of these organisations inside South Africa meant that the church had to re-define its role as a voice of the voiceless. Within this altered context, SACC committed itself to an active and prophetically critical solidarity with all processes promoting justice.

- The emergent trend of the politics of power resulted in a tendency for some politicians to seek to restrict the role of the church to the realm of the spiritual, consigning it to deal with issues that are not critical to the organisation of national life. SACC remains on guard against this marginalisation.

- On the question of the church's participation in politics, specifically its active participation in the constitutional negotiations, the church was to maintain a critical distance from party political events so as to exercise its authority without compromise and monitor the process of negotiations as a witness for truth and justice.

- While maintaining a distance from party politics, the church's concern for justice and the cause of the poor and the oppressed would continue to call it into international political action. The church's critical distance from party political activity would not mean a distance from politics *per se*. Politics affects God's people as all of God's creation, and for this reason, politics must be a concern of the church.

- SACC ministers to all and, within a context of political debate and competition, it should proclaim the truth of the gospel without currying favour with any political organisation, party or opinion. While remaining impartial, SACC would actively take sides with justice.

- Only when the church lives on guidance from biblical reflection and the empowerment of the Spirit of God can it be an effective partner in God's mission. SACC intended to work for the spiritual renewal and strengthening of the church to help it to be effective in undertaking God's mission in South Africa. Towards this end, the church was resolved to pray and work to equip its members at all levels of church life.

Out of these affirmations, under the initiative of its General Secretary, SACC devised for itself the following programme of action for its work in catalysing the church's ministry:

- Work to end violence and cultivate a culture of peaceful and democratic political activity.
- Maintain prophetic, vigilant monitoring of the negotiations process, putting in place a mechanism that will enable the church to intervene when necessary.
- Contribute the Christian ethical perspective to constitution-making and nation building.
- Ensure that a climate of freedom and respect for human rights is secured and maintained.
- Work to empower the public with knowledge of the workings of the negotiations process and the political machineries that issue from it and address the white right-wing problem.
- Contribute to the strengthening of the church's inner life.

In order to realise its programme of action and enact its mission perspective, SACC established broad-based task groups on economic matters, on political monitoring of the negotiations process, on violence, and on education for democracy.

Through these task forces, the church enlisted the knowledge of secular experts to help it deal with the uniquely complicated issues that the period of change had generated. Since the task forces' establishment in April, 1992, many of their valuable proposals have been used and implemented by SACC and its member churches. The perspectives on violence mentioned previously emerged mainly from the thorough work of the Task Force on Violence.

In the past, the church had focused its energies mainly on the destruction and/or frustration of the apartheid government, but in the period of transition it had to quickly adjust to making positive contributions to building a durable society out of the ashes of apartheid. This new task required more intensive and scientifically-based work than the work of the past. Throughout, the church has intended to ensure that its voice remains credible and respected by policy makers and those who are negotiating the new South Africa. The church has had to guard strenuously against the loss of the theological uniqueness of the nature and context of its involvement in matters of national concern. This obviously theoretical task on occasion has required more exertion than the actual issues.

Conclusion

The church has been able to serve in the role of mediator and facilitator largely because of the role it played in the pre-February 1990 period. It has been acceptable to the liberation organisations and other opposition political partners because of the respect it earned through its valiant opposition to the political evil of apartheid. On the other hand, the government also has accepted the church as a facilitator—albeit grudgingly —largely because it is known to be principled in its prophetic ministry. Throughout the period of struggle it counselled successive National Party leaders on the moral bankruptcy of apartheid and its inexorable demise, and it refused to support violence or any other form of opposition to the regime that it considers ethically irresponsible. In the course of its condemnation of the apartheid system, it also preached reconciliation to all South Africans.

During the period of political transition from apartheid rule to non-racial democracy, the church in South Africa has faced its most trying test. It is engaged in a ministry of mediation, prophetic witness and pastoral care within a political situation without precedent in the history of decolonisation and freedom struggles in Africa or anywhere else. It has been forced to learn, while at the same time performing with optimum expertise as occasioned by the process of political change. It is still premature to pass a verdict on its performance or provide a thorough appraisal of its role.

Notes

1. Since this chapter was written, South Africa held its first ever non-racial democratic elections in 1994. The African National Congress's Nelson Mandela now heads the country's new coalition government.

References

African National Congress (ANC). 1992. "Statement of the ANC's National Executive Committee Meeting." In *Negotiating a New South Africa*, edited by M. Mutloatse. Johannesburg: Skotaville Publishers.

Alberts, L., and F., Chikane (eds.) 1991. *The Road to Rustenburg: The Church Looking Forward to a New South Africa*. Cape Town: Struik Christian Books.

Chikane, F. 1988. *The Church and the Crisis of Apartheid in South Africa*. Johannesburg: SACC.

South African Council of Churches (SACC). 1988. "South Africa: Christian Faith and Resistance—A Memorandum." In *Political Legitimacy in South Africa*, edited by C. Lienemann-Perrin and W. Lienemann. Heidelberg: SACC & FEST.

———. 1988. *SACC National Conference Report*. Johannesburg: SACC.

11

The Demands of God's Faithfulness
A Case Study of Peacemaking in Mozambique

Dinis S. Sengulane and Jaime Pedro Gonçalves

Mozambique has been described in recent years as the poorest country in the world. The country has the highest infant mortality rate anywhere on the planet, essential goods and services are in very short supply, and human dignity is routinely disregarded.

Yet God's gifts to Mozambique are awe-inspiring. The country is big, with fertile soil, a good and varied climate, a long, lovely coastline with rewarding fisheries, and a persevering and beautiful people. Unlike many other African countries, Mozambique has no desert lands, and almost anything will grow there. Mozambique is said to be rich in mineral resources, but little has been done to assess their potential.

God has been generous and faithful in what he has bequeathed to Mozambique. Political leaders, however, have distracted Mozambicans from making use of their resources to improve their lot. And the church has not evoked a sufficient sense of the sacredness of these resources, nor of the great responsibility God has placed on Mozambique as stewards.

This is the story of how the churches in Mozambique came together to take up Jesus' call to promote peace in the country. All that has happened since 1984 under the auspices of the church to promote peace in Mozambique has been in response to God's faithfulness and his promises to guide, protect and sanctify.

Historical Background

Mozambique is located in Southern Africa and is bounded in the north by Tanzania, in the south by South Africa and Swaziland, in the east by the Indian Ocean and in the west by Malawi, Zambia and Zimbabwe. Its area is approximately 799,380 km^2, and its population is 16 million.

The map of Mozambique is the result of Portuguese occupation. By 1498, the Portuguese had already travelled along the Mozambican coastline on their way to India, and hence developed trade along the coast and eventually created companies to explore the interior. After the signing of the Berlin Treaty in 1885, the Portuguese were forced to definitively occupy the colony. To accomplish this goal, they fought the local tribes and established frontiers, resisting the English, who wanted to expand the frontiers of its nearby colonies in order to gain access to the sea.

The political instability that followed the proclamation of a republic in Portugal in 1910 weakened the Portuguese presence in Mozambique and gave the English the opportunity to create an economic structure in their own interest in the region, with the construction of railroads from Beira in Mozambique to Zimbabwe and from Beira to Malawi, as well as a bridge over the Zambezi River.

In 1928, Dr. Antonio Salazar took power in Portugal and ruled for forty years, during which he gave stability to Portugal and renewed the ideals of the Portuguese empire in the Time of Discovery in the colonies. The reconstruction of the Portuguese empire, in the pattern of the great colonising countries of the time, required a complex political and administrative process. The colonies became provinces and, later, states. Portugal became one and indivisible with its provinces.

This type of political system was in direct contrast to the African liberation movements of the second half of this century, which were often supported by the Soviet Union. Mozambicans organised the Front for the Liberation of Mozambique (FRELIMO) in 1962 to fight against Portugal's colonisation. After a ten-year struggle against the Portuguese, Mozambique became independent again in 1975.

The new FRELIMO government adopted a Marxist-Leninist system. Shortly after independence, another war—in which Mozambicans fought Mozambicans—broke out and raged for seventeen years. This war, fed by the geopolitics of the cold war, caused untold suffering and resulted in tens of thousands of deaths, millions of refugees and massive internal displacement of the population.

The Mozambican church, particularly through the Christian Council of Mozambique, played a catalytic role in the negotiations that led to the formal end of the civil war in 1992. It has since continued in its peacemaking role by working for reconciliation and reconstruction.

The Church in Mozambique

The first Christians to reach Mozambique were Roman Catholics who accompanied the first Portuguese; chaplains took part in Vasco da Gama's expedition on his way to India in 1498. The first eucharistic celebration in Mozambique took place on 11 March of that year, and hence the kings of Portugal sent chaplains to convert the "natives." During the 15th and 16th centuries, the Jesuits, Dominican and Divine Word orders and diocesan clergy carried out limited evangelisation. Nevertheless, their efforts were not fully organised; the Portuguese republic and the Masons were in the process of persecuting and expelling religious orders from Portugal, and this delayed organised mission work.

Intense and extensive evangelisation began in Mozambique only in the 1940s, when Portugal's government, under Salazar, signed a missionary accord with the Holy See establishing the first three dioceses in Mozambique. The new bishops then invited many new missionaries, even non-Portuguese, to the colony.

The missionary accord also determined that the Catholic church should open primary schools for the local people. The bishops and rectors of these seminaries were to be Portuguese. Understandably, then, not all of the church hierarchy accepted the colony's struggle for independence when the time came.

When Mozambique achieved independence, the country had nine Catholic dioceses and approximately 1.5 million faithful. The first African bishops were appointed at that time. Presently, there are twelve dioceses and three archbishops for about 2 million Catholics.

About a hundred years ago, other Christian groups including Reformed, Methodists and Anglicans arrived. In the course of this century, other churches also came, and independent Zionist or Pentecostal churches started their witness in Mozambique. All have enriched the Christian community with their multi-faceted contributions.

The Communist regime, however, brought difficulties to the life of the church. It nationalised missions, expelled missionaries and revoked religious freedom. Dialogue between the church and the government became almost impossible. Then, in December 1982, FRELIMO reversed its stance and officially announced that religious institutions had a place in the revolution as educators in ethics.

Today, many towns and villages show signs of the presence of the church, although Mozambique is the least evangelised country south of the Sahara. The number of denominations in Mozambique is growing, but this growth is not matched by the number of Christians in the country. Nevertheless, Mozambican culture, languages, understanding and presence can be found in international denominational and ecumenical Christian forums, and Mozambican Christians provide leadership at various levels of the church, at home and elsewhere.

The Christian Council of Mozambique (CCM) was founded in 1948 to promote unity and co-operation among Mozambican churches. At present, its nineteen member churches and two societies represent Anglican, Baptist, Reformed, Methodist and Independent church traditions. The Council's first full-time General-Secretary, the late Reverend Isaac Mahlalela, was elected in 1976. Since then, the CCM has grown in staff numbers and in relationships. In looking for an appropriate role for the church in the larger society, the CCM became involved in the pursuit of a lasting peace for the people of Mozambique.

The Roots of Conflict

The suffering of the people of Mozambique has had four major causes:

- Wars.
- Natural disasters.
- International economic demands and crises.
- Wrong policies.

Together with wars—the Mozambican War of Independence, the Zimbabwean War of Independence that followed and the armed conflict between RENAMO and the Mozambican government—floods, drought and plagues have caused great suffering. During the same period, the world economy suffered critical upheavals that impacted almost every country, not least Mozambique.

The 500 years of Portuguese rule did very little to ensure human dignity in Mozambique in a permanent and growing fashion. The country's post-independence constitution was attractive but not completely adequate for this purpose. The people have not benefited from self-rule, but this cannot be attributed wholly to the wars that followed independence. Other factors linked to planning, vision and accountability also have played an important role.

The Church's Response to Armed Conflict

The church has had a varied response to the three main armed conflicts that have had such drastic effects on Mozambique. During the War of Liberation, which lasted from 1964 to 1974, the World Council of Churches (WCC) gave moral and material support to FRELIMO through its Programme to Combat Racism. Pope Paul VI gave moral support by receiving leaders of the liberation movement in Rome. The Mozambican church made no official utterances concerning this war, but individual leaders took stands and spoke openly, even to the point of being misunderstood or rejected. Some Roman Catholic priests and other clergymen were expelled from the country, or left on their own in protest against Portuguese policies. Protestant ministers were jailed, some were killed and others were ill-treated in jail for associating with those who wanted change in Mozambique.

The Zimbabwean war, with all its political, ethical and financial implications, did not elicit a noticeable response from the church. This could have been because of its short duration (about three years) or because it was not officially directed against Mozambicans, although it affected and took the lives of many. Around this time, the new government also developed its hostile attitude towards the church, which seemed to be preoccupied with its own survival without asking the question, "Survival for what?".

In 1982, one church synod passed a resolution calling for abolition of the death penalty. It sent the resolution to churches of various denominations for comments and action. Their responses demonstrate well the churches' disarray at that time: one church declined to answer, saying that the subject was too complex politically. Another replied that it needed more time to consider the proposal. The head of one church reported to the secret police, although this was considered confidential. CCM never officially dealt with the issue, in spite of requests from the originating synod for a decision.

In May 1984, during the civil war, CCM for the first time publicly called for dialogue between Mozambicans caught in armed conflict—albeit in a confidential memorandum to the head of state. The reaction was equivocal. It repeated its request in July 1985, again to equivocal response. Informal requests at various levels continued for a few more months. In October 1986, President Samora Moisés Machel died, and CCM began directing its requests to his successor, Joaquim Chissano. Around December, 1987, the government indicated appreciation of the churches' initiative and sent a clear message that steps towards dialogue would not be interpreted negatively.

Subsequently, CCM started locating RENAMO representatives who could put it in contact with their leaders inside the country. Because the Roman Catholic Church was known to share this concern, CCM felt the time had come to join hands in bringing RENAMO and government leaders together. Towards this end, it organised a trip to the United States, at the invitation of its National Council of Churches, for a group of seven Mozambican church leaders including one Roman Catholic archbishop. Our hosts, who had not been aware of their visitors' intentions regarding RENAMO, turned out to be adamantly opposed to the idea. Their feeling was so strong that some felt they had been betrayed.

CCM's task in the United States therefore was not easy, and some people could not understand the purpose of the trip. A neutral person did eventually come forward and offer to put us in touch with people who could bring us into direct contact with RENAMO. With this promise, we returned to Maputo in February 1988.

In April and May 1988, CCM organised trips to Kenya for two Roman Catholic bishops and two CCM leaders with the help of Christian organisations in that country. This time we kept our numbers small in order to avoid attention. The Kenyans were informed about CCM's mission and made efforts to locate RENAMO leaders and convey our message. After many trips to both Kenya and Switzerland, in December 1988 CCM made contact with one person from RENAMO. At the end of this trip, some hope emerged.

Dialogue with RENAMO

In our first meeting with a RENAMO representative, we emphasised that we wanted to meet the movement's leadership inside Mozambique in order to share our concern about peace. We also made it clear that we represented the churches of Mozambique. Our contact promised to convey the message.

In February 1989, two RENAMO people from within Mozambique came to talk to us in Nairobi, where we had waited for almost two weeks. We told them that the churches were calling for dialogue with the government for peace because we were convinced that there were no alternatives. Clearly, neither side was benefiting from continued warfare, and the people were suffering. Above all, we explained, we considered reconciliation to be the vocation of the church. The RENAMO representatives agreed to an early meeting with the organisation's president.

Removing obstacles

After various abortive attempts, a RENAMO delegation, led by its President, made the journey to Nairobi to meet with church leaders to talk about our intent to press for talks. This first meeting between the two groups was held in August 1989. The press had circulated "news" that RENAMO would call for the withdrawal of all foreign troops as a precondition for dialogue, and that the government would tell RENAMO to stop fighting. In fact, both the government and RENAMO were holding out for dialogue without precondition, and the churches helped to dispel the rumours.

Another misunderstanding concerned the role of the church. The press said that the churches were biased in favour of the government. In response, we reiterated that we represented the churches of Mozambique and her suffering people, and that it was on this impartial basis that RENAMO had started talking to us.

The government took the occasion of our meeting to send a message to RENAMO offering twelve points on which dialogue could begin. We passed on the document without comment. RENAMO replied with a sixteen-point proposal, which we took to the government in Maputo. Whether these points found their way into the peace agreement is irrelevant. What *is* important is that this seems to have been the first written communication between the two sides, and it was this communication that led eventually to dialogue.

Meanwhile, the church refused to answer questions from the two sides about each other, insisting instead that the opposing parties address them directly. The church expressed its availability to facilitate further contacts, provided that such involvement did not violate gospel tenets. It was with this clarification of the churches' position that, later on, mediators were selected to continue to ensure conversation. The church, represented by the four leaders who made the first direct contacts with RENAMO, was never far from the peace process, although the four were not always physically present in one place.

Persuading others

It is not only the government and RENAMO that needed persuading that peace could only be attained through dialogue, but also some religious and secular groups inside and outside Mozambique who insisted that guns were the only solution to the country's political impasse. They felt that dialogue only served to legitimate what was illegitimate. CCM's answer was that Mozambicans were the legitimate seekers of peace for the country, regardless of the violent means that had been deployed previously. "Why talk to communists if there is no hope for change?", people asked about FRELIMO. "Why talk to bandits?", others asked about RENAMO. "Both groups are Mozambicans, capable of appreciating one another," was our answer. Some people in Mozambique, wounded by the deep pain of war, wondered whether a communication bridge was possible at all.

In spite of all the contradictory opinions, our group was sure of God's faithfulness and that he would "lead His church into all truth" (John 16:13) and "our feet into the way of peace" (Luke 1:79). Nevertheless, we felt the need to address the doubts and pain some of our countrymen felt at the prospect of negotiating for peace. We soon initiated a number of other activities in support of that peace.

Prayer

As soon as the need to engage ourselves in the search for peace was clear, we organised services to pray for peace in various rural and urban parts of the country. Later on, the churches agreed that each denomination would intercede for peace on the last Sunday of every month, and that ecumenical services for peace would be held every three months. In addition, some churches maintained their tradition of praying and fasting for peace every Friday.

Bible study

During Lent in 1985, CCM prepared a Bible study guide on peace that was sent to all churches. *Called to Peace*, designed for use by groups, individuals and seminaries, dealt with all four dimensions of peace: God, self, society and nature. Even today, studies using this guide continue as a means of challenge and encouragement. *Called to Peace* was also used in seminars preparing the people for peace from 1990 to 1992.

Children's toys

Christians in Mozambique are shocked that many crimes in the country faithfully imitate films and plays watched by both children and adults. Many toys given to children also are war-oriented and provide an efficient way of creating and perpetuating a violent mentality. Even Christmas toys teach Mozambican children to kill, when the message of the season is Peace on Earth, Goodwill to All. As a contribution to peace, CCM decided to advise children to bring their toy guns to church, where they would be smashed as a testimony of their devotion to the Prince of Peace; during one such service, the Head of State and the Executive Committee of the All Africa Conference of Churches (AACC) were present. Children who did not own such a toy were encouraged to buy one and explain to the shopkeeper that it was being destroyed as a sign of commitment to peace. This exercise made a remarkable impression on many children. They now advised others not to buy or use toy guns.

Meanwhile, people discovered gun symbols in many things including banknotes, flags and monuments. They began to ask, "Does the glorification of war really help anyone?".

An appeal for peace

Christmas 1989 saw the publication of an Appeal for Peace (see Annex 11.1). It was read in CCM churches and sent to the Head of State; the Prime Minister; the Ministers of Defence, Security, Interior, Commerce, Justice and Co-operation; and the Ambassadors of Nigeria, the U.S.S.R., the U.S.A., the U.K., Germany and France; and other people.

Meeting physical needs

Churches that had no connection with the colonial power arrived in Mozambique late in the last century. From the beginning, these churches were concerned with human dignity. In this context, people such as Eduardo Mondlane emerged to speak on behalf of the Mozambican people. The government met this initiative with suspicion and persecution, but it had the effect of opening the people's eyes.

After independence, the Portuguese no longer carried out their dehumanising policies of "Portugality" and "civilization," but persecution continued in revolution. The new government closed churches and imposed restrictions, and development of human dignity faltered. After eight years of such alienation, the churches finally received permission to assist the victims of war and natural disaster.

In 1984, CCM spent US$ 2 million in food aid, medicines and agricultural tools in support of human life and dignity. The following year, it used more than US$ 5 million in four provinces to assist victims in rural areas and two cities. By 1987, it had established emergency offices in all ten provinces to co-ordinate this assistance. In 1988, as the roads had become nearly impassable, it undertook a massive airlift programme involving 1,600 tons of relief supplies, bringing an end to certain grim statistics; in Gile, for instance, 45 to 55 people had died each day in 1989. In 1990, CCM spent nearly US$ 6 million to help alleviate the suffering of more than 260,000 people. These funds and goods came from the ecumenical family through the World Council of Churches and the All Africa Conference of Churches.

While needs increased in 1991, resources were diminishing as external partners found continued support for a country that showed no sign of solving its problems difficult to justify. Even so, CCM's ministry of compassion and sharing of resources to sustain life and promote human dignity has continued. Its emergency aid and development programmes employ ten people and provide vehicles, radios, telephones and other infrastructure in all of the country's provinces. About 500,000 people in the rural areas have benefited from this work.

Involvement of the ecumenical family

From the beginning, the ecumenical family has been interested in working towards peace in Mozambique. Without its support, the initial contact journey to the United States would not have been possible. Other steps, known and unknown, helped our efforts. Delegations from the WCC and AACC, as well as from national church councils and other ecumenical bodies, made themselves available to support, advise or engage in steps towards peace. In 1990, especially, ecumenical efforts had a noticeable impact in the form of:

- a seminar organised by the AACC and Nairobi Peace Initiative (NPI) to examine the experiences of Mozambique and Angola and identify commonalities and means of mutual support.
- direct contacts established between the AACC in Nairobi and CCM in Maputo to share information and counsel.
- the WCC Africa desk's more permanent role in sharing information and resources with external partners on the issue of peace.

Preparing the People for Peace (PPP) seminars

Although it is difficult to ascertain the exact date, it was already clear to us in 1990 that peace would come. CCM planned seminars to prepare people for this peace. Two initial three-week-long national seminars involved two people from each province. Pastors, lay leaders and people from the AACC addressed participants in these first PPP seminars, which led to ten additional two-week seminars, one in each province. Roman Catholics, representatives of the government and even Muslims participated in some of the seminars, which brought together old and young, literate and illiterate, clergy and laity, men and women, public servants and unemployed and privately employed participants in groups of thirty to eighty.

While CCM originally planned to conduct only in-country seminars, we were challenged to go to refugees outside the country. This we did, with seminars carried out in five Zimbabwean camps. Similar efforts were also targeted in Malawi, Kenya and South Africa, which also sheltered Mozambican refugees.

Ministering to refugees

Both CCM and the Roman Catholic Church continued to minister to people in refugee camps in neighbouring countries, initially through the PPP seminars.

Visits to the camps were mutually beneficial, resulting in the exchange of information and experiences and in mutual encouragement. We hope that these visits will continue until repatriation is completed. Meanwhile, we have also ministered to displaced people, or internal refugees, wherever possible.

General Guidelines for Preparing the People for Peace Seminars

THE BIBLE AS MESSAGE AND INSTRUMENT OF PEACE	THE FAMILY AS A CENTRE CAPABLE OF SOLVING CONFLICTS	LAND ISSUES	CHURCH HISTORY IN SOLVING CONFLICTS	THE YOUTH	REFUGEES AND DISPLACED PEOPLE
• The concept of peace	• The concept of family	• Land as property	• The church as an instrument of reconciliation	• The young people as victims of the conflict	• Who is a refugee?
• The dimensions of peace	• African families and towns and villages	• Land and eternity			
				• The youth as agents of the solution	• Who are the displaced?
• Turning swords into ploughshares	• Polygamy	• Land, the state, multinationals and others	• Culture and Christianity		• The role of NGOs
	• Single mothers		• Christian witness and social justice	• The young student, his present and future	
• Human rights	• Funerals and life after death	• Land and displaced people			• Repatriation
• Prayer vigils			• Church history in Mozambique	• Military service	• The refugee and his family
	• State protection				

Bringing the Peacemaking Process to a Close: The Rome Talks

The Mozambican government and RENAMO agreed to meet in Rome for peace discussions in 1990. Before the talks began, the church again offered itself for any appropriate role, and the Right Reverend Jaime P. Gonçalves, Archbishop of

Beira, and one of the four church leaders who had originally contacted RENAMO, became a mediator, along with representatives of the government of Italy and the St. Egídio Community, a religious order in Rome that offered to provide space and make other logistical arrangements for the discussions.

The talks in Rome were long and difficult. The greatest difficulty for the mediators was that while the dialogue went on and on, the war continued. It was impossible to convince the parties to cease their fire while the conversations took place. Lack of trust was the other great difficulty. Each side presumed bad will on the part of the other. Here, the church was very important in inspiring trust in the process.

The language used also presented problems. Not all the words that FRELIMO used were accepted by RENAMO, and vice-versa. The government was more interested in a ceasefire and RENAMO in solutions to political problems. The government was reluctant to discuss political problems with RENAMO.

In addition, the peace talks were very expensive, and it was not easy to get the government's part of the financing. The Community of St. Egídio gave part, but the majority came from Italy.

In September 1991, during an AACC Executive Committee meeting, the ecumenical family expressed interest in becoming more involved in the process. In a protocol call on the Head of State, CCM expressed its impatience with the slow progress of the Rome talks and offered to contact RENAMO about the issue. Our intention was neither to undermine nor replace the Rome talks, but to accelerate them. Permission was granted.

Petition campaigns, with signatures gathered in Mozambique, Italy and Portugal as well as prayers for peace, were a great help. We moved the diplomatic world, and this also helped. The European Community[1] supported the peace initiative and pressured the delegations to quickly arrive at an accord. We worked jointly with the American ambassador and the Holy See, and the governments of Kenya and Zimbabwe continued to help as well.

In August 1992, England, France, Portugal, Italy and the United States were admitted to the conversation table as observers. At this level, the United Nations also entered the process.

After a marathon journey in which we travelled in six airplanes, visited Malawi and Kenya and slept in South Africa and Zimbabwe, with only a short time to share our concerns with one side, a breakthrough occurred. In our next meeting with RENAMO, we read from Matthew 5:7 and 9 before talking about practical steps in the peace process. We said that now was the right time to show mercy to the people of Mozambique, and that we were there as peacemakers. We invited President Joaquim Chissano and the President of RENAMO, Alfonso Dhlakama, to be peacemakers also. We suggested that they meet to talk about a ceasefire. This suggestion was acceptable to both sides, so preparation, began. Two subsequent meetings between the parties culminated in the signing of a ceasefire agreement on 4 October 1992, with churches and other religious bodies invited to attend the ceremony

The Way Ahead for Mozambique

Peace in Mozambique is now a reality, and preparations for elections are underway.[2] The church played a key role in peacemaking by:

- initiating negotiations
- helping prepare people for peace at the grassroots and
- stimulating the peace process when it flagged.

Peace in Mozambique now needs to be consolidated. The church will continue in its active mode until peace has been fully secured and has penetrated the hearts, homes, institutions and way of life of Mozambicans and those who influence them. We suggest that Mozambican churches assist this process by:

- institutionalising peace, reconciliation and justice issues in their agendas. Ecumenical bodies should appoint full-time staff members to deal with this issue. The staff should work to motivate, challenge and encourage churches and society to undertake action on peace issues. Theological institutions should make peace an important aspect of their curriculums, including catechism and Sunday School.
- turning "swords" into "ploughshares" by making weapons, the instruments of death and domination, into tools that promote human dignity and sustain the sanctity of life.
- undertaking civic education to make people aware of human rights and their duties regarding elections.
- facing, as a matter of urgency, the land issue.
- holding regular services to pray for peace.
- being creative in providing gestures and/or symbols that inspire peace in the church and in society, replacing the culture of violence with

the culture of peace, and keeping in mind always the message of Psalms 34:12-34:

Peace with God,
Peace with ourselves,
Peace with our neighbours and
Peace with nature, God's creation.

New opportunities for African Christians to serve as peacemakers are being created, and resources in the form of personnel, advice and finance are frequently available. In our case, it was impressive to see a basically weak mediation end an armed conflict. The truth is that Italy is not a big country in the life of world politics, the community of St. Egídio is hardly known, the Archbishop of Beira is no one. Nevertheless, the church's initiative bore fruit. We must continue to prove our faithfulness to God by putting our spiritual vitality to use in the pursuit of peace and by administering the available resources effectively.

In working for solutions to armed conflicts, it is necessary to have patience and a method. We adopted the following practical principles in the search for peace in Mozambique:

- Look for what unites rather than what separates.
- Discuss problems step by step.
- In the beginning, it is necessary to develop a dialogue between mediators and each side rather than set up official meetings between the sides.
- Remember always the suffering that people endure during war.
- The mediators must work with the friends and supporters of both sides. This is fundamental.
- The mediators must not count it of much importance when one side accuses them of being in favour of the other side.
- The mediators must remember and insist on the ethical and religious aspects of peace such as reconciliation, justice, human rights, forgiveness and mutual trust.
- All the religious forces of a country in conflict must collaborate in the process of peace. The power of all the churches together is greater than one alone.

It is distressing to see how evil humankind can be, hating to the point of wishing death to one another. It is also true that human beings can change. This is what we saw. The RENAMO and FRELIMO men hated each other—yet little by little, they became compatriots, Mozambicans, brother, my brother.

A story from the life of Paul (Acts 27:31-44) provides a fitting conclusion to our consideration of peacemaking issues. On a long, dangerous journey, some of Paul's companions had become impatient and despondent; they threw some items overboard, threatening to kill those who were not important. But Paul saw the salvation of his fellow travellers in staying in the boat.

The boat in this story symbolises the church. Some people become impatient with the church and want to jump out or throw others out. Others want to give up their leading roles. But we can rest assured, if we are men, women and children of prayer, that we can stay in the boat and realise the full meaning of salvation.

True, people get impatient and expect to find meaning in political solutions to world problems. But the gospel provides a lot of room to address political issues from within the boat. I urge you all to stay in the boat and make a difference for the better as we work to construct a new Africa, an Africa of hope.

Note

1. Now the European Union.
2. Elections were held in 1994 and, although FRELIMO won, RENAMO has been accomodated in the government.

Annex 1: An Appeal for Peace

We Christians of member churches of the Christian Council of Mozambique (CCM) greet you with the Angelic message:

> Glory to God . . .
> Peace on Earth and
> Goodwill to mankind.
>   Luke 2:14

A. Glory to God

I. We rejoice that there are signs that the Glory of God is being proclaimed. Indeed, the decade of evangelism that our churches and others are observing, the growing number of ordination candidates and other ministries, the concern about the environment as God's creation for which we have to be accountable before Him, the solid and beautiful buildings erected in some places of our country for the worship of the Almighty God, the involvement of the church in the search for peace as her legitimate and timely role, the crowds to translate the Holy Scriptures and other events constitute sufficient reasons for us to "rejoice in the Lord" and say "Glory to God."

II. What worries us is the fact that there are many things which seek to seize the place of the glory, among which is the growing preoccupation with easy and dishonest wealth; drunkenness, not only among adults but also among youths; the lack of sensitivity towards other people's needs; the small percentage of those who know and worship God through our Saviour Jesus Christ in all our towns, villages and many rural areas; the number of Mozambican refugees in all our neighbouring countries and in others as well; and the internal displacement of population which is so high in such a way that "we have become a scandal for those around us, who say among themselves, Where is their God?" (Joel 2:17).

B. Peace on Earth

I. We rejoice for the peace initiatives through dialogue, both at national and international levels, which are beginning to bear fruit. We salute the efforts of all those who contribute to direct dialogue between the Government and RENAMO. We pray for the success of the same so that a just and lasting peace may be restored in our country, which has suffered so much.

II. Among other things, we are concerned with the following:

1. The fact that the manufacture, sale, distribution, buying or acceptance as gifts and use of weapons in their varied forms and sizes is not based on the idea of peacekeeping but rather on the possibility of war and not on the protection or salvation of people's lives, but rather on lives' destruction.

2. The fact that some leaders in the society, secular or religious, hold that the involvement of the church in matters of justice and peace is to interfere wrongly in political matters, which we should not do.

3. The fact that in quarrels, encounters or suspicions between people or groups of different convictions, the gun has first answer.

4. The fact that in our cities there are violent crimes of the same style as those shown in our cinemas and televisions, acts which uproot peace from the earth.

C. People of Goodwill

I. We rejoice for the signs of goodwill that we find as we endeavour to restore peace. There are several people who are ready to engage in dialogue that leads to peace, and others are ready to give their support to the process of peace. There is, generally, a favourable climate of goodwill, especially in our region. We know that there are many people who are praying and fasting for our country, interceding for peace.

There are people who are openly saying what their political convictions are for the sake of peace; these are Christians, people of other religions, and other men and women of goodwill.

a. Being inspired by the message of the birth of the Prince of Peace, the Emmanuel, God With Us.

b. Being encouraged by the signs of the people of goodwill, for whom human life is important and sacred.

Compelled the destruction of lives and infrastructure and the burden of refugees and the displaced inside our own country, all this caused by the war, which is sustained by circumstances that all of us can do something to eliminate.

Confident that you, to whom we address this message, are people of goodwill

1. We appeal very earnestly that you should not allow this war to continue, even if someone among you is taking personal material benefits or gaining prestige. To allow much blood is unacceptable.

2. We appeal to Mozambican Christians to pray even more for peace and to be instruments of peace in your day-to-day behaviour. Do have the kind of language and behaviour that expresses peace in the family, so that such peace may overflow into the society around you. Keep away from your homes and from your properties all symbols of violence.

3. We appeal to the manufacturers of war toys to stop making such toys because they inspire war and train children to formulate a mentality of war. Instead you should make toys that inspire the normal activities of humankind and emulate peaceful living, not war.

4. We appeal to those who own and sell war toys to stop importing these instruments, which train our children to think more about adventures that take away other people's lives and not about the dignity and holiness of those lives.

5. We appeal to parents and those who buy war toys to create, for the children and their little friends, an environment free of war mentality by not buying war toys and by not allowing their children to receive them as gifts from whoever may give them.

6. We appeal to the educators (parents, teachers and others) to tell children about the evils of war toys, and to replace them with toys of normal human activities and by entertainments that inspire peace and co-operation.

7. We appeal to the children, who are our wealth and most precious heritage, to understand that the use of war toys is to train them for their own suicide and for killing other people. Consequently, children must not accept any war toys, no matter how attractive and sophisticated they may look.

8. We appeal to the manufacturers of firearms, other weapons and other equipment of war to stop your business, whatever just reasons you may have for your activity: To provide employment to millions of people, to satisfy the orders long requested and paid for, to contribute to the progress of science, to balance military force. Hundreds of thousands of human lives have been eliminated in our country by instruments that you have manufactured, and millions of people live under sub-human conditions in and outside our country in fear of the instruments that you have made. We invite you to come and see at least, the graveyards of the victims of your instruments and to see vast areas of hundreds of square kilometres abandoned by the victims of the instruments that you made. Or you could make a visit to any of our neighbouring countries to see the people who have fled because of these instruments.

   Ask yourselves, as human beings, like the victims of your weapons, created in the image and likeness of God, Is it worth doing? Is it morally acceptable? Would I make these instruments to send them where my own son or daughter is? We are quite convinced that the armaments business is a bloody one, a business that claims millions of lives and sets back the progress of peoples.

9. We appeal to those who use guns or other weapons not to apply your guns as your first word (do not give it priority), rather do your best to avoid killing human life, whatever the political convictions of that life. We plead that it should not be yourself who is the author of the death of any person in Mozambique because human life is sacred. If you are a military participant in the battle, do remember that the gun over your have in your hand is primarily meant to avoid the shedding of blood and, consequently, avoid killing and persuade until you win you opponent. To kill is to lose. To kill is to waste. To those who are behind the ones who do the practical killing, we appeal that it is time now you sought to stop the suffering of the people and stop protecting your individual and petty interests at the expense of shedding blood. To all, especially the young, we say, If someone wants to lend or hire or offer or sell a gun to you, please do not accept it because if you do take it, you will end up killing someone.

   To all groups we say: Another person's life is as good and precious as yours, as sacred as yours.

10. To the artists, whatever may be your specialty: You have a lot of influence in society and on the behaviour of individuals. Your music, your films, paintings, theatre, sculptures and other works have been used for various ends.

    We appeal to you that your art should not contain aspects of violence that lead others, particularly the youth and children, to be involved in violence. It is regrettable that episodes of violence shown in cinemas and on TV are repeated in the life of our country by people who saw or heard about them. Recognizing that you are people of goodwill, we appeal for the use of your creative spirit to influence the minds of those who benefit from your art so that they can develop a mentality of peace.

11. To Christians and members of other religions and to all men, women and youth of goodwill, we appeal that "Everyone should turn back from your ways and from violence that is in your hands" and your heart (Jonah 3:8). We say this because our country is becoming more and more destroyed by violence on the roads, violence of the war, violence in the farms and in other public institutions. It seems that we find ourselves in a situation where many hearts are flooded with the spirit of violence.

May the Prince of Peace, Jesus Christ, bring in the heart of each one of you and to your homes and to the society where you live Peace, goodwill among people and Glory to God.

APPENDIX I

Summary of Discussions*

Symposium participants dwelt on a wide range of issues relating to the lives and circumstances of the citizens of African countries. A question that surfaced repeatedly was, How are the current changes to be directed so that they result in meaningful improvement in the conditions of these citizens?

Participants recognised that Africa is currently undergoing a wave of change and is poised between promise and uncertainty. In particular, participants focused on the ongoing debate on democratisation and its meaning and implications for Africa, peacemaking and reconciliation, and the life of the church. They noted that the continent of Africa has so far been poised in a reactive posture, reacting against slavery, colonialism, apartheid, dictatorship, etc. The continent now is being challenged to take on a more pro-active agenda. Church leaders, especially, were called upon to reflect on their role in forging a pro-active agenda. How can emerging conflicts be avoided? What can be done to settle raging conflicts peacefully? In cases in which agreements have been reached, how can former rivals be helped to learn to trust each other and build a common future?

On democracy, participants noted that the current debate and clamour for political change has emerged as a response to the excesses of the one-party state and the deprivation that has come with economic deterioration, with two implications. One is that people will hasten to change existing structures without much reflection on what to replace them with. Second, they will have the unrealistic expectation that democracy will automatically bring economic salvation. They need to be aware of the international context within which the current change is taking place so that they can set their expectations within reasonable and realistic limits. Participants were urged to reflect keenly on the fact that the drive for democratisation is accompanied by the drive for economic liberalisation and the establishment of laissez-faire-type market economies. Whose agenda is this? Who is going to benefit from these systems? Might this sudden reversal unleash another force for destabilisation and revolution by the poor and those who are going to be left out of these economic systems?

Participants expressed concern that democracy has come to mean multipartyism. In its turn, multipartyism has come to mean a winner-take-all competition for positions of leadership and brings to the fore the question of how winners and losers should relate. This relationship takes on important significance in countries in which ethnic relations are delicate and can be compounded by the formation of political parties along ethnic lines. More so in developing countries than elsewhere, political power is actually—but quite wrongly—linked to economic advantage. In the traditional context, there are provisions for relinquishing power through an accepted consensual process. This is not the case in current politics since current structures of governance have yet to find a wide consensus in the African community. Participants in the current change processes would do well to seek insight from tradi-

---

* Compiled by G. Wachira

tional practices on how consensus can be achieved in Africa today. In particular, they should realise that in-built norms and values in the African heritage minimise tension between winners and losers. Where borrowing becomes necessary, Africans should take care to borrow meanings rather than words such as *democracy* and *multipartyism*.

Participants also noted the importance of viable and functioning economies as requisites for stable democracies, although some cautioned against placing too much emphasis on economic determinism. Some aspects of the economy could be addressed hand in hand with issues of sound, accountable governance. Others, however, are determined from outside the continent and are intricately linked to Africa's colonial past. In this case, development of analytical expertise on international determinants is needed in order to address the issues effectively.

The church itself was a major subject of discussion. Who or what is "the church"? Participants agreed that the church should not be seen as only the more audible and visible senior leaders and heads of national and regional church groupings, but as its full membership at all levels of the community. The church's effectiveness in social-change processes will largely depend on how attentive it is to people at the grassroots. Participants heard how churches in Madagascar, for instance, made efforts to involve non-church members in church-sponsored regional forums leading up to a national forum. Participants noted, however, that it is not enough for the church to represent the grassroots; it must also make an effort to educate its congregations about their rights and responsibilities. Only an enlightened population can speak up for and defend its rights to freedom and peace. Conversely, oppressive leaders can be propped up by an ignorant population that is easily manipulated and divided along minor concerns. Because of its presence across all communities, the church can be a rallying point or unifying factor for different ethnic communities. It should take advantage of the cultural and religious plurality in Africa not only to forge a true inter-Christian ecumenical unity, but to reach out to members of other faiths, including Islam. In order to be able to participate fully in the lives of its members, the church needs to sharpen its analytical skills. The church was therefore urged to utilise the skills available in its own congregations—but always in a manner sympathetic to its values. Examples were cited from the experience of the Madagascar Christian Council.

Participants noted that African cultural and spiritual identity is stifled in the absence of economic self-sufficiency, leaving entire countries open to easy manipulation from outside. This greatly undermines the self-confidence of the African people and the church in the search for self-identity. How can existing African economic bases be strengthened? Examples were cited of African churches that have taken steps toward more economic self-reliance.

Much as the church was praised for standing up against oppression and dis-empowerment of citizens of African states, it was also pointed out that some of its leaders have been witting or unwitting collaborators with oppressive systems. Political leaders have never failed to seize upon an opportunity to sow and exploit divisions, particularly in an institution that poses a challenge to their power. Witting collaborators are easily bought off, while others accept rewards and favours (e.g., diplomatic privileges) that later compromise their objectivity as spiritual leaders. The result is usually confusion as the church is unable to speak with one voice and provide appropriate perspectives on issues of national importance. Participants regretted that, on some occasions, some church leaders have praised and defended actions and utterances of politicians that other leaders of the same church have censored and condemned.

With regard to its contribution to political processes, participants agreed that the church should not engage in partisan politics. It was noted that it is the duty of the church to provide ethical and moral nurture for all people, including politicians. The church certainly should nurture lay members who may be interested in running for public office. In this way, it may be able to foster and reinforce ethical and moral behaviour in politics. As it nurtures and encourages lay members interested in public office, the church also should educate the electorate about its rights and responsibilities and what to expect of their leaders.

Participants agreed that the church cannot be a model for good exercise of leadership if its leaders do not set examples in transparency, accountability and encouragement of full democratic participation by all members. The church is particularly lax in recognising the role (both actual and potential) of women, not only in the life of the church, but in such important processes as reconciliation, peacemaking and social renewal. In the same way, decision-making in the church remains very much the domain of the elderly, thus shutting out the youth and their spiritual needs.

Peace and reconciliation are a clear mandate for the church, not a choice, participants noted. The church should not be preoccupied only with reconciling human beings with God, but should foster reconciliation between human beings. It was pointed out that the Bible makes reconciliation between brothers and sisters a prerequisite for reconciliation between human beings and God. The church should play a bridge-building role between hostile and hurting communities, encourage dialogue instead of confrontation, and foster the search for mechanisms to understand and meet needs rather than wrangle over superficial political positions. The church should anticipate tension and engage in bridge-building well in advance.

Church leaders present agreed that although the current changes embody the hope and promise of a better Africa, wounds from past misrule and raging conflicts still need to be healed. This is a task and challenge for the church. Examples were cited of the church's involvement in the healing process in Ethiopia, Liberia, Mozambique and Sudan, among others.

With regard to the current resurgence of multiparty politics on the continent, it was noted that the approach works best in societies characterised by a strong social consensus in which issues of contention are marginal. When applied to African situations, characterised by (real or imagined) fragile ethnic relations and not-very-stable economies, possibilities for conflict are heightened. Here the politics of reconciliation comes in. The politics of reconciliation should encourage consensus-building and the quest for common ground. Particularly in societies struggling to put behind years of war and deep-seated mistrust, social healing should take precedence over organisation of competitive elections.

Participants agreed that the church should not be oblivious to political processes. Although it normally works outside political structures, activating spiritual and moral values at the grassroots, the church should not be afraid to be a force in building social consensus and injecting moral and ethical behaviour into political structures.

Summary of Specific Lessons and Key Issues

1. Lack of consensus within churches tends to destroy their overall effectiveness. The church is taken more seriously when it addresses itself to the problems of the day as one body. At the same time, the church should not openly align itself with political

parties or parties caught in bitter conflict. When the church remains non-partisan, difficult as this may be at times, it is able to be at the forefront in fostering reconciliation.

2. If churches collaborated across borders, they would learn a great deal from each other and avoid duplicating mistakes. For example, churches in Zaire and Malawi could look across the border to Zambia and learn how a united church was able to participate effectively in a change process.

3. The church is able to use a variety of means to reach both the people and political leaders. These include the mass media, pastoral letters, press releases and personal contacts. Churches in Burundi were able to put all of these to good use, while in Kenya the churches were not as successful. In instances in which the incumbent leadership was committed to peaceful change and fair elections, the role of the churches was easier.

4. Accords and peace agreements can be and are often signed between leaders of contending parties. But—as has been amply shown by the case of the Sudan (1972) and, recently, by the cases of Angola and Mozambique—the bigger challenge is usually how those agreements trickle down and find support and expression at the lower levels and how they are translated into action. The church can be in a position to help translate agreements downward once they are signed. Similarly, social-change processes are rendered ineffective if people at the lower levels are not empowered to own the change process, so that it translates to their best interests. Church institutions have launched programmes aimed at educating people about their rights and responsibilities as citizens. The gains have been modest, however, because of numerous obstacles thrown in their way.

5. The politics of reconciliation, defined in one symposium paper as a process of interest negotiation "in which there are no total losers and total winners but everyone wins something together," was attempted in Burundi, where the prime minister in the new government was picked from among the "losers" of an election. In addition, the former president, who lost in the elections, was accorded the full privileges (unlike in Zambia) of a retired statesman. Another fitting example narrated in the symposium is what happened in Benin. Benin is viewed as a case in which the process of change was better managed. Churches and other organisations were able to approach the head of state in confidence and, through a written agreement, assure him that he would have the full protection of the law, even if a new government took over. With church leaders as sworn guarantors of that promise of protection, the head of state allowed the national conference that people were agitating for, thereby possibly averting a violent confrontation.

6. Recognising all stakeholders in a change process and accommodating their concerns is important. For example, efforts to bring peace in Rwanda and Burundi would have to take into consideration refugees from both countries who are scattered in neighbouring countries and Europe.

7. Support of international bodies and partners can be very helpful in situations in which many years of persecution and systematic destruction of the church and its institutions leave it helpless. In this regard, the WCC and the AACC offered support to Ethiopian churches for more than seventeen years.

8. Mediation between long-time rivals needs a lot of patience, hope and perseverance. Only then can the parties cultivate the necessary trust and confidence. In the end, there is joy when patience bears fruit. As the Right Reverend Jaime Gonçalves, Archbishop of Beira (who was centrally involved in the Mozambican peace negotiations), observed, "I was convinced that people can change when I saw FRELIMO and RENAMO sign a document of reconciliation. I cried because I knew that these people hated each other to death. Be patient and know that people can change, and I think Africa can change also."

9. Church leaders also need to show respect to political leaders when they dialogue on national issues. Public confrontation may not always yield the intended results.

10. Church leaders' involvement in political matters and dialogue should not be seen to be divorced from their spiritual commitment. Indeed, spiritual commitment separates what is expected of them from what is expected of other politicians. There is need therefore for a clear theological discourse on social change, reconciliation and peacemaking, as well as an articulation of the role of the church and its leaders based on sound theological principles.

11. The question of consensus-building was very central in the symposium discussions. It was noted that national conventions and conferences (as employed in Madagascar and Zaire) can be important consensus-building mechanisms. The churches have been centrally involved in these.

12. The church has been involved in many areas during the change process, and it has become clear that expertise in diverse fields is necessary. The church will need to use expertise and informed input available from the laity and even outside its own community. The church's contribution should, however, be strongly founded on its moral and ethical values.

13. Links between church leadership and the grassroots need to be enhanced. The church risks doing no better than politicians if it does not have an effective and grounded link with the grassroots. Likewise, churches need to enhance links on the national, regional and international levels for purposes of networking and information sharing.

14. Involvement of women in the process of change, peacemaking and reconciliation, as well as in the life of the church, has in the past not been acknowledged or given adequate attention. Similarly, the youth and their aspirations have tended to be sidelined. Any institution that fails to cater for these member categories is not representative and lacks credibility.

15. There remains a real need for education/empowerment of the people, so that they know their responsibilities in the social-change and peacemaking processes.

16. Church leaders need to recognise and deal with the contradictions inherent in advocating democratic reform while thriving on undemocratic structures, as well as in its prophetic and mediation roles.

17. Church leaders need to be competently equipped to become facilitators with confidence and credibility. Only an equipped church can read the signs of the times and intervene appropriately.

18. African leaders were faulted because of their reluctance to discourage dictatorship in their midst. The OAU's red-carpet welcome to internationally renowned corrupt and dictatorial leaders during summit meetings makes a mockery of the institution and the values it stands for.

19. The symposium dwelt a great deal on the issue of leadership in Africa. The point was made that people seem to recall only the failures of African leaders and forget the achievements, which are possible building blocks. Even though past and present African leaders have failed in many respects, some have made meaningful contributions to their countries and to the continent. A careful re-reading of these contributions is needed.

20. The issue of ethnicity cannot simply be wished away since many atrocities have been committed on its account. Mechanisms that enable people to transcend parochialism are needed. It was suggested that the church/Christianity represents one form of transcendence since people of different origins identify with it.

Recommendations

1. Local Christian councils and episcopal conferences were urged to study and reflect on the ideas that came out of the symposium and see how they can implement them in their respective countries.

2. People should be empowered and educated to participate in political processes in meaningful and practical ways, so as to be able to effect change in their best interest.

3. The AACC and Symposium of the Episcopal Conferences of Africa and Madagascar (SECAM, the Catholic equivalent of the AACC) should initiate networking among churches so as to further the work of peacemaking. It was further recommended that the AACC and SECAM set up a data-resource base that will be available to church leaders engaged in peacemaking or other social-change processes.

4. A special follow-up committee should be set up to implement the findings of the symposium. This committee would facilitate continued consultation, common action, mutual support and information sharing. It would also identify groups involved in similar activities and devise ways of collaborating with them.

5. There should be continuing analysis of the biblical and theological basis for the church's involvement in social-change processes. Another symposium for theologians only should be called to articulate the theological basis for church involvement.

6. The symposium's host organisations should address ways and means of involving women and the youth at different levels in peacemaking and reconciliation. This should be in the form of workshops and seminars at the regional level.

7. The Nairobi Peace Initiative was recognised as a useful organisational structure for implementing most of the recommendations. It should transform itself to become the Africa Peace Initiative. It should be given a higher profile, more resources and more tasks. It should co-ordinate research and engage in training programmes.

8. Steps should be taken to infuse the spirit and substance of the discussions on peace, reconciliation and democratisation that are taking place among church leaders into political discussions. This way, the values and principles identified in Nyeri and in similar discussions could guide the goals and actions of politicians, as well as enhance the quest for common ground between the two groups of actors.

APPENDIX II

Joint Statement of Symposium Participants*

I. Introduction

1. This symposium is convened jointly by the All Africa Conference of Churches (AACC), the Association of Member Episcopal Churches in Eastern Africa (AMECEA) and the Nairobi Peace Initiative (NPI). Participants in the symposium came from sixteen countries in eastern, central and southern Africa and two European countries to consider the multiple changes currently underway on the African continent and in the neighbouring island countries. Partici-pants came from Angola, Botswana, Burundi, Ethiopia, France, Kenya, Madagascar, Malawi, Mozambique, Namibia, Rwanda, South Africa, Switzerland, Tanzania, Uganda, Zaire, Zambia and Zimbabwe.

2. Africa is under the influence of a "second wind of change" characterised by a restructuring of the political order. It is clear that changes such as the shift from one-party to multiparty political systems, the revision of constitutions and legal reform highlighting various aspects of social concern are benefiting Africa. These are welcome changes. We note, however, that these changes come at a time when there is renewed interest in the history of the carving up of Africa by colonial powers. The implications of that interest for current developments in Africa remain to be seen.

3. During the early 1960s, when most African countries became independent, Africa's leaders collectively accepted the boundaries drawn by the colonial powers. That acceptance constituted one of the basic provisions of the OAU. One of the main objectives of the OAU was to facilitate the liberation of those portions of Africa still under colonial or minority rule. Thus was post-Independence Africa committed to a reactive agenda, premised in great measure on the structures imposed by or inherited from the colonial period. But as the African proverb notes, "The log can be in water for a long time without becoming a crocodile." Africans will not become Europeans, even if we continue to work within European categories and structures.

4. It was against such a background that this symposium was called to consider the role of religious leaders in peacemaking and social change in Africa. More particularly, we have been called together to forge a pro-active agenda for this continent. Through the public media and by means of our ecumenical networking, we are all aware of the roles played by individual church leaders as well as church groupings in the current political reordering.

II. Democracy

Definition

1. We understand democracy to be a political, economic, social and cultural choice made by society, allowing for the implementation of a government constituted

---

* This statement was initially drafted by Jesse Mugambi and Harold Miller.

with the full participation of the people and accountable to the people. Additionally, we understand democracy to encompass the broad range of social institutions and movements that have their origins in initiatives taken by the people. In our discussions, it became clear that "democracy" makes its appearance in Africa as a response to the excesses of one-party and, in many cases, one-man rule. Additionally, the unsatis-factory political order has been exacerbated by economic decline with commensurate human suffering because of declining standards of living. People in Africa want change, with the expectation that a shift to more participatory governance will provide answers to the ills of their respective countries.

2. Africa is undergoing a "second liberation." One of the elements of this process has been identified as democracy. In this symposium we have been at pains to understand the concept, as it comes from outside the continent, and to define for our own purposes what it might mean for the church's engagement in the change process.

International Order

3. Additionally, there is an understanding that some portion of the current democratisation process is lodged in the shifting dynamics of the international order. In as much as the process of democratisation is perceived as imposed from outside the continent, it is manifest most explicitly as a new configuration of conditionalities with regard to both bilateral and multilateral aid.

4. In some of our countries, the democratisation process has come to be associated with what is now referred to as "multipartyism." Multipartyism, in turn, has been identified with pressure and agitation for national elections, with the attendant possibility of the respective political candidates to "win" or "lose." Although the democratic process is associated with multi-partyism, there is discussion underway to expand and enrich the meaning of democracy.

Relationship Between Winners and Losers

5. There was strong discussion regarding the demands of the win-lose matrix. We noted that within traditional African leadership patterns there is acceptance of and provision for losing and for the surrender of power to a person identified through an accepted consensual process. Relinquishing power, in many traditional contexts, is compensated with face-saving devices. Patterns of power management, together with the various manifestations of shared power and compensation, are situated within the context of a community-consensus process.

6. In contrast, post-colonial political regimes, whether based on single- or multiparty configurations, have yet to find their roots in widespread popular consent. Thus when a political figure loses (rather than relinquishes) office, the loss is total and, on occasion, devastating. Obviously, in such situations leaders are reluctant to leave office. They are tempted and often prepared to abuse power in order to retain it.

Popular Consent

7. If the current political process is to be carried out with some degree of legitimacy, it will be necessary to revise the national constitutions of African countries, which were, in any case, drafted without full consultation with the people. Any such revision, in the current situation, will require full consultation with and the consent of the people. Meaningful political change

can only be achieved on the basis of consensus. How is consensus achieved in Africa today? In the discussion, there was repeated appeal to insights from the African tradition.

8. We emphasise that Africans need not be taught about the win-lose matrix; this matrix has been present in Africa since time immemorial. However, in the African heritage, it did not yield unmanageable tensions owing to society's in-built values and norms. This insight has not been acknowledged or sufficiently appreciated by political leaders in the post-colonial period. In the African tradition, there is an understanding of unity in diversity, an affirmation of a certain kind of pluralism and a balance between the several components. A re-appraisal of this traditional understanding of the political process will greatly enhance the social transformation taking place in Africa today.

Government

9. The concept of government in Africa is still in formation. Existing models of government are informed by aspects of the colonial heritage, while the current democratisation process makes additional contributions. Good government is characterised by community, compassion and continuity. The church will do well to identify and incorporate into the consensus-building process value concepts that provide for stable but responsive exercise of power.

Economics

10. The economies of some countries in Africa have, for all practical purposes, collapsed. Many others are not viable. If the current democratic reordering of the political scene in Africa is to be sustainable, it will need to be undergirded by stable economies. We have noted that the economic issues need to be addressed on two levels: those that impinge on Africa from outside the continent and those within the continent over which Africans have control.

11. Economic issues within the continent can be further divided between those that governments control and those over which the people have control. We call for careful analysis and action by the church on all levels of economic concern. To the extent that some portions of local economies are viable, they are to be affirmed, strengthened and enlarged. However, wherever the constraints to economic reform are lodged in power centres outside the continent, the church should develop expertise to address the issues effectively.

III. The Church

Definition

1. We call for a critical review of our understanding of "the church." Who is the church? When we speak of the church addressing or interacting with political change in today's Africa, who is being referred to? Just as in the case of the word government, it is useful to reflect on the word church in the variety of African languages and our respective ecclesiastical traditions. In the public arena, the church has tended to be portrayed as the voice of senior church leaders and officers of national and regional ecumenical organisations. We question the adequacy of this understanding of the church. We urge that public advocacy by church leaders at all levels be premised on consensus and the unity of the entire church community. Collectively and individually, the leadership role of the church is called to be exercised in the posture of servant in its relation to the people at all levels.

Identity

2. African identity comprises a number of elements including a) politics—the distribution and management of social influence; b) economics—the distribution and management of resources; c) ethics—the system of values; d) aesthetics—beauty and e) metaphysics, or worldview, the most recognised instrument of which is religion. Obviously, the church in Africa has been preoccupied with metaphysics and religion. During this time of rapid and far-reaching changes, we call upon the church, additionally, to engage itself in the renewal of all aspects of African identity.

Ethnicity

3. Among other things, such engagement will call for a review of the ethnic character of African peoples. We need to examine critically the African ethnic reality as one of the potential building blocks of the new society. In this regard, it is incumbent on the church to participate in an affirmation of common and inclusive elements of ethnicity that in turn render the African identity renewed and strengthened. In one form or another, the church is present in nearly all ethnic communities across the continent. More than any other community or institution on this continent, the church is well placed to exercise a unifying influence over African peoples. Most critically, the church is challenged to address the question of authentic African identity and the related issue of African culture.

Religious Plurality

4. We emphasise that Africa has always been culturally and religiously pluralist. In the traditional African setting, this plurality has not generated tensions andconflicts, largely because of the in-built values and norms of tolerance and reciprocation. We urge that these values and norms be taken seriously, not only in building bridges of co-operation between churches and church organisations, but also in interaction with individuals, organisations and institutions of other religious communities, including Islam. We recognise that the unity of Africa will be greatly enhanced by the development of positive and constructive relationships at all levels.

The Church and Economics

5. Cultural and spiritual identity remain truncated in the absence of economic self-determination. As a colonised continent, Africa was by definition not economically self-determining. During the post-colonial era, African countries have not been able to assert their economic self-determination. Instead, continued economic dependency has served to undermine the self-confidence of African countries and communities including the African church. In our discussion groups, we have articulated the need for Africa's full and deliberate participation in the determination of its own economic future, in all aspects of life. Economic self-determination is an important component of a healthy self-identity.

6. The necessity of belt-tightening and sacrifice in the current economic crisis is understandable but not attractive. Every possible means must be identified to affirm and strengthen the viable sectors of the existing economic base in Africa. Already some churches in Africa have taken up the call for more deliberate action toward their own economic self-determination and toward greater participation in the respective economies.

Participation

7. We praise the churches for challenging, on occasion, all oppressive powers and structures. At the same time, we are cognizant of their unwitting collaboration. We affirm the church as an instrument of change in anticipation of the new society. In particular, the church must address the manner in which political power is claimed and exercised on the African continent. In the very first instance, within its own structures, among its own leaders and between leaders and the laity, the church must be seen to be modelling a unified witness in terms of equitable participation, trans-parency and accountability. In particular, we urge the churches to recognise the essential role of women in the life of the church and also in the processes of reconciliation, peacemaking and social change. This recognition should be supported by strengthening the participation of women at all levels. Likewise, we also urge the churches to further encourage the youth to participate in their programmes at all levels. To this end, we urge the churches to review their strategies in order to provide opportunities and resources for such participation.

Consensus Building

8. Additionally, the church must affirm and strengthen the unity of all peoples; it must help create an atmosphere of mutual caring and listening, enabling people to participate knowledgeably in the current change processes. Specifically, the church should encourage the selection, education and preparation of qualified candidates to run for public office and should, to this end, educate the electorate on its rights, duties and expectations of the holders of public office. Among other things, such expectations include the consent of the people for whom an elected representative speaks.

9. In periods prior to elections, the church should facilitate consultation and formulation of common goals among political candidates, educating them to the norms of transparency and accountability vis-à-vis their own electorate. For those who lose in the contest for public office, the church must offer its pastoral ministry, ensuring that such loss is neither total nor detrimental to the individual or community involved. Such principles apply to all levels of polity, including the continental level. In this regard, we urge continental church organisations such as the All Africa Conference of Churches (AACC) and Symposium of Episcopal Conferences in Africa and Madagascar (SECAM) to take seriously their observer status at the OAU.

Reliable Information/Expertise

10. If the church is to play its role in the public affairs of the continent effectively and efficiently, it must do so on the basis of reliable information and with the support of qualified personnel. In this regard, churches must utilise lay experts in various disciplines for collection, analysis and synthesis of relevant data.

11. To this end, it will also be necessary for the national, regional and continental ecumenical organisations to collaborate in the dissemination of relevant information and insights that facilitate the process of change in various parts of Africa.

12. Such collaboration should include strengthening the existing theological facilities and curricula, ensuring that the training of young church leaders will be attuned to the needs of the times.

The Church as a Healing Community

13. There is great promise of a more participatory society in Africa. There is also the dire need to heal the wounds of the past. In numerous countries across the continent, civil wars are raging. The church is called to minister to all conflicting parties and, of course, to the victims of conflict, working for the restoration of broken people and broken societies. The examples of church initiatives in this regard are many; in Mozambique, Liberia, Sudan, Ethiopia, Kenya and other countries, the church has demonstrated compassion and articulated a vision of a reconciled future. In limited fashion, and at times on a larger scale, the church has been able to beat swords into ploughshares.

IV. Reconciliation and Peacemaking

The Mandate

1. The church is mandated to be involved in peacemaking and reconciliation. The gospel presents this mandate as an essential element of the Christian witness. Biblical reconciliation has everything to do with wholesome self-identity, with integrated relationships with God, neighbour, community and nature. The whole world is God's world.

2. Ultimately, mature reconciliation is the product of interdependent relationships at all levels of society and with all people. In the quest for "right relationships," the church must exercise the role of bridge builder between hostile communities, of healing within and between hurting communities, of dialogue instead of confrontation, of an understanding of real needs rather than superficial political positions staked out by power brokers.

Reconciliation Politics

3. It is in governance and political life that the noble mandate of reconciliation politics is put to the test. As a beginning point, multiparty politics as presently practised in Africa takes a variety of forms. The definition of democracy must be open to contributions from all quarters, including the African tradition. If the goal of political change is a harmonious community, it does not necessarily follow that the politics of competition provides the means. The churches must become actively involved in the search for alternative democratic models appropriate to the respective countries, taking into account the African heritage, the colonial legacy and post-colonial pressures.

4. The church in Africa must affirm the wellbeing of political contestants, ensuring that the good of all participants in a changing political order is catered for. On a continent in which the exercise of power is often equated with "eating," the politics of reconciliation offers a daunting challenge and opportunity for the churches to serve Africa. Reconciliatory entry points are provided precisely by the strongest tension points; the church should keep pressure on political or military contestants at the points where apparently unresolvable differences surface. As the "servant of all," the church has no option but to be available wherever there is hurt or tension.

5. Even more urgently, the church should anticipate tension spots by engaging in consensus-building, ensuring that constitutional reform, elections and other public processes at all levels are carried out in a "win-win" spirit. Clearly, win-win possibilities are greatly enhanced when a basic consensus exists and when such consensus eventually takes the form of equitable laws for the benefit of all.

6. The church ought never be oblivious to the political process. But neither is the church bound to make its contributions solely within the confines of the publicly accepted political arena. Indeed, the church has the option and the mandate to work outside political structures, appealing to basic values and norms and building consensus on a broad range of issues. Indeed, consensus-building involves much more than political relations.

7. Consensus-building and education for participation in the political process is not carried out in a void. We recognise that the electorate knows what it wants. In this regard, consensus-building is carried out as a process that liberates people to fulfil their own felt needs. Toward this end, the church must foster reconciliation as dialogue with all sectors of the community—with protagonists, with antagonists, with all contestants in conflict—strengthening, meanwhile, all who have the gift of healing and reconciliation.

Nyeri, Kenya

23 July 1993

APPENDIX III

Description of the Sponsoring Agencies

All Africa Conference of Churches (AACC)

The AACC is a pan-African fellowship of 147 member churches and national Christian councils in 39 countries, founded in 1963. Its functions are

1. To keep before the churches and national Christian councils the demands of the gospel pertaining to their life and mission, in evangelism, in witness to society, in service and unity; and to this end promote consultation and action among the churches and councils.
2. To provide for a common programme for study and research.
3. To encourage closer relationships and mutual sharing among churches in Africa through visits, consultations and conferences and the circulation of information.
4. To assist member churches in identifying, sharing and placing personnel; utilising other resources for the most effective prosecution of their common task.
5. To assist the churches in their common work of leadership training—lay and clerical.

Under its general secretariat, the AACC has an international affairs desk. Through this department, the AACC worked with AMECEA and NPI to co-sponsor the symposium.

Association of Member Episcopal Conferences in Eastern Africa (AMECEA)

AMECEA is a service organisation for the national conferences of Catholic bishops in Ethiopia, Kenya, Malawi, Sudan, Tanzania, Uganda and Zambia. Founded in 1961, AMECEA enables the seven conferences of bishops to do together what they could not do alone and offers them the machinery to work together on a regional basis. Its aims are:

1. To maintain liaison between the member conferences of bishops;
2. To facilitate inter-communication;
3. To serve as the co-ordination agency for organising combined studies as required by the member conferences of bishops;
4. To execute projects and manage and/or direct any joint institutions agreed upon by the member episcopal conferences.

Although AMECEA deals primarily with inter-conference matters, it is also engaged in a wide spectrum of the church's apostolate in eastern Africa due to the many mandates it has received from its member conferences for regional undertakings. AMECEA also welcomes fraternal collaboration with ecumenical bodies and overseas mission partners.

Nairobi Peace Initiative (NPI)

NPI had its beginning in 1984 as a discussion and reflection forum to explore ways of addressing chronic conflicts plaguing Africa. Over the years, NPI has grown, undertaking direct peacemaking and reconciliation activities in many civil wars in Africa. Its activities fall under the following categories:

1. Undertaking *peacemaking initiatives* with continental, regional, and national actors by providing mediation and conciliation

assistance to political organisations or groupings engaged in violent conflicts.

2. Undertaking *peacebuilding activities* at the grass-roots level by promoting reconciliation between conflicting ethnic, religious or cultural groups by facilitating conflict resolution activities as well as by training and coaching actors in peacemaking and reconciliation process.

3. Contributing to *new understandings of conflict and conflict transformation processes in Africa* through organising symposia, conferences and workshops.

4. *Publication and dissemination* of action-oriented research, reflection, and case studies with the aim of widely sharing thoughts and experiences in conflict resolution and transformation in Africa.

APPENDIX IV

Aggregated Responses from the Symposium Evaluation Form

The questions that appeared in the symposium evaluation form are reproduced below. All responses received have been summarised. Clear, unequivocal responses are represented as percentages.

1. *Do you feel the objectives of this meeting were accomplished? Please explain.*
   - 68% were positive that the objectives of the meeting were achieved.
   - 20% thought that the objectives were mostly but not wholly achieved.
   - 8% thought that the objectives were not achieved at all because no concrete structures were set up for continuity and follow-up, as they had hoped.
   - 4% did not have any comments.

2. *What were the most positive aspects of the meeting for you?*
   - The experience of meeting and sharing with participants from different countries.
   - Opportunities to begin networking.
   - Good facilities: conference hall, audio equipment, accommodation and very good food.
   - Insightful papers and inputs from participants.
   - The "Peace Panel" with participants from strife-torn countries.
   - The symposium was an educative process.
   - The spirit of ecumenism.
   - Richness of interaction.
   - The openness and frankness of participants.
   - Unity of purpose shown.
   - The realisation that Africa's problems are a common concern and not one person's or one country's burden.

3. *What were the negative aspects?*

The negative aspects identified by 72% of the participants revolved around the question of the time available for the workload. Some stated that there was just too much to be covered in six days, while some thought the time available tended to be misappropriated by some speakers who took too long on the floor.

Other negative aspects identified were
   - Too much time taken up by paper presentations.
   - Inadequate time for conclusions and final report.
   - Inadequate women's participation.
   - Over-optimistic expectations by organisers.
   - Negative attitude of some participants towards women.
   - Refusal by some to be open-minded about democracy and party politics.

Aggregated Responses from the Symposium Evaluation Form

- Conference hall was too squeezed.
- Discussions tended to be academic contests at times, thus obscuring major concerns.

4. Please comment briefly on:

Arrangements (tickets, transport, communications, etc.)

Nearly all the participants thought that arrangements were excellent, especially the ticket arrangements, mail and telephone communications prior to the conference, and transfers from the airport to the hotels.

However, nearly all agreed that the transport from Nairobi to Nyeri was a complete foul-up due to uncomfortable buses, poor time-keeping and the length of the ride.

Facilities (accommodations, meals, etc.)

Here, all participants except two were positive, with special praise for meals and services. Comments ranged from "O.K." to "Good!", "Very Good!" and "Excellent!". Two participants felt that sharing rooms caused inconveniences, especially because there was only one key per room.

Content of meeting (themes, discussions, etc.)

- 60% were unequivocally positive that the themes and discussions were relevant and timely.
- 32% were positive but also pointed out some shortcomings:
  - Not enough time.
  - Some views were glossed over due to poor chairing.
  - Too many papers.
  - Some felt lost when discussions became academic.

- Limited time for all to participate.
- 4% answered in the negative and explained that whole programme was entirely too crowded.
- 4% did not comment.

Special events (evening programme, entertainment, worship, etc.)

In general, 96% had positive comments about the special events and thought they were different and educative, while the worship was simple, and meaningful. A number pointed out that the session with the "sages" was disappointing. 4% felt that the worship could have been improved. 4% did not comment.

Opportunities for networking

With the exception of 4% who answered in the negative and 16% who did not comment, all other participants (80%) thought they had ample opportunity for networking during the symposium. Among the positive respondents, 20% saw networking as a continuing challenge rather than an achievement.

Participation

- 64% said they had ample opportunity to participate.
- 8% qualified their approval by pointing out that there was not enough time for everyone to participate due to inadequate group discussions and language barriers.
- 8% thought that participation was lacking.
- 16% did not comment.

Other comments

- Not enough Catholic participants, especially from Kenya.
- A good selection of participants.

5. How would you describe the spirit of this meeting?

96% thought the spirit of the meeting was very good. 4% thought that the spirit of the meeting was negated by the workload and pressure of time. Comments included: ecumenical spirit, spirit of sharing, lots of humour, too much pressure, cheerful and lively, very sisterly, trés fraternal, serious and hopeful.

6. What suggestions would you make for the next meeting?

Most suggestions revolved around time, women's/youth participation, group work and involving other countries:

- Have a different country as a venue.
- Invite secular leaders other than religious ones.
- Include more women and younger people.
- Have a lighter workload.
- Have time for personal reflections.
- Include government people.
- Have more group discussions.
- Start from concrete situations (case studies?) and later have teams of theologians and social scientists reflect on the concrete cases to extract general principles.

7. What do you feel was the most important outcome?

- Church leaders' awareness that peacemaking and reconciliation is a calling.
- The opportunity for networking.
- Awareness of the existence and activities of NPI.
- The elevation of peacemaking and reconciliation to the top of the church's agenda.
- The successful bringing together of Catholic, Protestant and Orthodox leaders.
- The awakening of hope for a better Africa and the church's role in sustaining that hope.
- The realisation of the need for unity among all churches.

8. Please feel free to make any other comments in areas not covered below in this page.

- The organisers deserve to be congratulated for a job well done.
- Assignments should have been given to national councils and episcopal conferences as part of the follow-up.
- The Portuguese speakers should have been provided with interpreters.
- Not too many academics if issues are intended for practical application.
- Sincere congratulations to the staff of AACC, NPI, AMECEA.
- Include evangelicals next time.
- Good choice of venue (out of Nairobi) and good selection of participants.
- Organisers should work hard on the follow-up.
- Nairobi Peace Initiative (NPI) should transform itself into Africa Peace Initiative (API) and provide a resource base for churches in Africa.
- Two participants commented that participants should have been required to make a minimum monetary contribution to the symposium expenses.

APPENDIX V

Symposium Participants

1. Dr Agnes Chepkwony Abuom
   Church of the Province of Kenya
   P.O. Box 40502
   Nairobi, Kenya
   Tel: 254-2-714752

2. Prof Hizkias Assefa
   Nairobi Peace Initiative
   P.O. Box 14894
   Nairobi, Kenya
   Tel: 254-2-441444/440098/442533
   Fax: 254-2-445177/442533

3. Mr Emmanuel Bombande
   IYCS Africa Regional Coordination
   P.O. Box 44335
   Nairobi, Kenya
   Tel: 254-2-553029

4. Mr Job Chambal
   Director of Religious Affairs
   Government of Mozambique
   Maputo, Mozambique

5. Rev Dr Frank Chikane
   General Secretary
   South African Council of Churches
   P.O. Box 4921
   Johannesburg 2000,
   South Africa
   Tel: 27-11-4921380/96
   Fax: 27-11-4921448

6. Fr Alex Chima
   Cathedral Parish
   P.O. Box 19
   Mzuzu, Malawi
   Tel: 265-332108

7. Rev Emmanuel Chinkwita-Phiri
   Christian Council of Malawi
   P.O. Box 30068
   Lilongwe 3, Malawi
   Tel: 265-783499/721215
   Fax: 265-734987/652999

8. Mrs Eva Chipenda
   P.O. Box 14205
   Nairobi, Kenya

9. Rev José Chipenda
   AACC
   P.O. Box 14205
   Nairobi, Kenya
   Tel: 254-2-441483/443242
   Fax: 254-2-443241

10. Rev Augusto Chipesse
    Angolan Christian Council of Churches
    P.O. Box 1301,
    Luanda, Angola
    Tel: 244-2-330415/350493
    Fax: 244-2-39-3746

11. Ms Marcia Cruz
    AACC
    P.O. Box 14205
    Nairobi, Kenya
    Tel: 254-2-441483/441338
    Fax: 254-2-443241

12. Mr Kes-Yadessa Daba
    Ethiopian Evangelical Church
    Mekane Yesus
    P.O. Box 2087
    Addis Ababa, Ethiopia
    Tel: 251-1-553280
    Fax: 251-1-552966

13. Bishop Emilio J. M. De Carvalho
    United Methodist Church
    P.O. Box 68
    Luanda, Angola
    Tel: 244-2-390184

14. Rev Dr Sakala Foston Dziko
    Justo Mwale Theological College
    P.O. Box 310199
    Lusaka, Zambia
    Tel: 260-1-230852/229551
    Fax: 260-1-290285

15. Mr Dominic Gitau
    AACC
    P.O. Box 14205
    Nairobi, Kenya
    Tel: 254-2-441483/443242
    Fax: 254-2-443241

16. Archbishop Jaime Pedro Gonçalves
    The Archbishop of Beira
    P.O. Box 544
    Beira, Mozambique
    Tel: 258-3-322313/322883
    Fax: 258-3-327639

17. Rev Grace Imathiu
    United Lavington Church
    P.O. Box 25030
    Nairobi, Kenya
    Tel: 254-2-562908

18. Rev Anastacio Kahango
    Angolan Franciscan Province
    C.P. 3578
    Luanda, Angola
    Tel: 244-2-343686/345504
    Fax: 244-2-345504

19. Ms Kambale Kavuo
    AACC
    P.O. Box 14205
    Nairobi, Kenya
    Tel: 254-2-441483/443242

20. Mr Aba Kidane Mariam
    Secretary General
    Catholic Secretariat
    P.O. Box 2454
    Addis Ababa, Ethiopia
    Tel: 251-1-550300
    Fax: 251-1-553115

21. Dr Timothy Kiogora
    Department of Religious Studies (Social Ethics)
    University of Nairobi
    P.O. Box 30197
    Nairobi, Kenya
    Tel: 254-2-334244 Ext. 2441/2148 or 725922

22. Fr Renato Sesana Kizito
    New People Media Center
    P.O. Box 21681
    Nairobi, Kenya
    Tel: 254-2-567229

23. Fr William Knipe
    AMECEA
    P.O. Box 21191
    Nairobi, Kenya
    Tel: 254-2-566506/7
    Fax: 254-2-566065

24. Rev Dr Samuel R. Kobia
    General Secretary
    National Council of Churches of Kenya
    P.O. Box 45009
    Nairobi, Kenya
    Tel: 254-2-338211/2
    Fax: 254-2-224463

25. Rev Murombedzi Kuchera
    General Secretary
    Zimbabwe Council of Churches
    P.O. Box 3566
    Harare, Zimbabwe
    Tel: 263-4-791208/790100
    Fax: 263-4-706410

Symposium Participants

26. Rev Dr John Lamola
    The South African Council of Churches
    P.O. Box 4921
    Johannesburg 2000,
    South Africa
    Tel: 27-11-49-21380/96
    Fax: 27-11-49-21448

27. Fr Peter Lwaminda
    Secretary General
    AMECEA
    P.O. Box 21191
    Nairobi, Kenya
    Tel: 254-2-566506/7
    Fax: 254-2-566065

28. Rev Dr Laurenti Magesa, Jr.
    Bishop's Office
    P.O. Box 93
    Musoma, Tanzania
    Tel: 0196-17

29. Fr J. Mak'Opiyo
    Justice and Peace Commission
    Kenya Catholic Secretariat
    P.O. Box 48602
    Nairobi, Kenya
    Tel: 254-2-441112

30. Bishop John H. Mambo
    Church of God
    P.O. Box 30315
    10101 Lusaka, Zambia
    Tel: 260-1-248265
    Fax: 260-1-245425

31. Rev Dr Bodo Marini
    Vice-President
    Church of Christ in Zaire
    P.O. Box 4938
    Kinshasa-Gombe, Zaire
    Tel: 211-33077
    Fax: 211-2431234961

32. Pastor Dr Philippe Kabongo-Mbaya
    World Alliance of Reformed Churches
    P.O. Box 2100
    150 Route de Ferney
    1211 Geneva 2, Switzerland
    Tel: 33-83-32-0234
    Fax: 33-83-98-6365

33. Mr Harold Miller
    International Affairs Desk
    AACC
    P.O. Box 14205
    Nairobi, Kenya
    Tel: 254-2-441483/443242
    Fax: 254-2-443241

34. Fr Prof Daniel Joseph Mkude
    University Catholic Chaplaincy
    University of Dar es Salaam
    P.O. Box 35027
    Dar es Salaam, Tanzania
    Tel: 255-51-49051/48163

35. Mrs Florence Mpaayei
    Nairobi Peace Initiative
    P.O. Box 14894
    Nairobi, Kenya
    Tel: 254-2-441444/440098
    Fax: 254-2-445177/442533

36. Prof Jesse Mugambi
    Office of the Registrar
    University of Nairobi
    P.O. Box 30197
    Nairobi, Kenya
    Tel: 332651

37. Mrs Margaret Mukuna
    AACC
    P.O. Box 14205
    Nairobi, Kenya
    Tel: 254-2-441483/443242
    Fax: 254-2-443241

38. Rev Christopher Mtikila
    Liberty Desk
    P.O. Box 3885
    Dar-es-salaam
    Tanzania
    Tel: 255-51-34955

39. Mr Mutombo Mulami
    International Affairs Desk
    AACC
    P.O. Box 14205
    Nairobi, Kenya
    Tel: 254-2-441483/443242
    Fax: 254-2-443241

40. Ms Edith Dorah Mutale
    Christian Council of Zambia
    Women's Desk
    P.O. Box 30315
    10101 Lusaka, Zambia
    Tel: 260-1-229551
    Fax: 260-1-224308

41. Bishop Patrick Mumbure Mutume
    Imbisa Secretariat
    4 Bayswater Road
    P.O. Box 230 BE, BELUEDERE
    Harare, Zimbabwe
    Tel: 260-1-60909
    Fax: 260-1-724971

42. Mrs Faith Mwondha
    Church of Uganda
    Diocese of Busoga
    P.O. Box 1658
    Jinja, Uganda
    Tel: 256-43-20999

43. Prof Tshiyembe Mwayila
    9, Place de la Foret Noire
    54500 Van Doeuvre
    Les-Nancy, France
    Tel: 33-83-553594

44. Rev Dr Ngeno-Z K. Nakamhela
    Council of Churches in Namibia
    8 Mont Blanc Street
    P.O. Box 41, Windhoek 9000, Namibia
    Tel: 264-61-213303/217621
    Fax: 264-61-62786

45. Mr Alfred J. Ndoricimpa
    United Methodist Church
    P.B. 97, Gitega, Burundi
    Tel: 257-40-2171/2058

46. Rev Canon James Ndyabahika
    General Secretary
    Ugandan Joint Christian Council
    P.O. Box 30154
    Nakivubo-Kampala, Uganda
    Tel: 256-41-270218/9

47. Rt Rev Silas S. Njiru
    Catholic Diocese of Meru
    P.O. Box 14
    Meru, Kenya
    Tel: 254-0164-20261

48. Ms Elizabeth Otieno
    Ecumenical Support Program (ESP)
    P.O. Box 14894
    Nairobi, Kenya
    Tel: 254-2-446966/448142
    Fax: 447015

49. Ms Jennifer Margaret Potter
    Deputy General Secretary
    Botswana Christian Council
    P.O. Box 355
    Gaborone, Botswana
    Tel: 267-351981

50. Pastor Josoa Rakotonirainy
    General Secretary
    Christian Council of Churches in Madagascar
    P.O. Box 798
    101 Antananarive, Madagascar
    Tel: 261-2-29052
    Fax: 261-2-25914

Symposium Participants

51. Rev Père Adolphe Razafintsalama
    Dean of St. Michael College
    B.P. 3832,
    Antananarivo, Madagascar
    Tel: 261-2-20961
    Fax: 261-2-35397

52. Bishop Dinis Sengulane
    Diocese of Lebombo
    Anglican Church
    P.O. Box 120
    Maputo, Mozambique
    Tel: 258-1-734364
    Fax: 258-1-401093

53. Mr Lal Swai
    World Council of Churches
    150 Route de Ferney
    P.O. Box 2100
    1211 Geneva 2, Switzerland
    Tel: 41-22-7916111
    Fax: 41-22-7910361

54. Archbishop Timotheos
    Ethiopian Orthodox Church
    P.O. Box 1283
    Addis Ababa, Ethiopia
    Tel: 251-1-553566

55. Mrs Leah Tutu
    Bishopscourt Claremont
    7700 Cape Town, South Africa
    Tel: 012-712531
    Fax: 012-429-3332

56. Rev Michael Twagirayesu
    Presbyterian Church in Rwanda
    B.P. 56
    Kigali, Rwanda
    Tel: 250-76929

57. Rev Fr Joseph Ukelo
    Diocese of Torit
    P.O. Box 52802
    Nairobi, Kenya
    Tel: 254-2-743855/748523

58. Ms Gretchen Van Evera
    P.O. Box 14894
    Nairobi, Kenya
    Tel: 254-2-442533
    Fax: 254-2-442533

59. Mr George Wachira
    Nairobi Peace Initiative
    P.O. Box 14894
    Nairobi, Kenya
    Tel: 254-2-441444/440098
    Fax: 254-2-445177/442533

Interpreters

1. Mr Eloi Assogba
   P.O. Box 60804
   Nairobi, Kenya
   Tel: 254-2-500164

2. Mr A. R. Rumongi
   P.O. Box 30605
   Nairobi, Kenya
   Tel: 254-2-717681
   Fax: 254-2-713172

3. Ms Awinda Oleche
   P.O. Box 39951
   Nairobi, Kenya
   Tel: 254-2-441303/444792

4. Mr P. King-Ondoua
   P.O. Box 60804
   Nairobi, Kenya
   Tel: 254-2-500164

Translators

1. Mr Pipien Hakizebera
   UNESCO
   P.O. Box 30592
   Nairobi, Kenya
   Tel: 254-2-230800/520600
   Fax: 254-2-215991

2. Ms Dorothy Lusweti
   P.O. Box 61139
   Nairobi, Kenya
   Tel: 61139

Technicians

1. Mr John Kairu
   Cameraman
   Alwan Communications Ltd.
   P.O. Box 51841
   Nairobi, Kenya
   Tel: 254-2-211213/212809
   Fax: 254-2214129

2. Mr V. Ngarabe
   Symposia Consult
   P.O. Box 30605
   Nairobi, Kenya
   Tel: 254-2-717681
   Fax: 254-2-713172

3. Mr James Wasonga
   Cameraman
   Alwan Communications
   P.O. Box 51841
   Nairobi, Kenya
   Tel: 254-2-211213/212809
   Fax: 254-2-214129

Index

Action Chretienne pour Madagascar (ACM-France), 159
adolescence, 45
Adubia, 114
adulthood, 45
Adventist Church, 157, 171
Afigbo, A.E., 76
Africa
  colonisation, 11, 24
  economic growth, 42, 62, 64, 83
  ethnic violence, 106
  governance in, 24
  governance, 37, 42, 52
  heritage, 34
  human rights in, 88
  modernisation, 62, 64
  post-colonial state, 25
  re-membering, 29
  social change, 72
  social reconstruction, 34, 82
Africa Must Unite, 14
The African Heritage and Contemporary Christianity, 40
African Leadership Forum, 29
African National Congress (ANC), 180, 181, 184
African Recovery Unit, 88
African text, 26
The Africans: A Triple Heritage, 39
Agrippa, King, 73
Ajayi, 9
Alberts, Dr. Louw, 180
All Africa Conference of Churches (AACC), 1, 3, 129, 131, 199, 200, 201
Amba, J. Ileo, *see* Ileo, Joseph
Andriamanjato, Pastor Richard, 168
Anyona, George, 98
Association of Member Episcopal Conference of Eastern Africa (AMECEA), 1, 3
Attoh-Ahuma, 14

Batungwa, Father Ives, 124
Bazinga, Dr., 137
Berdyaev, Nicolai, 73
Beyond, 101
Birindwa, Faustin, 148
Bodo, Pastor Marini, 143
Bokeleale, Monseigneur, 136, 140, 145
Botha, P.W., 181
Buhlmann, Walbert, 76
p'Bitek, Okot, 40

Called to Peace, 199
Casely-Hayford, 14
Castro, Emilio, 188
Chikane, Frank, 186
childhood, 45
Chiluba, Fredrick, J.T., 125, 127, 128
Chissano, Joaquim, 196, 203
Choma Declaration, 121
Christian Churches' Monitoring Group (CCMG), 126
Christian Council of Churches in Madagascar (FFKM), 153, 154, 155, 156, 157, 158, 159, 160, 169
Christian Council of Mozambique (CCM), 193, 195, 196, 197, 199, 200
Christian Council of Zambia (CCZ), 123, 127, 136, 142
Christian humanism, 121
Church Missionary Society (CMS), 75
Church of Christ of Zaire (CCZ), 130, 131
Church of Jesus Christ on Earth (CJCSK), 130, 131, 137
Church of the Province of Kenya (CPK), 101, 105, 107, 112
church in Africa, 72
  advocacy, 91
  and democratisation, 130
  and education, 75, 84

and state, 74, 77, 98, 112
dependence, 87
fundamentalism in, 90
in social reconstruction, 79, 101
mediation, see conflict resolution
pluralism, see religious pluralism
post-independence role, 75
prophetic role, 73
shortcomings, 112
youth in, 92
Commission de Theologie, 154
Commission des Affaires Nationales (FIEFIP), 154, 157, 158, 159
Commission Oecumenique Nationale de Theologie (FET), 155
community, 36
Concilium: Revue Internationale de Theologie, 177
Conference Intermissionnaire de Madagascar, 155
conflict resolution, 46, 90
Congolese Sovereign Naitonal Conference, 139
La Conscience, 141, 145
Conseil Supreme de la Revolution, 156
Constantine, Emperor, 75
Constantino, Renato, 10
Convention for a Democratic South Africa (CODESA), 187

democracy, 17, 30
 and statehood, 37
 concept of, 16
 community and, 36
 churches and, 34
 culture and, 38
 in Africa, 7-22, 15
democratisation
 church in, 20
 in Kenya, 95-116
 in Zambia, 123
 multipartyism, *see* multipartyism
 religious leaders in, 72
develoment, 29
Development Dialogue, 16
Development Education Leadership Teams in Action (DELTA), 99, 108
Dhlakama, Alfonso, 203

Diangienda, 137
Diop, Chiekh Anta, 20
Dumont René, 9

The Economist, 12
Ecumenical Commission for Social Affairs (FEMES), 155
Education for Participatory Democracy, 109, 11c
education in Africa, 23
Eglise Anglicane Malgache, 154 *see also* Society for the Propagation of the Gospel (SPG)
Eglise de Jesus-Christ a Madagascar (FJKM), 155
Eglise du Christ au Zaire, *see* Church of Christ of Zaire
Eglise Lutherienne Malgache (LMS), 155
Electoral Commission of Kenya, 105
Etsou, Archbishop, 138, 142, 145
Evangelical Fellowship of Kenya (EFK), 96, 100
Evangelical Fellowship of Zambia, 127
Evangelical Lutheran Church (ELC), 154, *see also* Eglise Lutherienne Malgache (LMS)

Fanambana Contract, 175
Federalist Christian Democrats (FCD), 141
Federation des Eglises Protestantes de Madagascar, 155
Federation Protestante de France, 159
Forces Vives, 154, 163, 164, 165, 166, 167, 168
Forum for the Restoration of Democracy (FORD), 103, 110
Friends Foreign Missionary Association (FFMA), 155
Front for the Liberation of Mozambique (FRELIMO), 193, 203
Front Nationale pour la Defense de la Revolution, 153

da Gama, Vasco, 194
Gandhi, Mahtma, 44
God, Humanity and Nature in Relation to Justice and Peace, 40
Gonçalves, Right Reverend Jaime, 202
Gott, Richard, 9
government, 29
 for community, 30
 for compassion, 31

Index

for continuity, 31
state government, 37
Granjow, Sandra, 178
Guardian Weekly, 9

Hall, John, 186
Hani, Chris, 187
Hempstone, Smith, 103
Hobbesian view, 59
Howard, R., 32
human behaviour, 45
human rights, 81, 88
Hyden, Goran, 39

Ileo, Joseph, 141, 144
Infinde, Busonga Loombe, 141
Inkatha Freedom Party (IFP), 184, 185
International Monetary Fund (IMF), 153
The Inventions of Africa, 38

Jong, Bishop Dennis de, 124
Justice and Peace Commission (JPR), 109, 110
Justice et Liberation, 145
Justice, Peace and Reconciliation Department, 110
justice, 66, 85

"The Kenya We Want", 102
de Klerk, Frederick, 156, 182, 184, 186
Kalonji Mutambayi, 142, 143
Kapwepwe, Simon, 119
Kariuki, J.M., 99
Karl-I-Bond, Nguza, 144
Kaunda, Kenneth, 26, 27, 117, 120, 122, 126
Kenya
    challenges, 113
    church and state, 98
    churches in, 96
    churches' activism, 101, 107
    democratisation process, 95-116
    electioneering, 105
    ethnic violence, 106
    Inter-party Symposia, 106, 109, 111
    Kasarani, I, 102
    Kasarani, II, 103
    multiparty democracy, 100

    one-party rule, 97
    Second Interparty Symposium, 106, 109
Kenya African Democratic Union (KADU), 97
Kenya African National Union (KANU), 96, 97
Kenya Episcopal Conference, 105, 107
Kenya People's Union (KPU), 97
Kenya Social Alliance [KSC], 98
Kenya Television Network (KTN), 106
Kenyatta, Jomo, 99
Kiernan, V.G., 7
Kiliku, Hon. Kennedy, 106
Kiliku, Report, 106
Kimbangu, Simon, 131
Kimbanguism, *see* Church of Jesus Christ on Earth
Kiogora, T.G., 36
Kobina-Sekyi, 14
Korten, D.C., 66
Krapf, Johann Ludwig, 75
Kuria, Manasses, 101, 102

Law Society of Kenya [LSK], 96
Leopold, King of Belgium, 11
Les Amis de Nelson Mandela, 145
London Missionary Society, 154
Lord's Prayer, 48
The Lords of Humankind, 7
Lubumbashi Massacre, 140, 142
Luchembe, 123
Lugard, Lord Fredrick, 11
Lumumba, Patrice, 131
Luntadila, Pastor, 141
Lutheran Board Mission, 154, *see also* Eglise Lutherienne Malgache (LMS)
Lutheran Mission of Norway, 154, *see also* Eglise Lutherienne Malgache (LMS)
Lutz, M.A., 65
Lux, K, 65

'Marxism, Humanism and Christianity', 121, 128
'Mvunga, Commission Report,' 124
Machel, President Samora Moisés, 196
Madagascan Socialist-Revolutionary Charter, 153
Madagascar
    church in, 154

convention of 31 October 1991, 167, 167, 170
dinka santatra, 165, 166
FFKM activism, 156
fihavanana, 155, 157, 169, 175
First National Convention, 157, 160, 161
National Forum, 169, 170, 172
natural resources, 175
new constitution, 174
political crisis, 165
Second National Convention, 163
Second Republic, 153, 169, 174
Third Republic, 154, 157, 169, 177
transitional authorities, 169
Tripartite Committee, 166
Magoba, Bishop Stanley, 186, 187
Mahlaleha, Reverend Isaac, 195
majimboism, 104
Malula Foundation, 138
Malula, Cardinal Joseph, 77, 138, 139
Mambo, Bishop John, 127
Mandela, Nelson, 181, 182
Masamba, Professor Jean, 141
Matiba, Kenneth, 102
Mazrui, Ali, 39
Mbiti, John, S., 30
Mbiya-Mulumba, Pastor, 140
Mboya, Tom, 99
The Merchants of Venice, 86
Mission Protestante Francaise (MPF), 155
Mobutu Sese Seko, Marshal, 131, 132, 133, 136, 141, 142
modernisation, 62, 65
Mogojo, Khoza, 187
Moi, Daniel arap, 99, 101, 103
Moke, [Bishop], 138
Mokolo, 133
Mondlane, Eduardo, 200
Mosha, Raymond, 76
Mousengwo, [Archbishop], 138, 142, 143, 145, 150
Mouvement Militant pour le Socialisme Malgache (MMSM), 165
Mouvement Populaire de la Révolution (MPR), 133, 141
Movement for Multi-Party Democracy (MMD), 124, 125

Mozambican War of Independence, 195
Mozambique
  Appeal for Peace, 206
  church in, 194
  conflict in, 195
  independence struggle, 93
  Portuguese in , 193
  PPP seminars, 201
  refugees, 201
  Rome talks, 202
Mpolo, Professor Jean Masamba Ma, *see* Masamba Professor Jean
Mudimbe, V.Y., 38
Muge, Right Reverend Alexander, 101, 102
multipartyism, 89
Mulumba, Professor L., 142, 143
Mumba, Stephen, 124, 125
Mung'andu, Archbishop Adrian, 124
Mutale, Bishop, 128
Mutambayi, Kalonji, *see* Kalonji Mutambayi
Mutumbayi, Kalonji, 141
Mvunga Commission, 124
Mvunga, Professor, 124

Nairobi Peace Initiative (NPI), 1, 201
National Council of Churches of Kenya (NCCK), 96, 99, 101, 105, 106, 112
National Democratic Front, 141
National Ecumenical Civic Education Programme (NECEP), 107, 109, 113
National Federation of Christian Democrats (FENADEC), 141
National Party (NP), 181
Nelson, John, 46
neo-colonial axis, 8, 10
neo-colonialism, 7
Ngoma, Professor, 141
Njoroge, Ciugu, 104
Njoya, Reverend Timothy, 101,103, 110
njuri-njeke government, 29
Nkonga, Bennet, 124
Nkrumah, Kwame, 14, 20
No Shortcuts to Progress, 39
Nyerere, Julius, 14, 26, 27
Nyong'o, Professor Peter Anyang, 103

Index

Obasanjo, General Olusegun, 29
Odinga, Oginga, 97, 98
Okolo, Chukwudum B., 77
Okullu, Henry, 101, 102, 111
Omoniyi, 14
Organisation of African Unity (OAU), 2
Ott, Marvin C., 90
Oyugi, E., 113

Pan Africanist Congress (PAC), 180
Pasinya, Monseigneur Monsengwo, 122
Paul of Tarsus, 73
Paul VI, Pope, 84, 196
peace, 42
  and peacemaking, 50
  concepts of, 42
  of reconciliation, *see* reconciliation politics
  values and principles of, 44
peacemaking, 49, 50, 72, *see also* conflict resolution
  in Kenya, 110
  in Mozambique, 192-210
  in South Africa, 179, 191
peacemaking-and-reconciliation, 59, 66, 67
Permanent Committee of Catholic Bishops, 133
Pobee, John, 82
politics, 38

Rahantavololona, Mrs Andriamanjato, 166
raiamadreny, 157
Rakotanirina, Manandafy, 168
Ramahatra, Colonel, 165, 166
Ramakavelo, General, 167
Ratsiraka, Didier, 153, 154, 156, 168, 173, 175
Razanamasy, Guy Willy, 167, 168
Rebmann, Johann, 75
reconciliation politics, 56
reconciliation, 42, 46
  churches and, 51
  concept of, 50
  dimensions of, 46
  implications, 49
  in Kenya, 110
religious leaders, *see also* church in Africa
  ecclesiastical powers, 77

in advocacy, 91
in independence struggle, 74
in Madagascar, 157
social status, 88
religious pluralism, 89
RENAMO, 195-198, 202, 203
Roman Catholic Church (RCC), 130, 154
Rubia, Charles, 102

"second liberation" of Africa, 2, 95, 100, 128
Saba Saba (July 7) Uprising, 102, 103
Sacred Union, 142, 143
Saitoti Review Committee (SRC), 102
Salazar, Dr. Antonio, 193, 194
Santa Ana, Julio de, 177
scientific socialism, 121
Second Vatican Council, 83
Seme, Pixley, 14
Sese Seko, Marshal Mobutu, *see* Mobutu Sese Seko, Marshal
Shakespear, [William], 86
Shamwana, Edward, 123
Sharpville Massacre, 180
Simuchomba, Philip, 124
sir-kali, 37, 38
Sisulu, Walter, 182
Social Christian Democratic Party (PSCD), 141
social change, *see also* democratisation
  in Madagascar, 153-178
  in South Africa, 179-191
  word of God in, 84, 89
social reconstruction, 39
Society for the Propagation of the Gospel (SPG), 154
Soja, General, 167
'Song of Lawino', 40
'Song of Ocol', 40
South Africa
  church in, 179
  church struggle, 180, 191
  constitutional negotiation, 183
  Harare Declaration, 182
  Koinonia Minute, 188
  National Peace Accord, 186

National Peace Committee, 186
State of Emergency, 181
   violence in, 185
South Africa Council of Churches (SACC), 179, 180, 184, 185, 186, 188, 189, 190
Sovereign National Conference (SNC), 142
state government, *see* government
statehood, 59
structural adjustment programmes (SAPs), 83, 153
structural violence, 43
Study Programme of Christians in Apartheid Society (SPROCAS), 182

Target, 105
Thiong'o, Ngugi wa, 10
TOT (Training of Trainers), 108
Tshiamalenga, Father, 139
Tshibangu, [Bishop], 138
Tshisekedi, Etienne, 143, 147, 148
Tutu, Archbishop Mphilo Desmond, 79, 187

Ujamaa, 26 27, 30
Union for the Total Independence of Angola (UNITA) 55, 56
Union pour la Démocracie et le Progés Social (UDPS), 132, 142
United Democratic Front, 181
United National Independence Party (UNIP), 117, 188
United Nations Universal Declaration of Human Rights, 81

Wanjau, Very Reverend George, 106
Watcher, P., 63
Wehr, Paul, 91
Were, Gideon, 9
Wina, Sikota, 118, 119
World Bank, 153, 157
World Conference on Religion and Peace (WCRP), 179
World Council of Churches (WCC), 181, 188, 195, 200, 201

Zafy, Professor Albert, 154, 165, 166, 169, 175, 177
Zaire
   churches in, 130, 149
   democratisation process, 130-152
   High Council of the Republic (HCR), 147
   Lubumbashi riot, *see* Lubumbashi Massacre
   multiparty system, 132
   socio-political transformation, 132
   transition crisis, 144
Zambia
   coup attempt, 121
   independence struggle, 117
   multiparty democracy, 117-129
   religious leaders in, 127
Zambia Elections Monitoring Co-ordinating Committee (ZEMCC), 126
Zambia Episcopal Conference (ZEC), 123, 124, 127, 148
Zambian humanism, 121
Zimbabwean War of Independence, 195
Zulu, Grey, 119

About the Contributors

A.C. ABUOM, an historian by training, received her PhD from Uppsala University, Sweden, in 1987. She consults on the role of NGOs and churches in development and she is currently working for the (Anglican) Church of the Province of Kenya as its National (Provincial) Development Coordinator.

H. ASSEFA, Director of the Nairobi Peace Initiative (a Kenya-based African peacemaking organisation), has been involved in mediation and peacemaking efforts in many civil wars at high political levels and at the grassroots. He holds an LLB and Master's degrees in law, economics and public management as well as a PhD in international affairs. He is the author of numerous articles and several books and has taught law, conflict resolution, international affairs and management at Addis Ababa University, the University of Pittsburgh and LaRoche College (also in Pittsburgh).

J.P. GONÇALVES is the Catholic Archbishop of Beira in Mozambique. He was an official church mediator during the Rome peacemaking process that led to the cessation of hostilities in his country.

P.B. KABONGO-MBAYA, a Zairean sociologist and historian, is currently pastor of a congregation of the Reformed Church of France in Melun, France. He has served as the External Representative of the Conference of Reformed Churches of Zaire to the World Alliance of Reformed Churches in Geneva.

T.G. KIOGORA, Associate Professor of Ethics at Eastern Kentucky University, has taught at the University of Nairobi and at Asbury Seminary, U.S.A. After completing undergraduate studies in theology at St. Paul's Theological College, Limuru, Kenya, he earned an MA in theology from Southern Methodist University, and a PhD in ethics from the University of Denver, both in the United States.

J.M. LAMOLA, Head of the Department of Justice and Social Ministries of the South African Council of Churches at the time he wrote his paper, is now Vice-president of the Progressive People's Party, an opposition party in apartheid-free South Africa.

L. MAGESA, a Catholic priest of Musoma Diocese in Tanzania, holds a PhD degree from the University of Ottawa and a DTh degree from St. Paul University,

Canada. His main areas of interest are social ethics and African theology. He has taught in universities in Africa and the United States and is the author of several books.

J.N.K. MUGAMBI is Professor of Philosophy and Religious Studies at the University of Nairobi. While on official leave of absence from the University, he is in charge of development and research at the All Africa Conference of Churches, Nairobi. He has been involved in the ecumenical movement for many years and is the author of several books on theology and philosophy.

K.K. PRAH, a Ghanaian pan-Africanist, is currently Professor of Sociology at the University of the Western Cape in South Africa. He has taught in universities in many countries including the University of Amsterdam, Heidelberg University, the University of the Cape Coast (Ghana), the University of Botswana, and the University of Namibia.

J. RAKOTONIRAINY, currently General-Secretary of the Christian Council of Churches in Madagascar (FFKM), received his training from Theological College, Ivato, Madagascar, and the Faculté de Theologie Protestante in Paris. He is pastor of Avaratr'Andohalo, a reformed parish in Antananarivo. In 1990, Rakotonirainy was moderator of Madagascar's National Conference Steering Committee and took active part in the rewriting of his country's constitution in 1992.

F.D. SAKALA has been Principal of Justo Mwale Theological College in Lusaka for the last seventeen years. He studied history and sociology at the University of Zambia and received an MA in theology with a major in church history from Fuller Theological Seminary in U.S.A.

D.S. SENGULANE, Anglican Bishop of Lembombo in Mozambique, was intensively involved in the peace and reconciliation process in his country.

G. WACHIRA is Programme Officer with the Nairobi Peace Initiative, where he has worked since 1989. He holds a BA degree in government and anthropology from the University of Nairobi and an MA in international peace studies from the University of Notre Dame, U.S.A. He has been involved in peacemaking and peace building initiatives in several African countries.

www.ingramcontent.com/pod-product-compliance
Lightning Source LLC
Chambersburg PA
CBHW071350290426
44108CB00014B/1492